PRAISE FOR
The Introvert's Guide to Professional Success

"Introverts, you've earned your place at the front of the line and this remarkable, eminently practical book shows you how to use your own unique qualities to get there. It could help you bypass years of professional struggle and transport you to your highest goals.

In a recent meeting with a longtime client, she suddenly grew teary-eyed and apologized for her display of emotion saying, 'It's just that sometimes I feel like such a fraud.' My mind instantly went to this book and its discussion of the imposter syndrome. Here was a respected and successful physician in the prime of her career, tapped by her organization consistently to lead business units, new projects and other special assignments on top of her other professional demands, and she feels like a fraud! Because I had read this book, I was able to say to her, 'You're not a fraud, you're just an introvert.'

Just as I recommended this book to my client, I highly recommend it to other introverts, and especially those who sometimes might feel like 'frauds' or misfits in their professional lives. This book can give you the confidence and the ideas that you need to move forward toward your highest aspirations—a must-read!"

—**Robert Priddy,** *President,* third_Evolution, Non-Clinical Careers for Physicians

THE INTROVERT'S GUIDE to PROFESSIONAL SUCCESS

how to let your quiet competence be your career advantage

A PROGRAM TO LEVERAGE YOUR STRENGTHS

Joyce Shelleman, Ph.D.

SNOWY RIDGE STUDIO
Wiscasset, Maine

The Introvert's Guide to Professional Success

Published by Snowy Ridge Studio
PO Box 234
Wiscasset, Maine 04578-0234
www.snowyridgestudio.com

Names and identifying details have been altered to protect the privacy of the real persons mentioned in this book.

ISBN: 978-0-983108-40-5

Library of Congress Control Number: 2011902086
Library of Congress subject headings:
Introverts
Success in business
Leadership
Leadership skills
Introverts-Vocational Guidance
Career development
Introversion

Printed in the United States of America

*To the quiet dreamers everywhere
who create outside the limelight
because it is simply what they do.*

CONTENTS

Part IV Build Your Internal Capability

Part V Choices and Challenges

INTRODUCTION

I pulled into the parking lot and briskly crossed the green lawn with its fragrant flower beds to the modern three-story brick office building. Entering, I paused to locate the escalator that would take me to the conference registration, then took a deep breath and ascended. There were clusters of people at the top, but no one looked familiar. Making my way to the registration table, I wound past tote bag-carrying individuals who were chatting in pairs or small groups, amiably and without apparent self-consciousness. I smiled slightly and nodded hello to one or two. After picking up my packet of handouts and the conference agenda, I approached the auditorium, where the first session had already begun. Outside the door, I listened to the drone of the speaker and the smattering of applause, feeling the familiar dread mount my spine as I anticipated entering. Suddenly, with only the briefest of pauses, I strode to the end of the hall where a large red exit sign beckoned at the mouth of a stairwell. Within minutes I was back in my car, thinking, "Not today." I just could not face the throng of people, the introductions, and the small talk at lunch. Feeling guilty yet curiously relieved, I headed back to my office.

This story illustrates the extent to which introversion can influence our professional lives. If you have ever done—or wanted to do—something similar to what I did that day, then you know the power of this personality trait to shape our responses to situations involving other people.

But introversion is not a bad thing. It isn't a flaw that must be submerged, disguised, or denied if you are to achieve professional fulfillment. Despite the times when you have wanted to retreat, your introversion has served you well by enabling you to acquire professional skills that you apply to your career. Your thoughtful, quiet competence is an asset. Now you need only learn how to let it take you to the next level of success.

Introverts bring enormous strengths to their careers. They are the workhorses outside the spotlight, who engage deeply with their professions and innovate new pathways to success for their organizations and their clients. Focused and thoughtful, introverts perform independently. What many—perhaps even you—fail to see is that the quiet competence of introverts *complements* the warmth and enthusiasm of extroverts and is equally as valuable. Introverts can see details and implications of alternatives that are overlooked by extroverts, who think so well on their feet and express their ideas so eloquently. Introverts are deliberative, careful, and attuned to nuance—invaluable qualities that, nevertheless, are often undervalued in a workplace culture that frequently reserves its highest accolades for splendid form over this less flamboyant but more practical substance.

Because introverts are often misunderstood and overlooked, you *can* miss out on the career success that comes readily to highly visible extroverts. It's a fact that introverts are less likely than extroverts to reach the top of their organizations or to make as much money. *But this need not be your destiny.* This guide will show you how to actively deploy your introverted strengths to *your* career advantage.

My life experience as an introvert was my first step toward writing this book. The second step was my training in organizational behavior[1] and psychology, which included study of professions and unique dynamics of professional careers and workplaces. As I put my knowledge base together with my personality and experience as an introvert, I also realized that many of the concepts I was teaching to aspiring *leaders* had a special potential to guide *introverts* toward professional success. Inspired by Dr. Marti Laney's book, *The Introvert Advantage,* which focuses on issues largely outside the workplace, I began sharing *my unique perspective* on the *career and work life issues* faced by introverts. I learned more as I applied my insights to mentor others. As the pieces began to fit together like a puzzle, I formulated the model for achieving success that you will read about in this book. While the framework itself is an innovation, every part of it is based on solid evidence.[2]

Who Will Find This Guide a Great Fit?

If you're an introvert in a professional career, or who is aspiring to one, this guide is intended for you. Its principles will apply whether your field is accounting, administration, arts, education, engineering, information technology, journalism, law, medicine, nursing, science, social work, or any of a wide range of other fields that require rigorous training and dedication to a set of professional standards. My objective is simply to help you be the best you can be in the practice of your profession or, if you aspire to it, to expand your oversight of projects or people in a formal leadership role. What matters is that:

- you are seeking to advance your career with a practical, organized *strategy* that can be flexibly tailored to your unique situation

- you are committed to taking a series of concrete *actions* that build on your strengths as an introvert to get results

- you are open to learning *ideas* that may be new to you and trying different approaches

- you are willing to engage in a *process* that could take time to pay off and require you to search out additional help if needed for certain issues

Who Will Not Find This Guide a Great Fit?

This book is not for everyone. If a quick fix, a piecemeal approach, or *all* the answers is what you want, you should look elsewhere. This guide is not a great fit for you if you're looking for counsel *from* an extrovert on how to succeed with methods that work best *for* an extrovert. It will not give you advice on getting along with your significant other, or tips from celebrities, or extended case histories of former clients of mine, or inspirational slogans, or a detailed how-to in every possible area of your work life. Sorry if this is disappointing! The strategies I include in this book are for professionals who take themselves and their careers seriously and want a systematic and serious guide to a set of concrete behaviors and actions that, if implemented consistently, yields positive career outcomes.

How to Use This Guide

The conceptual framework at the heart of this guide is designed to be implemented sequentially. Follow the steps as outlined to derive the greatest benefit from the program. Actions that you take initially not only set the stage for those that follow but also take longer to produce results. That's why they come first.

If you're like me, you may be impatient to read specific sections that relate to your pet interests or challenges, such as networking. I love nothing better than to browse and skim a book extensively before I settle down to a sequential reading, if I ever do. If you too have a gadfly nature, feel free to indulge yourself. Just be aware that undertaking the whole program step by step in its recommended sequence is the path to greatest benefit.

As an introvert you are reflective, so I provide opportunities for you to reflect on concepts. In my website at www.TheIntrovertsGuide.com, you will find exercises to help you sort out the implications for your own situation and begin to think through how you can apply what you are reading. (Use the pass phrase "insightful expert" to access the exercises.) These hands-on exercises can build your expertise in the concepts covered in this book; together, the dynamic pairing of book and online exercises creates a learning experience grounded in your own personal situation and professional experience.

Since this guide is written for introverts, I make no effort to provide balance with a corresponding focus on extroverts, though I mention them from time to time. The singular emphasis on introverts and introversion at work is intentional. This is meant to be *your* guide.

Be prepared to discover straight talk throughout. I share my personal perspective, based on my experience as a specialist in human behavior in organizations *and* my life experience as an introvert. You will get ideas on what *not* to do as well as what *to* do, and on how to proceed. Here's a promise: I won't try to make you into an extrovert. Despite a business culture that favors extroversion, you can remain true to your nature as an introvert and do well, no matter what stage of your career you are in right now. You simply have to know how and be willing to expend some effort.

The detailed Notes in the back of the book provide background sources and insights to allow you to investigate topics further. But since this guide is intended to be practical, you can skip these if you choose and get to the heart of what you want to know.

Because you don't wish to waste time—or you don't have the time *to* waste—your ability to *apply* the information presented here is a primary goal. My aim is to improve your entire life by making its professional component easier and more successful.

PART I

Claim Your Identity

CHAPTER 1

Are You an Insightful Expert?

Bryn likes to be alone whenever she can. She seeks solitude at the end of a day of helping her clients. Although Bryn's work is of the highest caliber, she shies away from networking and promoting her professional practice. Her career suffers accordingly because Bryn doesn't get the number of referrals for new clients that she needs to keep her practice full.

Justin excelled in graduate school and long ago landed a position with a top-notch firm. Because he's quiet, however, he tends to be overlooked in meetings and in his supervisors' plans. As colleagues win promotions and advance into leadership roles, he wonders when his expertise will be rewarded with more challenging assignments.

Do you see yourself in Bryn and Justin?[1] Both are highly skilled, competent professionals who also happen to be introverts. Their introversion holds them back from accomplishing their deepest aspirations for career success and meaningful professional achievements.

Introverts like Bryn and Justin are *Insightful Experts*, a term I've coined to describe professionals who combine expertise in their work with the benefits of introversion. Their expertise is evident in their education, professional values, knowledge, and results. As introverts, they bring qualities of introspection, deliberation, and thoughtful insight to their work. They are an asset to any organization. While extroverts love to be among people, make lively conversation, and take instantaneous action, introverts like Bryn and Justin prefer the background, focusing

on tasks rather than relationships with others. They are stellar perform-
ers who are invigorated by time alone, accomplishing great things.

Yet, despite such capabilities, introverts are often handicapped on the
career ladder, as Bryn and Justin are learning the hard way. The obstacles
they encounter may be nearly invisible—never identified by colleagues
or in performance reviews—but they are real. If you identify with Bryn
or Justin, this book may be the help you need. Now is the time to begin
to look at your career differently; by changing your perspective, you will
learn how to retain and build upon the many strengths of introversion
while sidestepping the potentially adverse consequences. You will find
new ways to let your introversion work to your advantage—and to the
advantage of those around you.

See the Gestalt

Picture a mountain sunrise. Distant purple hills let the russet sun
emerge bit by bit and then, all at once, burst into full view with a cascad-
ing radiance. Rays of lemon-gold light peek around green boughs and
dance in the dewy grass, and a rich aroma of pine needles fills the air.
Sunrise is a multidimensional phenomenon—on the one hand a triumph
of nature, a complex miracle adhering to the laws of the physical uni-
verse; and on the other hand a delight for the human senses, an exquisite
drama that seems to unfold in a realm of poetry, not science.

Like a sunrise, your career experience is multidimensional. Have you
heard the story of the hotel manager who had problems with an elevator?[2] Although the elevator worked fine, Ben received many complaints
from hotel guests who felt that they were facing unacceptable wait times.
As complaints rose, Ben asked the elevator manufacturer's technician to
take a look. The technician informed Ben that he should install a new,
faster elevator. Facing budget constraints, however, Ben sought a less expensive solution. He mentioned his dilemma to a psychologist friend,
and she visited the hotel for a couple of hours, riding the elevator herself
and observing hotel guests. Afterward, she recommended that Ben hang
a large mirror at each elevator landing. Given the low cost of implementing her suggestion (compared with a new elevator!), he did so right away,
and immediately, to his great delight, complaints decreased markedly.

What's the moral of the story? The way we view situations is critical.
In this case, the least expensive and perfectly effective solution was a human one, not a technical one. A faster elevator (the technical solution)

was unnecessary if hotel guests could be distracted while they waited (the human solution).

A similar technical/human multidimensionality is at work in your professional career. On the one hand, you undoubtedly possess an impressive technical expertise founded on education and training and honed by your apprenticeship in your chosen profession. Your technical skills and knowledge of your profession can take you far. And yet, on the other hand, a toolbox of equally advantageous interpersonal competencies is required to advance to the heights of many professions. And it is there that an introvert is often at a disadvantage.

These two dimensions—technical expertise and human expertise—combine to create the full picture of your career potential. Think of it as a gestalt. With only one component, you are handicapped from achieving your highest aspirations. With both components and some hard work, you can accomplish any goal you choose at the senior levels of your field. Like a sunrise, the whole of your career will be greater than the sum of its parts.

Human expertise (what I sometimes call interpersonal competency) is not learning to make witty small talk. It is mastering the ability to use your quiet competence to get ahead within a community of other people. It involves constructing relationships with integrity and learning to apply your influence strategically.

This guide gives you the "how-to" to understand and develop the human aspects of your professional career, so that those abilities will stand alongside and complement your technical competencies. This is the path to leadership as well if that is your goal.[3] Introverts are often disadvantaged not so much by a lack of skills as by the failure to understand the importance of the human element. They might not know *how* to take advantage of their interpersonal abilities, or they might even erroneously choose not to engage with others at all.

Such failures matter in at least two ways having bottom-line consequences for your career. First, a failure of interpersonal practices can inhibit you from achieving positions of status that come with more pay, prestigious titles, and noteworthy achievement. Studies show that introverts make less money on average than extroverts, receive fewer promotions, and are less likely to end up in leadership roles.[4] Second, and of at least equal importance, is that a failure to leverage your relations with others can mean that you don't get to tackle (and therefore accomplish!) the very sort of professional challenges that create the greatest meaning for you—solving problems, helping clients and patients, building bridges, publishing, launching products, winning cases, and more. A career full of meaning affords a life well-lived.

This book will help you, an Insightful Expert, find your way through the human maze that constitutes the organization within which you work—whether a professional practice or partnership, a corporation, a university, a hospital, a governmental agency, a professional association of your peers, or a private nonprofit—and emerge a winner. You will discover new approaches and learn how to apply concrete strategies that leverage your strengths as an introvert (or simply a shy person).[5] And you will do this not by escaping your introversion, but by building on its unique strengths. In doing so, you will be freed to optimize your professional training and technical ability to *their* highest potential.

The Path from Insightful Expert to Third Eye Expert

This guide is unique in presenting a holistic framework for success that is grounded in established principles from applied behavioral and organization science. What it *doesn't* do is tell you how to masquerade as an extrovert. Rather, it focuses on deepening your understanding of your situation, exploring your options, and showing you how to take a long-term, step-by-step approach to leveraging your career capability at strategic points of influence. The framework is a strategic roadmap to professional success, including leadership.

This perspective breaks down the process of leveraging your professional strengths into three distinct phases, or levels of action, as shown in the diagram, *The Third Eye Framework for Introvert Success in Professional Interactions*: (1) *Create Impetus* by building sustainable relationships; (2) *Structure Interfaces* to manage your interactions; and (3) *Build Your Internal Capabilities* by acquiring and developing interpersonal skills.

> **Impetus.** Building sustainable relationships in organizational and professional settings allows you to create momentum that permanently alters how others perceive you. This requires an understanding of organizational behavior in general and explicit attention to your professional contacts and your organization in particular. This peripheral vision, often overlooked, gives you a valuable grounding and context for the other steps you will take. You can forge lasting bonds with others in a profes-

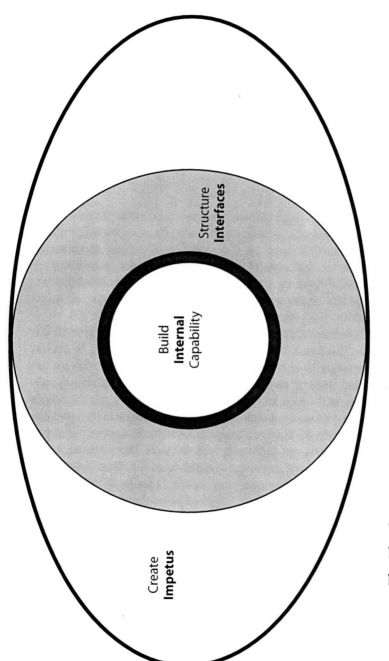

The Third Eye Framework for Introvert Success in Professional Interactions

sional world frequently biased toward extroversion. Trusting, authentic relations built on face-to-face interactions lead to positive perceptions in a way that superficial self-promotion tactics can never do.

The creation of impetus is a long-term endeavor, so it constitutes the outer layer of the model and the first that requires your attention. In this phase you will learn the fundamentals of influencing others from an introvert's perspective, even when you lack formal authority. You'll learn how to leverage your expertise and your unique personal attributes in a mutually beneficial way.

Interfaces. Structuring interfaces focuses on how you can manage your interactions with other individuals to your advantage while remaining genuine. If you fail to take steps to structure situations to match your predispositions as an introvert, they will inevitably be set up to accommodate the personal characteristics and preferences of extroverts instead. That's just a fact of modern professional life.

Your interactions will typically include working with clients (or patients), intraoffice exchanges, supervision of others, participating in meetings and task forces, dealing with an extroverted boss or partner, sales and marketing activities, networking, and more. In short, all of your working relations with others in professional settings constitute interfaces that you can learn to manage. This book explains simple homework that you can do so as always to be prepared for such interactions, and it will show you how to set the ground rules for situations so that they better accommodate your needs as an Insightful Expert. By taking charge of the settings and ways that you engage with others, you set the stage for positive relations. These techniques constitute the intermediate layer of the model.

Internal Capabilities. At the core of the model—though no more important than the outer layers—is the process of building your internal capabilities. The focus of this phase is on fostering your self-confidence, which will arise from and be accompanied by enhanced communication skills, assertiveness, emotional intelligence, leadership, team management ability, networking, and more. You'll learn tactics for how to manage any social anxiety you might experience, and you'll learn how to manage nonverbal messaging and skills. (Did you know that nonverbal signals communicate 60% of our messages?)

Mastery of the Third Eye Framework Transforms You into a Third Eye Expert

The Third Eye Framework for Introvert Success in Professional Interactions is your insight taken to the power of three! Its three elements are complementary lenses on your professional life that have an exponential effect when combined. Your understanding and application of the framework gives you power akin to your Third Eye, the mythical location of extrasensory insight, which is often associated with the pineal gland (which plays a role in your body's response to light). In Chinese medicine, the Third Eye location in the center of your forehead constitutes one of three major power centers, or *dantian*. Your Third Eye will see the gestalt of a situation and tell you how and where to intervene in the professional system within which you work and you will be able to respond. With mastery of the three elements of the Third Eye Framework in your toolkit, you can fully leverage your professional potential and achieve the meaningful challenges and career milestones that you deserve as an Insightful Expert. You will be an Insightful Expert cubed—a Third Eye Expert!

This Book Is Written for You, the Insightful Expert

In Chapter 2 I explain how your status as an Insightful Expert, an introverted professional, creates challenges for you. This will help you see how and why your career is different from others, and how your introversion may have handicapped you. In Chapters 3, 4, and 5 we'll investigate introversion itself. What is it? What does it mean, practically, in its effects on work life? How are we different from extroverts?

Parts II, III, and IV (Chapters 7 through 31) are the heart of the book. These take you in detail through the three main elements of the Third Eye framework, building a strategy for advancing your professional career and improving the quality of your professional life and thus your life as a whole.

In addition, there is a chapter (Chapter 33) on the management of other introverts like you. Even an Insightful Expert can be at a loss when faced with the need to supervise or work with another introvert, including an introverted boss! And Chapters 34 and 35 will help if you happen to need guidance for making an introvert-friendly career choice or exploring a change of professions. Finally, Chapter 36 will describe for you exactly how what you learn here applies if you want to be a leader.

Please know that you *can* do this. As an Insightful Expert, you're bright, capable, and thoughtful. You have within you at this moment all that you need to move forward. The rest is simply a matter of implementing a strategy that shows you where to begin and what to do. Let's get started.

Milestones Along the Journey

Below are a few of the key ideas related to this chapter with a couple extra bullet points for you to fill in. I'd like to hear other ideas that may have resonated for you or were stimulated by what you read. Go to the website www.TheIntrovertsGuide.com to share with me those that have special meaning for *your* personal journey.

- Career and professional success depends on both technical and human expertise.

- The strategic sequential phases of action to build success are: (1) creating impetus for yourself, (2) structuring interfaces, and (3) developing your internal capabilities.

- Mastery of the Third Eye Framework enables you to let quiet competence drive your career success.

- _____

  _____

- _____

  _____

CHAPTER 2

How Being a Professional Creates Challenges for an Insightful Expert

As professionals who are also introverts, Insightful Experts face unique challenges. In a professional job, which often places a premium on teamwork and communication skills, the effects of introversion can be magnified. Further, you may have taken little time while developing your deep technical expertise and focus to work on "corporate" interpersonal skills and self-insight, and you may be deficient in these areas as a result. It's likely that such uses of precious time have held no great attraction for you.

Professional training rarely includes a substantive focus on people skills, much less on how to navigate leadership, manage conflict, or develop political acumen. You can be a crackerjack engineer, programmer, researcher, accountant, physician, or even an executive and lack these abilities. They're simply not part of the curriculum! Yet, as a professional, you face high expectations. As you are likely to have discovered already, when you're good at what you do you're *expected* to manage the people in your office, take charge of project teams, and win new clients, among many other things.

Unique Features of Professions

Researchers in organizational behavior, sociology, and social psychology have studied the roles of professionals in work organizations. Professions and professional careers differ from other jobs in a number of important ways that can create difficulties for you, an introvert.

Careers in a traditional profession such as accounting, engineering, law, or medicine are the most subject to these differences, so if you're in one of those fields, pay special attention to this. Differences include:

- a high degree of autonomy
- high expectations
- a high degree of geographic mobility
- increased opportunity for those who are best able to cultivate mentors and networks

I will explain each of these in turn.

Autonomy. By definition, professional jobs come with autonomy. Because you are highly educated and have undergone extensive training, peer review, and practice in order to enter the ranks of your profession, you are granted exceptional levels of trust and autonomy. Autonomy means the freedom to determine how you accomplish your tasks, and working alone feels comfortable, providing a good fit for your introversion. You enjoy being alone and not being required to consult others frequently (though you may wish to do so on occasion).

If you're like some other introverts, however, you may find that you sometimes feel a paradoxical loneliness. On the one hand, you enjoy autonomy and working alone. On the other hand, because you're an introvert, you may not know how to ask for help when you need it or how to ask for collegial advice when you want that. The job autonomy that comes with being a professional can keep you locked in this conundrum and cause you to miss out on important growth that comes from insights from others.

High Expectations. The high professional expectations placed on you by others can likewise make you miss out on essential interpersonal connections. Professionals are often so busy doing excellent jobs that they fail to surround themselves with social support from others. Introverted or not, we all need human contact and emotional support, in addition to professional advice, that is not conditioned on how well we do our jobs.

Anne is a physician who was embarrassed recently to run into one of her patients at a Weight Watchers™ meeting. Consequently, she now darts in and out quickly for her weekly weigh-in and skips the meeting sessions altogether, missing the important support from the group that research suggests is a large part of the Weight Watchers program's success.

The expectations that others place on professionals can lead you to this kind of loss because you are not as likely as an extrovert to overcome the social distance that professional role expectations can create. Social connections are important not only for the emotional support they provide in the workplace, but also for networks that help lead to career achievement.[1]

Geographic Mobility. The mobility of most professional work can also create challenges. One effect of those long hours as a student was to indoctrinate you in the values of your chosen profession, and that socialization can make you more loyal and committed to the profession than to the particular organization that employs you or even the particular community or region in which you live. As a result—and because most professions can be practiced anywhere—professionals in many fields tend to move a lot in pursuit of career opportunities, especially early in their careers. Moving frequently and switching employers can sever professional as well as personal relationships, although of course it also offers the potential for creating a wider network over time. This rootlessness can bring you, as an introvert, more isolation than serves you best.

Mentoring and Networks. Finally, the intensive education, training, and apprenticeships that prepare one for professional credentialing and work create a strong culture of mentoring and networking. In part because professional work is based on cognitive processes (e.g., diagnosis, innovation, problem solving) that are invisible to an outsider, the support and endorsements of your professional network and mentors may well be critical to opening opportunities and advancing your career.

David is an Insightful Expert who holds a prestigious chaired professorship at a major U.S. university. Yet he struggled in his doctoral studies at two universities before finding, in a third university, a powerful mentor who was well-known in David's field. With this mentor as his advisor, David developed the research skills, the publishing record, and the high-level network that allowed him, through hard work, to achieve his prominent position just over a decade after earning his doctorate.

David's rapid trajectory to the top of his profession speaks to the power of mentors and networks, but the personality traits of an introvert—as discussed in the next chapter—lead you to prefer your "inner-world" work to the work of developing strong interpersonal bonds. This is not to say that mentors and networks are impossible for you, but rather that you must learn how to nurture them and pay explicit attention to doing so.

It should be clear by now that being an Insightful Expert can pose a unique challenge. Professional career success almost always depends on more than technical competence, requiring, in addition, interpersonal abilities to win clients, promotions, partnerships, etc. The autonomy, high expectations, geographic mobility, and emphasis on networking that characterize professional work all intensify the challenge for an Insightful Expert like you. Mentors may never emerge. Close collegial relations can be elusive.

What you learn in this book will help you surmount these challenges. But first, it can be useful to examine the nature of introversion and learn what it means to be an introvert. In the next chapter we'll do just that.

Milestones Along the Journey

Below are a few of the key ideas related to this chapter with a couple extra bullet points for you to fill in. I'd like to hear other ideas that may have resonated for you or were stimulated by what you read. Go to the website www.TheIntrovertsGuide.com to share with me those that have special meaning for *your* personal journey.

- Professional roles pose unique challenges for introverts.

- A mentor and a strong network often are necessary assets for professionals.

- The high expectations that professionals face and the autonomy that they enjoy can be accompanied by isolation and lack of social support.

- _____

  _____

- _____

  _____

CHAPTER 3

What is Introversion?

I have heard so many unflattering comments about introverts that I sometimes wonder, when I admit to being one myself, whether I'll be viewed as if I carry a communicable disease. Such is the bias against introversion, at least in U.S. culture, that confessing to it puts you at risk of being stigmatized.

A ready sense of humor goes a long way toward preventing this, but it's hard to laugh about something that you're not yet comfortable with. To put others at ease, first get comfortable with yourself. You can become more at ease with introversion by developing an understanding of how and why you're different, and that's what I'll discuss in this chapter. But before I do...

Hold the Value Judgments

Being different is a good thing. The Taoist concept of yin and yang recognized long ago that differences are complementary.[1] Yin and yang represent the opposing predispositions and characteristics on a continuum that makes up the whole of life. Yin is more passive and withdrawn, while yang is more active and outgoing. Each is necessary for the completion of the whole. The calendar year includes the cold, dark, enfolding winter as well as the expansive, bright summer, and neither is inherently better.

Chinese philosophy holds that within yin there is yang, and within yang there is yin. No matter which pair of opposites we might have in mind—deliberate or impulsive, thoughtful or heedless, careful or reck-less, fearful or bold—we are never wholly one or the other. We are usu-ally closer to one pole than the other, but never to the complete exclusion of the opposite characteristic. So it is that an extrovert sometimes is quiet and listens, and an introvert in a crowd sometimes laughs aloud with unself-conscious joy.

It is liberating to realize that introversion is merely one side of a nec-essary duality on a continuum of human nature. We introverts are not just okay—we need to be here. I invite you to think about that for a while. As an introvert, you are *essential* to balancing the force of extroversion in your profession and in the world at large. Professional organizations need your perspective, and grasping this can help to give you purpose and needed energy when, for example, you face an important event that you just don't want to attend.

Here's a brief exercise: What thoughts come to mind as you reflect on the idea that one of your purposes is to provide a balance to extroverts? What would happen to your workplace if it contained only extroverts? Record your thoughts below or on a sheet of paper that you can then tuck beside this page.

How Are Introverts Different?

Although you no doubt just "know" that you're different, a better understanding of *how* you are different will help you develop strategies to become more proficient in the human dimensions of your career. Self-insight and awareness are important.

First, what traits do introverts have that extroverts do not? We'll explore this in greater depth later, but briefly, here are a handful of key attributes: If you're an introvert, you tend to enjoy solitude over people and action, you need time to think before responding, and you are quiet. In contrast, an ex-trovert is someone who thrives on social interaction, often talks continu-ously, and takes action without needing a great deal of reflection.

Introversion is a dimension of your personality. Personality is a rela-tively stable set of characteristics that affects how each of us behaves, thinks, and feels. There are said to be more than 1,500 adjectives describ-ing personality, which suggests how large a role personality plays in our lives and how central it is to how we think about ourselves and others.

Personality traits have been conceptualized and assessed in many different ways by psychologists, but introversion is present, albeit sometimes under another name, in nearly all such frameworks. Since psychologist Carl Jung was a forerunner in naming introversion as a distinct trait, I focus here on his approach. Jung, the founder of analytical psychology,[2] first identified the personality dimensions that include introversion and extroversion in his book *Psychological Types,* published in 1921. Since then, these traits have been studied in a wide range of situations and settings.

Jung suggested that people are predisposed by nature and nurture to certain preferences in the ways that they think and reason, and these preferences make up their personal cognitive style. Although introversion and extroversion exist on a continuum, they comprise a core duality in Jung's concept of personality.

In part from observations of children, Jung identified two distinct orientations among people: a subjective orientation and an objective orientation. He noted that introverted children are more cautious, while extroverted children quickly take risks and play freely with objects in their surroundings. Thus, in Jung's conception, the introvert's subjective personality orientation makes him or her a perceiver of the surrounding world. In contrast, an extrovert, according to Jung's notion of an objective orientation, focuses on the outside world without taking time to cognitively process it prior to full engagement. Jung concluded that all people seem to gravitate toward one or the other of these two distinct ways of interacting with the world.

Introverts thrive on privacy and need time to think. Being alone enables them to process their thoughts and emotions more effectively. They are most in touch with their preferences and their feelings when they are away from others. Extroverts, however, revel in contact with other people and in being active.

Another way of conceptualizing Jung's perspective on introversion and extroversion is as preferences for the things that motivate and invigorate us. Introverts tend to become exhausted from large amounts of interaction with others, such as during social events. They are animated by solitude. If you're an introvert, you will feel more rested in quiet and solitude. In stark contrast, extroverts are enlivened by interaction.

Jung wrote that each of us carries each tendency, like the Taoist yin-yang. While he advocated therapy as a means of integrating these disparate sides into a whole person (after all, he was a psychoanalyst), Jung also believed that we function on a continuum of intro/extroversion, adapting best when we can flexibly move back and forth. He called this *ambiversion*. He did *not* advance extroversion as the "healthy" norm. Instead, he regarded either introversion or extroversion as perfectly all right, even though his own notion of the ideal was flexibility.

Further, Jung recognized that we have innate preferences and that it is detrimental to children to push them outside the natural ranges of their temperaments. A great deal of energy can be expended in diverging from one's natural predisposition. Jung believed that simply being aware of the introversion/extroversion continuum can improve our adaptive ability by giving us the *option* to shift our behavior according to circumstances. As you may have discovered for yourself, however, this is usually easier said than done. Although many introverts are capable of acting as if they are extroverts for short periods of time or even only at work, it is exhausting.

Why Are Introverts Different?

The origins of personality are not certain, but there appear to be several influences. Biological makeup and genetic inheritance provide each of us with a baseline of predispositions. The way we are socialized by our families, communities, and national culture influences how and to what extent our biological predispositions are expressed. Finally, we are shaped by our life experiences and situations. All of these influences—and our perceptions of them—lead us to our unique behaviors and personalities.

In recent years, psychologists who study personality have learned that there are physiological differences that distinguish introverts from extroverts. By mapping brain activity, researchers discovered that introverts actually exhibit greater cerebral activity and are more prone to speedy reactions to stimuli from the external world. For this reason, introverts are quickly overstimulated by events that extroverts take in stride. Extroverts' need to talk and be active can even be viewed as a search to attain the levels of stimulation that come naturally to the introverted brain. It's not hard to imagine that in today's fast-paced workplaces, introversion creates a continual and relentless energy drain for workers seeking to shut out what, for them, is an excess of stimulation.

This insight from modern research helps to explain Jung's earlier observations about children. Because the introverted child is more sensitive to stimuli, he is more cautious around people and things. The less aroused extroverted child, however, can more readily explore her environment without forethought.

Cultural Bias Against Introverts

Jung seemed to be on a mission to show that introversion is perfectly healthy and normal. He made the point that while an introvert's behavior, being driven by his or her internal perceptions rather than external reality, might seem idiosyncratic, it is only *perceived* in that way because our culture is extroverted in its orientation. In short, Jung recognized that Western cultures are biased toward objectivity and extroversion.

This bias is no less evident today than it was in Jung's time. Psychologist Colin DeYoung has called it the "cult of extraversion."[3] In this national context, those who are able to express themselves well and boldly are rewarded with accolades such as "energetic," "able to think on his feet," and "possessing an outgoing personality." Employment advertisements routinely seek candidates who display these qualities. It is often deemed odd to stop the action and simply reflect quietly. In this environment, introverts often blame themselves. Surely, they are wont to think, it must be an individual failing that leaves them stammering for words and unable to perform well among strangers! Nearly 100 percent of introverts in one study reported feeling "maligned" for being themselves.[4]

Introverts of Note

It's difficult to be certain, but a number of prominent individuals, both past and present, have been identified as introverts. Past figures include President Abraham Lincoln and Nobel Peace Prize Winner Mother Teresa. Today, President Barack Obama, Secretary of State Hillary Clinton, author J.K. Rowling, entertainer Lady Gaga, Facebook founder Mark Zuckerberg, and Microsoft founders Paul Allen and Bill Gates are all believed to be introverts.

An Introvert's Strengths

In the following chart, I have summarized some of the personal qualities that are strengths of introverts. For contrast, I've also summarized some of the traits that are strong suits for extroverts. Keep in mind that these are *tendencies* based on global personality differences; they do not imply mutual exclusivity.

Introvert strengths are firmly rooted in the arena of thoughtful, quiet competence. Because their engagement is more with mental activities than social interactions, introverts tend to be careful, deliberative, and thoughtful individuals. This does not mean that they are insensitive to those around them; quite the contrary, introverts may be even more sensitive to nuances of behavior and intonation because of their high levels of awareness and keen listening skills. They prefer a slower pace than do extroverts, who are excited by action. The advantage of a slower pace is that it allows time to perform tasks well, avoiding errors that result from hasty completion.

When introverts choose to communicate emotions, they tend to be honest. This, along with trademark careful listening, is an enormous benefit in helping build others' trust in them. Their focus and full engagement with a task is also a crucial professional asset. These strengths—focus, deliberation, thoughtfulness—foster inventiveness and help introverts generate solutions to problems.

As you can see in the chart, extrovert strengths include many interpersonal and communication skills. Easy conversationalists, extroverts tend to be witty, charming, and articulate. They can radiate interpersonal warmth.

Extroverts enjoy being the center of attention. They think out loud and love to talk. They are able to take charge and be totally at ease in nearly any situation involving other people. Comfortable and confident, extroverts gain a lot of energy from being the center of attention and on-stage, whether giving a presentation or networking. Always busy thinking of their next sentence, they are rarely at a loss for words. They tend to be perceived as having high energy and being highly productive because they are so open and effusive. Good on their feet, extroverts are usually quick decision makers, with little patience for slower folks.

Introvert Strengths

- ✓ Attuned to tasks more than social relationships
- ✓ Careful
- ✓ Deliberate and analytical decision maker
- ✓ Diplomatic
- ✓ Does not seek attention without good reason
- ✓ Engages fully with concepts and ideas
- ✓ Expresses written concepts well

- ✓ Fact-finding and research
- ✓ Focused
- ✓ Gives honest endorsements
- ✓ Good listener
- ✓ Independent; neither needs nor wants oversight and constant affirmation
- ✓ Introspective
- ✓ Keenly aware of nuances
- ✓ Maintains confidences and the confidentiality of client and company information
- ✓ Quietly effective
- ✓ Reserved demeanor in professional situations
- ✓ Respectful of others' territory
- ✓ Responsible
- ✓ Succeeds by diligence and hard work, not political gamesmanship
- ✓ Thoughtful

Extrovert Strengths

- ✓ Articulate
- ✓ Attuned to social relationships more than tasks
- ✓ Charismatic
- ✓ Charming
- ✓ Confident presenter
- ✓ Direct and open
- ✓ Displays ready wit
- ✓ Easy conversationalist
- ✓ Enjoys meeting new people
- ✓ Excited by a fast pace
- ✓ Exhibits personal warmth
- ✓ Interpersonally assured
- ✓ Likes gatherings of people and enjoys working closely with others

✓ Persuasive

✓ Quick

✓ Rapid decision maker

✓ Responsive

✓ Thrives with attention and the limelight

✓ Talkative

These sometimes dramatic personality differences between introverts and extroverts can lead to conflict, mutual frustration, and misunderstanding. Psychologist Marti Laney pinpointed several key differences that often lead to misconceptions about introverts[5]:

1. *"Introverts think and talk differently."* Because introverts are less spontaneous, need more time to gather their thoughts, and are not as quick in conversation as extroverts, extroverts tend to assume that introverts are passive and intentionally lacking in forthrightness. This perception of introverts as holding back can lead to damaging assumptions that they are willfully uncooperative.

2. *"Introverts are unseen."* Because the conversational style of an introvert is slower, and because an introvert tends not to interrupt others and is less expressive both in speech and body language, extroverts tend to think that introverts have little to add to a conversation. This leads to an overall discounting of introverts, and they often report feeling "invisible" to others. Blank faces—which often merely mask a lively internal thought process—may lead others to exclude introverts from a conversation.

3. *"Introverts pressure extroverts to stop and think."* Introverts exert their influence to slow down conversations and decisions. This frequently leads to better decisions, but it also deeply frustrates extroverts. They would rather be done and move on to the next thing.

Because the culture is extroverted, as discussed above, the negative brunt of these differences is borne primarily by introverts. Despite the origins of introversion in a necessary duality in a continuum of humanity that is derived from human physiology, introverts end up feeling like misfits, somehow defective. This can lead to even further withdrawal from interactions with others, escalating possible negative career effects. Sadly, both extroverts *and* introverts prefer extroverted leaders and would themselves rather be extroverted![6]

It is this phenomenon of being out-grouped as second class that creates the need for the Third Eye Framework. If it helps you realize your introverted strengths and fully claim them as your own, you can then leverage them to succeed in an extroverted professional world—*without* struggling to become something or someone that you are not—an extrovert.

So far, we've merely been assuming that you're an introvert. In the next chapter, let's examine where *you* are currently on the introversion-extroversion continuum.

Milestones Along the Journey

Below are a few of the key ideas related to this chapter with a couple extra bullet points for you to fill in. I'd like to hear other ideas that may have resonated for you or were stimulated by what you read. Go to the website www.TheIntrovertsGuide.com to share with me those that have special meaning for *your* personal journey.

- Introversion and extroversion are complementary personality differences at two ends of a continuum. Neither is inherently better.

- Introversion and extroversion are rooted in physiological differences.

- Because the dominant Western culture places its highest value on extroversion, introverts are forced to find their own way to thrive within it.

- _____

  _____

- _____

  _____

CHAPTER 4

Introvert or Extrovert?

Now that you know more about introversion, you may be curious to see what point on the introversion/extroversion continuum you inhabit. Are you more introverted than extroverted, or vice versa?

How Introverted Are You?

The questionnaire below will help you assess the degree to which you are an introvert in your social interactions. Introversion also includes your inner world—tapped in more depth in the Introversion at Work Questionnaire that follows this one. Please use the rating scale to describe how accurately each statement describes you. Think of yourself as you generally are *now* in *most* of your interactions, not as you may wish to be in the future. Consider how you are across all areas of your life, not just at work. Please read each statement carefully, and then circle the number that most closely represents the degree to which the statement describes you.

Very Inaccurate	Moderately Inaccurate	Neither Inaccurate Nor Accurate	Moderately Accurate	Very Accurate
1	2	3	4	5

1.   I don't talk a lot.1 2 3 4 5
2.   I keep in the background. 1 2 3 4 5

3.   I have little to say. 1 2 3 4 5
4.   I don't like to draw attention to myself. 1 2 3 4 5
5.   I am quiet around strangers. 1 2 3 4 5
6.   I find it difficult to approach others. 1 2 3 4 5
7.   I often feel uncomfortable around others. 1 2 3 4 5
8.   I bottle up my feelings. 1 2 3 4 5
9.   I am a very private person. 1 2 3 4 5
10.   I wait for others to lead the way. 1 2 3 4 5

Source: International Personality Item Pool, 2008.[1]

Scoring:
Add up your total score. _____

Interpreting your score:
If you scored between 40-50, you are a strong introvert socially.
If you scored 30-40, you are moderately introverted socially.
If you scored less than 30, you may have some strong introvert tendencies, but you also exhibit extroverted behavior.
If you scored 15 or less, are you sure you're not an extrovert? If you're sure you're an introvert, it may be that you are currently in a very comfortable situation that allows you to interact much as an extrovert does.

If these findings don't seem to match what you thought before you took the test, the upcoming questionnaire may provide a better view. You may also want to check your results by taking one of the other common assessments of introversion (discussed on page 239).

Introverted at Work Questionnaire

Now let's consider your work life specifically. Here are additional questions to consider. Answer "yes" or "no" to the following.

_____ Yes _____ No Do people often see you as being aloof or "standoffish?"

_____ Yes _____ No Do you find that you often think of what to say long after the moment has passed?

___ Yes ___ No In meetings, do you find it hard to break into the conversation?

___ Yes ___ No Do you sometimes wish you could go on at greater length about a topic when you are asked for your opinion?

___ Yes ___ No Do you dislike working in an open public area?

___ Yes ___ No Do you resent having to respond or share your work before you've had a chance to fully develop your ideas?

___ Yes ___ No Do you find that you need quiet downtime to be alone when you attend all-day meetings and conferences?

___ Yes ___ No Do you find that others ask you to speak up?

___ Yes ___ No Are you happiest when you work alone?

___ Yes ___ No Do you focus intensely when you're working on a project or listening to a client?

___ Yes ___ No Do you dislike being queried about your work or opinions?

___ Yes ___ No Do you disdain small talk, flattery, and grandiose monologues?

___ Yes ___ No Does it take you time to sort through new information?

___ Yes ___ No Do you notice details that others miss?

___ Yes ___ No Do you find yourself apprehensive when you're under a lot of deadline pressure?

___ Yes ___ No Do you procrastinate on tasks that require you to speak with and interact with others?

___ Yes ___ No Do you avoid using the telephone but instead rely on e-mail as much as you can?

___ Yes ___ No When your work involves working closely with other people, are you drained more than usual at the end of the day?

___ Yes ___ No Do you prefer work that doesn't involve lots of stimulation and excitement?

___ Yes ___ No Do you avoid or dread attending networking events and large gatherings?

___ Yes ___ No Do you want to be a full participant in meetings but find that you are often overlooked?

___ Yes ___ No Do you often keep your thoughts to yourself?

___ Yes ___ No Do you have a very limited number of contacts whom you consider trusted colleagues?

___ Yes ___ No Are you known for your ability to complete tasks and projects?

___ Yes ___ No Are you annoyed by colleagues who seem to say a lot without much substance to back it up?

___ Yes ___ No Do you sometimes withdraw into yourself and let your thoughts wander when you're in a lively professional gathering?

___ Yes ___ No Are you irritated by people who waste time talking rather than accomplishing something tangible?

___ Yes ___ No Do you hate to be interrupted when you are working?

___ Yes ___ No Do you feel that many of those with whom you work don't know you very well?

___ Yes ___ No Is your enthusiasm or commitment ever questioned when you simply have been lost in thought?

___ Yes ___ No Do you find that you often forget someone's name the first time you're introduced?

___ Yes ___ No Do you bring new ideas and approaches to your work?

___ Yes ___ No Are you at your best when your work demands problem solving that you can do on your own?

___ Yes ___ No Do you find that you are trying to think and talk at the same time so that you sometimes stammer over your words or talk more slowly than you would like?

___ Yes ___ No Are you ever exasperated by the expectation to multi-task?

___ Yes ___ No Do you sometimes feel "out of step" with the expectations of all that seems required for professional success?

Scoring:
Add up your total "Yes" responses. _____

Interpreting your score:
If your total is between 28-36, you are a strong introvert.
If your total is 17-27, you are moderately introverted.
If your total is 8-16, you may have some strong introvert tendencies, but you also exhibit extroverted behavior.
If your total is 7 or less, are you sure you're not an extrovert?

A "yes" response to these questions indicates introverted tendencies. The more of these that you checked "yes," the more introverted you are. You're not alone. There are many other introverts like you who experience some of the same things in *their* professional lives. Your personality is not a weakness, even though it may seem that way at times. You have many strengths—even in an extroverted work culture.

How Extroverted Are You?

Now, just for the fun of it, let's see how extroverted you are in your social interactions. Below are phrases describing people's behaviors. Please use the rating scale to describe how accurately each statement describes you. Think of yourself as you generally are *now* in *most* of your interactions, not as you may wish to be in the future. Consider how you are across all areas of your life, not just at work. Please read each statement carefully, then circle the number that most closely represents the degree to which the statement describes you.

Very Inaccurate	Moderately Inaccurate	Neither Inaccurate Nor Accurate	Moderately Accurate	Very Accurate
1	2	3	4	5

1. I am the life of the party. 1 2 3 4 5
2. I feel comfortable around people. 1 2 3 4 5
3. I start conversations. 1 2 3 4 5
4. I talk to a lot of different people at parties. 1 2 3 4 5
5. I don't mind being the center of attention. 1 2 3 4 5
6. I make friends easily. 1 2 3 4 5
7. I take charge. 1 2 3 4 5
8. I know how to captivate people. 1 2 3 4 5
9. I feel at ease with people. 1 2 3 4 5
10. I am skilled in handling social situations. 1 2 3 4 5

Source: International Personality Item Pool, 2008.[2]

Scoring:
Add up your total score. _____

Interpreting your score:
If you scored between 40-50, you are a strong extrovert.
If you scored 30-40, you are moderately extroverted.
If you scored less than 30, you may have some strong extrovert tendencies, but you also exhibit introverted behavior.
If you scored 15 or less, you may be more of an introvert than an extrovert.

Higher scores on this assessment indicate greater degrees of extroversion. Can an introvert score highly on it? Yes, because the items measure beliefs, feelings, and behaviors. Some introverts have *learned* how to be comfortable in situations where they might not otherwise be at ease, and some introverts have developed the skills of appearing and behaving like an extrovert. Such responses are consistent with Carl Jung's ideal of flexible movement along the introversion/extroversion continuum, i.e., ambiversion, as discussed in Chapter 3. There are two situations in which this typically occurs. One is when an introvert feels particularly comfortable with his or her companions. For example, within your nuclear family you probably talk as much and as animatedly as any extrovert. Many introverts are very much at ease within their families, with charismatic personalities, and this comes naturally. The second situation in which an introvert might behave like an extrovert is when forced to do so in order to thrive. Because of this, many introverts behave like extroverts when they are at work.

Here's an example. An information technology executive revealed to me that he does not experience many of the issues that plague other introverts, such as feeling unseen and unheard. Our subsequent conversation uncovered that early in his career he learned that he had to *act as if* he was an extrovert in order to get ahead. He has done so successfully for the past 40 years. His repetition of the role of extrovert led him over time to be comfortable in that role, just like an actor mastering a theatrical part. For him, it has worked exceedingly well.

Many other introverts, however, are likely to discover that, even if they can act like extroverts, the effort exacts a tremendous toll of exhaustion at the end of each day. Acting can also lead to a sense of lost meaning in one's work, as if your genuine self is not only devalued but somehow lost. Some people end up asking, "Is this all there is?" with respect to their careers, because their habitual acting divorces them from what makes them unique. Their diminished contribution reduces their ability to make an impact. Rather than bringing their highest selves to their work, they are forced to play a part that allows only a segment of their genuine competence—their Insightful Expert competence—to come forth and shine.

You're reading this book because you're really most interested in how your introversion affects your profession and your work. Now that we've settled which you are—introvert or extrovert—let's examine the additional evidence that has been discovered about introversion at work.

Milestones Along the Journey

Below are a few of the key ideas related to this chapter with a couple extra bullet points for you to fill in. I'd like to hear other ideas that may have resonated for you or were stimulated by what you read. Go to the website www.TheIntrovertsGuide.com to share with me those that have special meaning for *your* personal journey.

- Introverts tend to be quiet, private people who frequently avoid interaction with others.

- Extroverts tend to be talkative, friendly people who are socially skilled and at ease around others.

- In situations where they are extremely comfortable, introverts will be virtually indistinguishable from extroverts.

- Introverts can learn to behave like extroverts at work, but if it is not comfortable, it usually comes at a high cost.

- _____

  _____

- _____

  _____

CHAPTER 5

Introversion
in the Professional Workplace

I f you want to rise to or reside at the top of your organization, being an introvert stacks the odds against you. Consider that an astonishing two-thirds (65%) of top managers believe that introversion is an obstacle to corporate advancement.[1] In fact, just 6% say that introverts make better chief executive officers (CEOs), whereas nearly half (47%) of the 1,542 managers who responded to an informal survey for *USA Today* think that extroverts make better CEOs.[2]

In order to better understand the issues that Insightful Experts face, let's examine the known facts about introversion-extroversion dynamics in the professional workplace, including how the fundamental characteristics of organizations themselves can be biased against introverts. *Warning: The following discussion may be a little dry for some readers. If it's not your cup of tea, skip to the next chapter.*

The Dynamics of Introversion and Extroversion

In this section we'll review some of the most interesting research on the dynamics of introversion and extroversion with respect to career and work. Although data are not available for all professions, introverts outnumber extroverts in some better-known professional groups, including accountants (63%), engineers (62%), lawyers (59%), software engineers (57%), university faculty (55%), and doctors (53%). In contrast, other occupations such as management consultants (42%), human resources personnel (41%), top executives (40%), and life insurance agents (26%) are predominantly extroverted,[3] as are college students (43%).[4] Whether or not introverts are in the majority, however, if you are one, you face a set of common issues.

Imposters? Introversion has been shown in a number of studies to be associated with the imposter phenomenon.[5] First identified by researchers Pauline Rose Clance and S.A. Imes, the *imposter phenomenon* is the belief that one's success is not due to one's actual ability. Instead, you might feel that it's due just to hard work, luck, or a boss not seeing you for who you really are. The imposter phenomenon was first identified in groups that included professionals and college students who just could not see themselves as having earned the achievements they had attained. In short, the imposter phenomenon makes someone feel like a fraud. Clance and Imes claim that an introvert's focus on his or her inner world of experience may lead to a separation from what happens in the outside world, in essence causing low self-confidence. The imposter phenomenon can cause you to forgo opportunities you've earned.

Communication Preferences. The preferences of introverts for solitude and reduced communication with others can affect workplace relationships. A study of British physicians revealed that they were more introverted than the general population, and this was especially true of male physicians. Because patient complaints center around communication rather than professional competencies, the study's authors recommended that communication training be given to help bridge this gap.

While introverts' communication styles typically include briefer sentences, a quiet voice, and pauses, an extroverted style is much louder, more extended, and more prone to interrupting others.[6] It's important to differentiate between *adapting* to another style and *adopting* another style. Although it would be *un*desirable for introverts to take on the attributes of extroverts, especially in a helping relationship such as medicine, increasing their awareness of alternative styles and the possibilities for miscommunication could allow them to communicate more effectively.

Communication preferences and styles are central to group and team work in organizations. Teamwork skills, including communication, can be developed in the formal education of professionals, often in cooperative learning exercises. It's not surprising, however, that introverted accounting students show less preference for cooperative learning in college than extroverts.[7]

Attractive Situations. Similarly, research suggests that introverted job seekers are more attracted to organizational cultures that are supportive and in which information is shared and good performance receives praise. In contrast, extroverts are attracted to organizational cultures displaying a strong collaborative team orientation.[8] Apparently, introverts display their inclination for self-sufficiency and solitude by avoiding workplace situations that require a lot of teamwork. What is not clear from the available studies is whether working in *established* teams—in which relationships have been forged over time (and consequently where introverts might feel more at ease)—is equally as distasteful to introverts.

Electronic Meetings. The responses of introverts and extroverts to electronically supported meetings have likewise been examined,[9] and the results suggest that higher levels of participation and a more egalitarian distribution of opportunities for participation emerge from computer-dependent communications. Despite their discomfort with group communications, introverts appear to prefer a computerized platform to face-to-face meetings as a way to contribute to a discussion. All participants, both introverts and extroverts, produce more innovative solutions in a computer-mediated meeting. *It is possible that synergy emerging from the increased comfort and participation of introverts in the electronic setting is one of the reasons why overall innovation goes up.*

Job-Related Behaviors. In more general job-related behaviors, some extroverts tend to be more self-interested than introverts, less frequently helping others or simply getting along well with others in organizations.[10] Henry Moon and his colleagues systematically reviewed the scholarly literature and identified studies relating extroversion to higher levels of turnover, absenteeism, and lack of consistent effort at work. Still other studies link extroversion to better career decision-making capability and greater efficacy in job searches, interviewing, networking, and so forth. Obviously these are all necessary skills if one is changing jobs more frequently than average, as extroverts appear to do.

Performance and Rewards. A selective review of the vocational literature on personality revealed that higher levels of extroversion predict better performance in roles that require interpersonal skills, such as managers, salespeople, and police.[11, 12] Related research shows that extroversion predicts better performance at sales than introversion when explicit rewards are offered.[13] This result supports the theory[14] that extroverts favor external, material rewards such as pay and promotion, whereas an introvert's performance is driven more by intrinsic satisfaction with the work.

Increasingly, studies of psychology in the workplace show that it is a combination of personality traits rather than any one trait in isolation that leads to better job performance. For example, a study of health and fitness center employees (including many in sales/customer service roles that required interpersonal interaction) revealed that extroversion alone had no effect on performance, but employees who were both extroverted and emotionally stable performed better according to their supervisors' ratings.[15] Someone with this constellation of traits might be described as enthusiastic and happy, and a positive mood is associated (in the research literature) with a range of behaviors such as cooperation, motivation, a high energy level, and likability.

Even more revealing is that across a spectrum of jobs, and unrelated to the types of rewards, conscientiousness is more often associated with high levels of performance on the job. Conscientiousness is also related to finding a job. Even though extroversion is closely associated with many of the *activities* in a successful job hunt (e.g., setting goals, planning, and analyzing personal skills and performance), conscientiousness—which appears unrelated to the introversion/extroversion continuum—has been shown to have a direct effect on the number of job offers an applicant receives.[16] This shows that, in the end, even though extroversion would appear to be an asset, it is not the final determinant of success in landing a job any more than it determines success on the job.

Hiring Preferences. Putting actual performance aside for the moment, it is interesting to note differences in hiring preferences among a couple of professional roles. In a study of managers' personnel decisions involving applicants for positions, extroversion was deemed an important personality characteristic for sales agents but not for nurses, a job that also necessitates a high degree of personal interaction.[17] This suggests that there is indeed a hiring bias, not necessarily embedded in actual performance, toward hiring extroverts in business-related roles, a bias that does not appear to function in social service hiring.[18]

The Introverted Leader

Because Insightful Experts often take on or aspire to leadership roles that flow naturally from their professional roles, it seems especially relevant to be aware of what research has revealed about introversion among those in upper management and executive positions. In fact, it's often when professionals transition to leadership roles that introversion comes to be perceived as a handicap rather than the asset that it was to reach that point. The new demands of dealing with direct reports, high-level executives, or boards of directors, and/or the increased pressure to acquire new clients, can strain an introvert's energy reserves and interpersonal capabilities. Being human, we like to avoid what we don't like to do!

Higher-level managers appear to show a greater tendency toward extroversion,[19] though the actual incidence seems to vary widely, depending on the setting. In a review of existing studies, researchers William Gardner and Mark Martinko reported a range of extroversion in top managers from 77% for executive educators to 66% for other executives. We don't know whether this is because extroverts are more likely to be hired for managerial positions or, alternatively, whether introverts withhold themselves from upper-management applicant pools. Given the belief of top managers that introversion is a management handicap, however, it is likely that there is some preference shown for extroverts in leadership selection processes—i.e., recruitment, interviewing, and hiring decisions.

Executive Communication. In a striking testament to the power of the business norms that sanction extroversion, a study of Fortune 1000 executives suggests that many introverts adapt their natural style of communication to match workplace expectations for extroversion. At home, 72% were extroverts and 28% introverts. But a surprising 88% of survey respondents reported *more* extroverted communication in the workplace. Just 5% were equally introverted at work and at home. Communications expert Edward Brewer, author of the study, interpreted his results as support for the proposition that one must be extroverted to succeed as an executive, with the burden for adaptation on the introvert.[20]

Charisma and Performance. Some prominent contemporary views of leadership focus on leaders as inspirational figures. According to this thinking, charismatic leaders influence their followers by expressing a vision for a better future, demonstrating a willingness to take personal risks, responding to followers' needs, and acting in ways that are perceived as unconventional.[21] Martin Luther King, Jr.'s leadership in the American civil rights movement, for example, was widely acknowledged as charismatic. Nevertheless, the common belief that charismatic leaders are more effective is not supported by objective measures of company performance.[22]

One possible explanation for this is offered by research showing that CEOs of large companies are not much involved in the day-to-day running of their businesses. Instead, they focus on analysis of divisional performance and reallocation of resources. The advantages of charisma—whatever they may be—make little difference to a CEO who seldom interacts with or is visible to others in the organization.

Further, a study of charismatic leaders among early to mid-career managers revealed that although extroversion is correlated with charisma,[23] a proactive personality is more important than extroversion for predicting a superior's perceptions of one's charismatic leadership quotient.[24] A proactive person takes initiative to influence his or her environment. Although it may come more naturally to extroverts, both introverts and extroverts can be proactive.

Despite a prevalence of extroverts at the top of the managerial hierarchy in many organizations, leaders with extroverted qualities may perform no better than introverts after all.

Virtual Team Leadership. Another study of leadership compared the effects of team members' introversion and extroversion in virtual team settings with traditional face-to-face settings. Within the virtual teams, unlike traditional settings, the extroverts were not perceived as being the leaders.[25] Instead, members' levels of *participation* and their *written contributions* were most closely associated with perceptions of their leadership in the virtual teams. As with the ability to take initiative, these inputs seem well within the reach of most introverts, who typically are at ease in an online environment.

Behavior Differences. In other research, no major differences have been found between introverted and extroverted senior managers' behaviors. Behaviors examined include relationship management, provision of feedback, inventiveness, ethical behavior, strategic thinking, overall effectiveness, and customer focus.[26] Among minor differences, extroverts tend to rate themselves more highly than they are rated by others. Additionally, introverts are perceived by their peers to be more ethical managers than extroverts. Introverted managers also appear to spend

THE INTROVERT'S GUIDE TO PROFESSIONAL SUCCESS   45

more time on problem solving and less time on socializing and politick-ing than extroverts.[27]

Similarly, project managers' success is unrelated to their degree of extroversion.[28] In contrast, unrelated personality traits such as conscientiousness and openness *do* affect their success.

Clearly, introverts bring qualities to managerial roles that are valuable to their organizations, despite the popular perception that introversion is a liability when moving up to higher levels of management, and despite the challenges that introverts themselves may experience as they adjust to their new roles. In fact, because there are so few major differences in actual behaviors, management expert Seth Berr and his colleagues caution against bias toward either introverts or extroverts in managerial roles.[29] Specific attributes of extroversion, such as assertiveness and easy social skills, produce complex, sometimes conflicting outcomes[30] and further support the premise that sweeping generalizations are unwarranted.

Management expert Brad Agle and his colleagues reached conclusions similar to Berr's about selection criteria that value qualities related to extroversion (such as charisma): "—[T]he long-term corroborating evidence from objectively assessed CEO performance suggests that the search for charismatic CEOs may be based more on implicit theory or halo effects than on solid evidence that charisma really does make CEOs more effective."[31]

Executive Development. Some executive-level management positions include high levels of social interaction that are easier for extroverts to navigate because of their natural predispositions. However, companies can take developmental steps to ensure that introverts do equally well in those roles. A study of new executives revealed that introverts with strong relationships with their supervising senior executives had higher-rated job performance and showed less inclination to leave (i.e., lower turnover) than those who lacked the benefit of a close relationship with their boss. In a striking statement, the researchers concluded that, "for an introverted executive, a [strong relationship with his or her superior] seems *essential* for success"[32] (emphasis added).

This finding supports the approach recommended in The Third Eye Framework (see, for example, Chapter 16).

Career Outcomes

Despite the evidence that introverts perform just as well as extroverts in most professional roles, the deck seems stacked in favor of extroverts in Western organizations. Extroversion correlates with career success as measured by higher salaries, promotions, higher-status jobs, overall career satisfaction, and job satisfaction.[33, 34, 35, 36, 37]

While the mechanisms by which this occurs have not been fully studied, some current research suggests that it may be due to extroverts' highly developed social skills and predisposition for socializing. These provide them with higher visibility as well as expanded influence over others as a result of the relationships they build. The active orientation that many extroverts take also is believed to help them find a viable fit between their career goals and talents and an employer's needs. In addition, extroversion is related to traits such as dominance that are associated with leadership[38] in Western cultures. Our unconscious assumptions about how leaders should behave predispose us to see a leader in an extrovert.

Additional research into the workplace effects of introversion for professionals would be useful. Management experts Gardner and Martinko write that despite pervasive attention to the introversion/extroversion dimension of personality in the field of psychology, "*Management researchers…have virtually ignored it*"[39] (emphasis added). Others have echoed their conclusion.[40] It is in the management literature that we would expect to find studies of the career dynamics of many high-aspiring introverts—i.e., Insightful Experts—who assume leadership roles in their organizations—and there is precious little there.[41]

Challenges Faced by Introverts: Anecdotal Evidence

The challenge posed by introversion in career situations is a vibrant topic in online social and information-exchange forums. The discussions suggest that introverts often struggle to find their place in an extrovert-friendly business culture. Comments like these are not uncommon:

> *It's just such an introvert-unfriendly place out there in the work world. To have an introvert-friendly job that you enjoy, that you look forward to each day, is priceless.*

It's easier to define yourself by your job, if you're an extrovert in an extrovert world, because the workplace is such an extrovert invention, most of the time.

I was part of a different list, also introverts, and one of the most common repeating threads was "what kind of career is good for an introvert" and oh my how they obsessed over this. So many people are unhappy with their careers.

When people think you're quiet, they think you're weak and that people can run over you.

An informal, unscientific survey of working professionals that I conducted among people visiting my website confirmed some common difficulties. (It is important to keep in mind that respondents self-selected, so there is no assurance that they represent all Insightful Experts. We also don't know their individual professions, their career stages, or their current organizational levels and positions.) I asked, "Frequently, introverts face challenges in their professional lives. To what extent are the following issues a challenge for you personally?" In descending order, the most challenging issues reported by the introverts who responded are:

✓ Networking events
✓ Acquiring political power in my organization to get things done
✓ Finding a role that fits my personality
✓ Building a strong professional network
✓ Being recognized for my accomplishments
✓ Advancing in my career
✓ Having energy for my professional interactions

Networking events, acquiring power, and building a strong network are all related to interacting with others in ways that benefit introverts. Being recognized for accomplishments and career advancement are closely related to these. Without strong relationships built on personal power and carefully constructed networks, it is difficult to advance in a profession. (The Third Eye Framework addresses these issues on many fronts, but especially with its first step, *Create Impetus by building sustainable relationships.)* Finding a role or career path that is introvert-friendly reflects the extroverted work culture that introverts confront.

This issue is closely related to the survey respondents' difficulty in maintaining sufficient energy to deal with their professional interactions with others. Energy is difficult to sustain when your role forces you to behave in more extroverted ways.

Organization Design and Culture

Because the ways in which people behave are a function not only of who they are but also of the situations they are in, it's important to focus on the workplace itself in our considerations of introversion at work. The settings and organizations in which introverts work affect how introversion is received and whether it is sanctioned. Many organizations, though certainly not all, have fundamental norms and structures that are antithetical to introverted preferences for quiet introspection, time to reflect carefully, and reserved approaches that allow for second thoughts.

Instead of an introverted approach, most modern Western business culture is isomorphic with the broader Western social culture, which emphasizes decisive leadership, rational decision making, and thinking on one's feet. This outwardly directed, brazen style is more characteristic of extroversion than introversion. It has evolved historically from traditional bureaucracies such as the military. Classic business models that idealize organizations as top-down bureaucracies in which leadership entails simply planning, organizing, and controlling[42] replicate this extroverted pattern for business and organizational life. These blueprints for organizing and leading pervade mainstream management thought and are apparent in all sectors of the economy, including many non-profits and governments.

Although the dominant paradigm appears to be slowly shifting to flatter, more fluid, network-oriented organizational structures, the top-down organization continues to dominate. When I ask groups of thirty or more professionals if they work in a loosely structured network organization, just one or two raise their hands. Introverted, reflective ways of interacting are shunned in most organizations in favor of rapid, decisive action, where decisions flow downward and information flows upward. Often only very small and entrepreneurial businesses and true professional partnerships are exceptions. In short, the very design of Western business organizations establishes a bias against introverted behaviors and, consequently, Insightful Experts.

These basic rules for interaction inherent in organizational design are also the most fundamental influences and artifacts of the corporate culture. They establish the norms for working and communicating with others to accomplish goals. Norms for rapid thought and decisions disadvantage introverts from the start, because they fly in the face of evidence suggesting that introverts' physiological processes simply are not wired for instantaneous certainty.[43] What's more, extroverted norms are so pervasive that even smaller organizations, such as professional practices, struggle to balance collegial collaboration against clear "take-charge" solutions. *It's no wonder that, as an Insightful Expert, you may feel that achieving a position of greater influence and career perks demands something beyond your current capability.*

One of the contradictions that can be seen in the research evidence is that some introverts avoid collaborative situations (for example, college students who avoid cooperative learning and job seekers who avoid strongly collaborative organizational cultures), yet it is in network organization designs and collaborative cultures that introverts have the greatest opportunity to be heard. An understanding of the power dynamics that underlie organization design sheds insight on this. In a bureaucratic organization (i.e., an extroverted culture), the fundamental basis of power is in legitimate authority, the leverage that comes from one's formal position in the hierarchy. But in a networked, collaborative organization (i.e., more introvert-friendly), the fundamental basis of power lies in *expertise and personal relationships*, not someone's formal position.[44] Things get done and decisions are made on the basis of competence and ability to communicate ideas in a way that others understand rather than by edict.

Collaboration requires many things: self-confidence, communication skills, conflict management skills, and others, all of which can be challenging if you just want to retreat from people into your rich inner world. Some introverts may find bureaucracies more comfortable because there they need not put forth the energy to collaborate interpersonally to get things done. (Collaboration requires more energy of an introvert than an extrovert because of the nature of introversion.) A bureaucracy can allow some introverts to retire to the metaphorical cubicle and just do their jobs.

Ironically, career advancement is more likely to the extent that an Insightful Expert can demonstrate a broader range of competencies, something that is likely to be easier in a collaborative environment, but only *after it becomes familiar and he/she learns how to thrive within it.* Collaborative organizations, such as a long-standing team, can become more comfortable over time. Yet some introverts, perhaps lacking the tools and the belief that they can prosper there, avoid such situations rather than giving themselves time to settle in and be at home.

Implementation of the Third Eye Framework will provide the capabilities needed to engage fully in a networked, collaborative environment. No small part of this is the development of power and influence founded on expertise, quiet competence, and one-on-one relationships. While the natural tendency of an introvert is to retreat, retreat seldom leads to achievement of the career milestones that many Insightful Experts want.

Implications

Evidence from the applied research literature, combined with anecdotal reports and a deeper understanding of organization design, suggests that introverts in professional and managerial roles can face significant obstacles to career ascendancy. They report less satisfaction, gain fewer promotions, and have lower salaries than extroverts. There is a pervasive bias against introversion and a popular stereotype that extroverts make better leaders—a stereotype that is largely unsupported by hard data. The odds are further stacked against introverts by organizational cultures and structures that favor extroverted behavior. Yet there is little evidence that introverts perform any less effectively than extroverts when objective behaviors and measures of performance are considered.

Foremost among the challenges that introverts face is building strong relationships with others, especially extroverts. Unless they find mentors and advocates who believe in and promote their leadership capabilities, introverted professionals can find it difficult to advance their careers within and beyond technical roles. Relationships are highly relevant to career advancement.[45] One bright spot for introverts is the increase in virtual communications currently underway; this is a setting in which Insightful Experts can do well, building on the quiet strengths of introversion.

Adrift in a business culture that reveres extroversion, some introverts also lack self-confidence and self-efficacy, the belief that they can succeed. The imposter phenomenon is an example of this. Resultant feelings of inadequacy may lead them to forego career opportunities. Some may also avoid social situations that produce anxiety (e.g., networking), further solidifying their sense of being outsiders who are incapable of ascending to upper-level positions. Increased self-efficacy in professional situations can also help introverts better manage their energy by being more assertive about their needs for space and time alone.

Some introverts fail to polish their professional communication and interpersonal skills. While introverts need not mimic extroverted communication styles, better management of their communication, physical presence, and conflict management abilities could enhance interactions and dispel some misperceptions. As with self-confidence, development of these skills can also diminish stress and anxiety and help introverts conserve and replenish the energy that social interactions otherwise drain from them. Introverts sometimes experience communication apprehension,[46] related to what career specialists call "negative career thinking."[47]

This chapter reviewed evidence on how your introversion may affect your experience in the workplace. The Third Eye Framework is designed to address many of these issues and to help you develop the strategy you need to achieve professional success. It's time to move on to how you can take action to overcome some of the obstacles we've uncovered so that you can achieve *your* goals. That comes next.

Milestones Along the Journey

Below are a few of the key ideas related to this chapter with a couple extra bullet points for you to fill in. I'd like to hear other ideas that may have resonated for you or were stimulated by what you read. Go to the website www.TheIntrovertsGuide.com to share with me those that have special meaning for *your* personal journey.

- Extroversion is associated with higher levels of career success in the form of salary, promotions, high status jobs, career satisfaction, and job satisfaction.

- The popular stereotype that extroverts make better leaders does not appear to be supported by hard data.

- _____

  _____

- _____

  _____

CHAPTER 6

The Third Eye Framework: A Strategic Roadmap to Professional Success

R ealizing that you're an introvert—as you've already done—and work-ing with your introversion to build your professional success are two different things. You wouldn't go to a conference without knowing its location, planned program, and speakers. Similarly, it makes little sense to try to learn how to succeed as an Insightful Expert on the basis of random tips. The Third Eye framework is an organized approach. It pro-vides you with a process that is logical, strategic, committed to long-term authentic changes, and grounded in your unique professional situation.

Dual purpose, this process applies whether you aspire to leadership roles or simply to attain your highest potential in the practice of your chosen profession.

Just as an academic program coheres around a curriculum that builds on itself sequentially, your program of self-development will also benefit from an organized and logical approach. Which actions should you do first? Second? What will provide the biggest payoff given your present situation? How do you get started? Describing a big picture and a plan can help you budget your energy and time in a way that is wise, and even more important, strategic.

Because the changes you'll make require effort and time, a strategic approach can help you apply your energies to critical points of leverage—inflection points—timing them to your greatest advantage. The word strategy derives from the Greek word *strategia,* referring to the plans of generals during war. Strategic action requires advance planning and iterative reassessment of your progress. What's more, if you're interested in long-term success over the remainder of your career, you want more than short-term tactics. You want new and authentic ways of interacting with others that enable you to build your ideal career on the foundation of your values and hard-won expertise.

The three-step Third Eye framework ensures that the changes you make to leverage your Insightful Expert potential are more than superficial. Experience with human and organizational change tells us that real and lasting change rarely happens overnight. Kurt Lewin, a social scientist and expert on change in organizational settings, showed that we first have to unfreeze past behaviors, then learn new ones during a time of flux, and then finally cement into place or "refreeze" those new ways of being and interacting with others. A successful change effort requires each of these phases. Real change in your behavior and in the ways that others perceive and interact with you (i.e., *their* behavior) is not amenable to a quick fix.

As a lifelong introvert, you are likely to find—when you begin to alter how you work and interact with others in a professional setting to make more prominent use of your introverted strengths—that it takes time for others to notice and to begin to behave differently toward you. You *may* see a difference in days, but it could take weeks or even months. You may also require some trial and error to find the approaches that work best in your situation. Change *will* happen, but it won't always be immediate. You must have faith and stick with it.

Todd works in a nonprofit with several other professionals, all of whom are extroverts. In a prior position in a large company, he managed a hundred employees and reported to an introverted vice president. His experience as an introvert in the two situations has been vastly different. In his prior position, where his introversion was supported by his boss, he was a rising star who simply had the challenge of developing a stronger network to build his career for the long haul. Among the extroverts in his current job, he constantly struggles to be heard, rewarded, and to get growth assignments. In either situation, Todd can apply the Third Eye Framework to get results by changing his emphasis slightly.

By taking your professional milieu into account, you can choose actions that unfold within your day-to-day routines in a way that best accomplishes your aims. Each workplace is dynamic and unique as a result of its resident variety of individuals and groups with differing expectations, values, and goals.

The open nature of the Third Eye framework incorporates the simple idea that you depend on this context—your professional environment—for resources (e.g., help from others, promotions, new clients, etc.), and that your behavior must satisfy the standards and desires of those on whom you depend. So, for example, if you wish to make partner in your firm, your performance, both technically and interpersonally, must meet the explicit and implicit criteria for achieving that rank that are operative in your firm.

In Part II of this book, you will learn how to create impetus for yourself as an Insightful Expert. Because this approach is not a quick fix, it's important to develop a preliminary career development strategy before proceeding. Your will begin by formulating a plan. But before we do that, let's examine what the Impetus portion of the model is all about.

Begin with Impetus

The word impetus originally meant to attack, to generate force, and to use passion and vigor.[1] Impetus is momentum toward your goals. It is the first layer of the Third Eye Framework—the critical beginning that sets the changes you are undertaking to achieve professional success in motion for you. While its capstone is the creation of sustainable relationships, in order to get to that point you must first take a series of important steps. Here is an overview of the journey you are embarking on during this phase.

Develop Your Plan. You will begin by initiating the construction of a personal strategic career plan (Chapter 7). Your plan will identify your vision of success, your goals, your strengths and weaknesses, and a strategic analysis of your opportunities and the factors that threaten your success. With this in hand, you can begin to strategize ways to accomplish your goals as you follow the subsequent chapters in this book. Your professional development plan is pivotal to the Third Eye Framework. You should come back to it again and again, modifying it as progress toward your goals evolves.

How Planned Change Happens and Muster Courage to Take Action. In Chapter 8, you will learn more about how the change process that you are undertaking works. By knowing what to expect you are better prepared to overcome setbacks. Mustering courage to take actions that may be unfamiliar to you comes next in Chapter 9. Instead of affirmations that accent the positive, you will learn a different approach to staying on track with your career development.

Values = Meaning (and Motivation). Next a big surge in impetus comes from contemplation of your values (Chapter 10). Surfacing our most closely held preferred ways of being in the world is like rocket fuel to guide our behavior—a potent source of energy. The career change that you undertake with the Third Eye Framework works because it is connected to your values—how you want to live your life. Once identified, these values can be used to return to the work you did for Chapter 7 and reorient and revise your strategic career plan.

Raise Your Self-Awareness. Self-awareness is crucial to optimizing your career. Without knowing how you come across to others, especially as your introversion is perceived by others—both extrovert and introvert— you don't know what you are doing well, much less where you may be going astray in your day-to-day interactions at work! By beginning to become more aware of the human dimension in your professional interactions, you begin to move toward your goals.

From Experience Comes Confidence. This movement toward goals will be accelerated as you take action. Your experiences with the human side of your professional career—in light of your new knowledge and your plan—will build your confidence to *continue* moving forward. This is outlined in Chapter 12.

No Longer Hidden and Blind: Self-Disclosure as a Path to Connection. In Chapters 13 and 14, you learn how to begin taking concrete steps to modify your interactions with others. To this point, you will have been focusing on a lot of internal work—planning, learning, thinking about values, assessing interactions and so forth. But now, you will begin to create momentum for your career changes for the better by gradually changing how you interact with those around you. As an Insightful Expert, you tend to be a private person and that need not change. But beginning to connect with others by doing just slightly more self-disclosure is a path to building the strong relationships that will lead to career success.

Emotional Intelligence: The Insightful Expert's Secret Tool. The process of connecting with others is accelerated by developing your emotional intelligence (EI) and applying it in your daily professional dealings.

Get to Specifics: Identify and Target Your Stakeholders. With the "baby" steps in place, you will learn to further elaborate on your strategic career plan by identifying your stakeholders (Chapter 15). This is the last piece needed to move to the final and most important phase of creating impetus for yourself and building sustainable relationships—exercising your power and influence with others.

Learn to Exercise Your Power and Influence Others. This is the culmination of the creation of impetus for your career changes. With what you learn in this chapter, *you apply what you have learned and you explicitly use your introversion as your distinctive competence!* It is only possible to begin to influence others after you have: (1) decided what you want and how you wish to proceed (your values and plan), (2) understood the process, (3) evaluated how you're currently doing (your self-awareness), (4) gathered courage and gained some experience, (5) become open and attuned to developing stronger relationships (self-disclosure and EI), and (6) targeted *with whom* you need to have strong relationships (stakeholders). With this final step that you learn in Chapter 16, your momentum is at full sail. The relationships that you develop provide a network of human support for your other efforts.

With all of the steps to create impetus in place, you will be well on your way to achieving your goals. With just a few subtle changes and a good plan, you will be poised to move to the next phase of the Third Eye Framework, structuring your interfaces. *Now* we are ready to begin!

Milestones Along the Journey

Below are a few of the key ideas related to this chapter with a couple extra bullet points for you to fill in. I'd like to hear other ideas that may have resonated for you or were stimulated by what you read. Go to the

website www.TheIntrovertsGuide.com to share with me those that have special meaning for *your* personal journey.

- The Third Eye Framework is an approach that focuses on long run career success through the creation of a social context where your introversion can thrive.

- Efforts to attain professional goals work best when they are tailored to your unique situation.

- Substantive change takes time.

- Momentum is created as you take action. Each chapter in Part II builds on the preceding one, culminating in you learning to exercise your power and influence.

- _____

  _____

- _____

  _____

PART II

Create Impetus

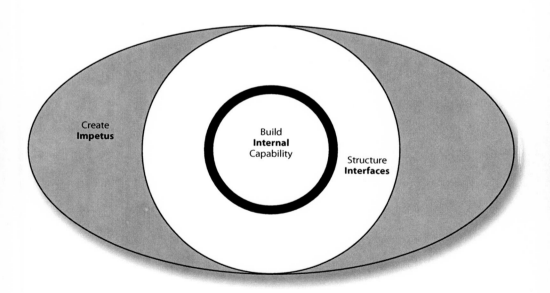

CHAPTER 7

Develop Your Plan

By creating impetus, you provide a supportive environment for yourself that sustains you through the hard work of all the other actions needed to achieve professional success. Impetus is a critical element of the Third Eye Framework, and the first step toward creating it is to develop a strategic plan of action.

As you embark on the process of allowing your quiet competence as an Insightful Expert to shine, use your planning as an occasion to think systematically about your future. Consider the other professionals with whom you compete for clients or promotions, your values and your goals, the threats and opportunities within your organization (or professional milieu), and your current interpersonal competencies. Your plan will evolve and change with changing circumstances and with your progress, but it's nevertheless essential at the outset of any major personal change effort. Not only is the plan itself a handy way to record where you're headed, but the very process of planning focuses your attention on key factors and issues you might otherwise overlook. With time and practice, your evolving plan becomes a strategic mind-set centered around your career.

Vision: How do I see myself?

Begin your plan with a vision of your desired future once your career potential is fulfilled. In Chapter 10 we talk about values, and the exercise there will help you flesh out this thinking, but for now, begin with a vision for you and your career two years, five years, or even ten years from now. What dream do you wish to accomplish? Do you want to be famous, well-respected, a division chief, a partner, a guru, or what? What aspiration would constitute your career apex or a major step toward it?

After almost twenty years as a scientist, Helen wants to be a research manager in charge of new product development, with a number of research scientists reporting to her.

Goals: What do I want to accomplish?

Next, plan a series of intermediate goals en route to your ultimate aspiration.

Helen set one major goal to start with: To achieve a stellar performance rating from her boss this year.

Inventory: What are my strengths and weaknesses?

With broad goals in place, you will want to consider the strengths and weaknesses that you bring to this stage of your career. Inventory strengths and weaknesses from both the technical and the human dimensions of your career. As you progress through the Third Eye Framework, you will learn more about how to expand your self-awareness (Chapter 11) and conducting that assessment will inform this section of your plan.

Your strengths are your personal attributes, relationships, and other assets that may allow you to be successful in achieving your career goals. Weaknesses are either personal deficiencies that may impede you or issues with which you struggle as an Insightful Expert. If your goal is to gain a promotion (for example, to become a partner in the firm), your assets might include acquired experience, long-term clients, training, and advanced educational credentials. Your weaknesses might include your communication skills and your influential network. Record this information as you brainstorm so that you don't forget any key items later.

Helen decided that her current strengths and weaknesses are as follows:

Strengths:
Her experience
Her intellectual capacity for problem solving

Weaknesses:
Her last project was unsuccessful in the marketplace
Her peers perceive her as an oddball
She has few trusting relationships with her peers
She doesn't dress the part of a manager and has been told that her appearance doesn't fit the corporate culture
Her communication skills need polishing

Assessment: What are the opportunities and threats that confront me?

Having completed a preliminary pass at identifying your strengths and weaknesses, you will next want to evaluate opportunities and threats in your work environment, now or potentially in the future, that may either aid or impede your progress toward your goal(s). If you've been involved in planning for your organization or department, you may recognize this process. In business jargon, it's called a SWOT analysis: S=strengths, W=weaknesses, O=opportunities, T=threats. The same assessment that applies to an organization applies to your personal development as well.

To identify opportunities and threats, you will want to consider objective conditions and, especially, long-term external trends in your work, career, or professional environment. Possible career opportunities and threats include changes in the number of people in different specializations within a profession; declining or rising levels of resources; impending retirements; organizational changes such as expansion, contraction, or ownership changes; competitors for your desired position and status in the field or your firm; etc. Many external factors can affect your ability to achieve your goals and realize your vision for your career, and any of these can change at any time. Be sure to devote sufficient reflection to this portion of your plan, because it offers you guidance for where and how to focus your personal development efforts as you compare your strengths and weaknesses to the challenges you may face.

Your SWOT analysis is ultimately about fit—the fit between your personal strengths and weaknesses and the opportunities and threats in your environment. If the fit is unfavorable, you will need to develop your skill set or consider alternative goals. If the fit is decent, your SWOT analysis will confirm that you're on the right track and tell you where to focus your efforts. Your SWOT may reveal, for example, opportunities that build on your technical skills or threats for which you need to develop your interpersonal skills.

As you follow the Third Eye Framework, you will be able to consider where your skills may fit into your personal development plan. For example, you'll learn about relationship building. Your SWOT will help you identify the specific relationships that are crucial to your success and, of equal importance, *why* they are important. It should also help you refine your efforts and make more effective use of your time by highlighting which relationships are *not* important.

Helen's SWOT revealed that currently there are few opportunities for advancement in her company. What's more, several other engineers are at a similar career stage and may compete for management positions (a threat). These limited opportunities for upward mobility will require strong communication skills and a viable personal network throughout the company. Currently Helen has neither, and she's perceived as a bit of a free spirit.

Objectives: What specific objectives will guide me toward my goals?

With the completion of your personal SWOT, you are ready to develop specific objectives with measurable outcomes and time-frames. What might these be? You might wish to build a relationship with a certain important colleague, to develop team leadership skills, to communicate better face-to-face, and so on. It depends on your situation. Whatever the objective, take the time to figure out how to measure your progress toward it and how to know when you've achieved it. For example, how long will it take to develop team leadership skills, and how will you know when you're there? How many fewer complaints can you achieve, and how soon can you achieve this? When will a major project be implemented successfully? When and on what dimensions of performance can you get feedback from your team members, achieving an average score of 6 on a seven-point scale? I'm not kidding here. While it's easy to go overboard, it's equally easy to forgo this step. And neither option is a good one, because concrete information regarding your success or failure (in achieving your personal objectives) can help you by motivating you and/or suggesting actions to take next.

Here is one of the objectives Helen selected to get started toward her goal:

To develop strong relationships with at least two other engineers in her division over the next six months, as evidenced by the frequency with which they talk and go to lunch together.

For Helen, going to lunch with someone twice a month is a good place to start. It's ambitious but doable.

Strategy: How will I accomplish my objectives?

How you accomplish your objectives should remain open to improvisation. This is your strategy. It could involve changes in your behavior and in the ways that you interact with others. It may require enlisting support from others, and it may involve workshops, reading, trial and error, systematic approaches, and more. I'll present you with a variety of potential actions in subsequent chapters, but how these can best be applied in your situation is impossible to generalize. So, if you're working through this process as you read, you'll probably want to leave your strategy open for now. You'll come back to it as you begin to add details to your plan.

Your personal development does not mean that you must act like an extrovert. Rather, you must learn to get along in an extrovert-focused world, and that's a different thing. It's simply a matter of figuring out how best to use your unique qualities.

Helen decided that her strategy to accomplish her aims would be to work with me, an organizational behavior consultant, for six months to analyze her interpersonal interactions at work and to learn and practice her communication skills. She also began making sure that she wears a lab coat when in the lab to keep her clothing clean. And she began to initiate short, informal conversations with a couple of her fellow scientists.

Evaluate: How am I doing and what needs to be updated?

There are two final steps in your personal planning process. First, assess your progress toward the objectives you set for yourself. And second, with this progress assessment in mind, reexamine and update your personal SWOT: your strengths and weaknesses, their fit with changing opportunities and threats, and so on. It's an iterative process that remains relevant until you've accomplished the career vision you set out for yourself.

As time passed, Helen refined her strategy by rearranging her office so that she could get the privacy she needed as an introvert yet still keep the door open, maintaining visibility and contact with her peers and boss. She also set a new objective to improve her presentation skills and began practicing presentations more carefully. She did not discard her original objective and strategy, since she was able to see that she was making good progress and building key relationships that would help her accomplish her goal in time. Soon Helen received high marks on her performance and was well positioned for the next opening as a research manager. What's more, she was poised to move should an opportunity open up in another company.

Beyond planning, there's more to understand and do to prepare yourself for big changes. You need to know a bit about what to expect as change begins, you need to garner courage, and you need to make sure that what you do reflects your core values. In the following chapter, you will learn more about how change happens.

Milestones Along the Journey

Below are a few of the key ideas related to this chapter with a couple extra bullet points for you to fill in. I'd like to hear other ideas that may have resonated for you or were stimulated by what you read. Go to the website www.TheIntrovertsGuide.com to share with me those that have special meaning for *your* personal journey.

- Your strategic plan is your first important step toward realizing professional success.

- Developing a plan to let your quiet competence be your career advantage gets you thinking about what is important: what you want to accomplish, what you have to work with, and the features of your situation that can help or hinder that process.

- Set measureable objectives that are realistic and as they are accomplished add new ones to keep momentum.

- As you read subsequent chapters and take actions based on them, come back to your plan and update it with new information.

- _____

_____

- _____

_____

CHAPTER 8

How Planned Change Happens

Let's take a brief side trip to examine how human change in career-related settings occurs. As you implement your plan to let your quiet competence be your career advantage, you are launching changes in the ways in which you interact with others in your work life. By knowing in advance what to expect, you will be better prepared for what happens.

As mentioned a few chapters ago, Kurt Lewin's study of organizations revealed that effective behavioral change takes place in three main stages within an organization, and these correspond broadly to the stages of change in individual behaviors as well.[1]

In stage one, it is necessary to unfreeze the old ways of doing things. What's the first step here? Being *aware* of how you're currently doing things! If you don't know and have no insight into what is or is not currently working for you, you can't know what to change or how to begin that process. Typically, unfreezing old behaviors involves learning about yourself, followed by reframing the situations you face so that you see them in a new light. First and foremost, you need to know what's happening in your interpersonal exchanges and how these interactions can become more effective.

How do we gain this knowledge? In our professional lives, it may come from a failure, such as losing a major client or case. It may come from disappointing ourselves and wishing that we had been better able to communicate, lead our team, promote a desirable outcome, or prevent a negative outcome that, as an Insightful Expert, we knew was coming. Insight may also come from the formal evaluations we receive from supervisors, colleagues, clients, or employees.

This unfreezing stage can be dramatic and even unsettling. Consider the socialization process that military recruits undergo in basic training. It includes new living arrangements, a serious haircut, a uniform, long hours, vigorous workouts, and the imposition of strict authority—in short, the near total reorientation of a recruit's previous life. All of these elements are designed to unfreeze the recruits' mind-sets and habits so that they can be transformed into effective soldiers. A medical residency that exposes new doctors to 36 hours without sleep is a similarly unfreezing process to socialize them into their new profession.

The process you go through will not be nearly as severe. Still, as you consider your career aspirations and your progress toward them, the insights you glean from introspection and from objective feedback can be quite unsettling.

A lifelong introvert, Sam underwent his unfreezing process while participating in a support group at his local hospital for people who had suffered abuse. A National Merit scholar and university honors graduate, Sam was working on a farm milking cows because he didn't wish to engage with other people all day long. When he went to the support group, he found himself forced to introduce himself the very first day. Chagrined, he did it nevertheless and even kept going back for an entire year, several times a week. He had never experienced such an atmosphere. Soon the unfreezing process that emerged from these simple group sessions enabled him to seek a job as a substitute teacher, interacting with others all day long. This set his process of change in motion. I'll tell you more about Sam shortly.

As we contemplate change, we confront ourselves and begin to evaluate our place in our professional environment. What exactly is going on in your professional organizations and interactions? How often do you "fail" your own goals? How severely do introversion and its effects on your behavior appear to hold you back, and in what contexts and ways? How is your introversion an asset to you? As you develop your plan and consider your strengths and weaknesses alongside opportunities and threats, you will start to get a handle on these questions.

You begin to see how important self-awareness can be to unfreeze your old behaviors and leverage your strengths as an Insightful Expert. Working with a professional who specializes in organizational behavior is one of the best ways to enhance your self-awareness. Your sessions will expand your self-awareness through your responses to carefully selected standardized assessment instruments[2] that evaluate your efficacy in interactions with others, interviews, and fact-gathering dialogues. I discuss self-awareness in greater depth in Chapter 11.

Once your current and past behaviors are evident and their effects become apparent, it is easier to undertake stage two, the actual process of change. In stage two you begin taking steps to achieve your aspirations. This is a positive, hopeful time. Having formed your plan (Chapter 7), you're ready to begin the change process.

During your program of change, you'll learn and practice new behaviors and put them into action. In later chapters you'll learn many of the actions you may wish to take to become more effective as an Insightful Expert.

New behaviors, however, will quickly fade away without further intervention. (How many New Year's resolutions have you abandoned?) This is one reason why I emphasize that achieving your career aspirations takes time. Some time is needed to learn and practice new behaviors, but even more will be required to cement the new behaviors into place in your routines. It may take a year or two before you feel confident of this.

In stage three, called "refreezing," you institute reinforcement mechanisms to sustain your new behaviors, such as saying "Good morning" to your employees. When we train a dog, we give him a treat when he performs as instructed, and this positive reward is meant to refreeze his habits into a new pattern. For you, refreezing may be as simple as the positive feedback you receive from others in your work environment. It may be accomplishing a desired promotion or getting a coveted position, or it might be a reward you devise for yourself such as a trip or a pleasurable activity. I think, though, that you will find sufficient reward simply in how much more effective you feel and how much more satisfying your professional life becomes when you acknowledge your quiet competence as an Insightful Expert and learn to leverage it to your advantage.

Remember Sam? After teaching for several years, he realized how much more he wanted to do with his life. Having gained confidence in dealing with others, Sam continued his process of change by applying to medical schools. He was accepted by and completed a prestigious program. Now Sam has a private practice, working from a home office at his own pace, caring for people with health problems. Each year his practice grows. Sam has learned how to excel as an Insightful Expert. The rewards that he gets from exercising his intellect to help his patients help to anchor his new behaviors into place.

An understanding of the change process reveals why self-awareness is so important to success. You cannot begin to change without self-insight. Well, you can, but you won't know *what* to change in your professional interactions. You can't complete your personal SWOT (see Chapter 7) without information. With appropriate self-insights you will know what to target in the unfreezing, change, and refreezing process.

We'll get to that soon. But what if you aren't sure you can do this? What if you lack confidence that, as an introvert, you can ever achieve your vision? In Chapter 9 you'll find a new way of thinking about leveraging your Insightful Expert potential.

Milestones Along the Journey

Below are a few of the key ideas related to this chapter with a couple extra bullet points for you to fill in. I'd like to hear other ideas that may have resonated for you or were stimulated by what you read. Go to the website www.TheIntrovertsGuide.com to share with me those that have special meaning for *your* personal journey.

- Your plan from Chapter 7 helps you manage the changes that you undertake to advance your career.

- Think of changes in how you interact with others as water unfreezing, moving, and refreezing.

- Dramatic career change is possible with intention, motivation, action, and positive reinforcement.

- _____

  _____

- _____

  _____

CHAPTER 9

Muster Courage to Take Action

I have found that some Insightful Experts feel isolated professionally and don't realize that there are many others who share their discomfort in an extroverted professional culture. When I lead workshops for introverts seeking to more fully realize their professional capability, one of the most powerful moments comes when participants learn that they are not alone in experiencing the effects of introversion. One participant, Dan, said later, "I found many of my classmates' informal stories about their experiences insightful and helpful." Another participant, Amy, said simply, "It was enlightening."

Many Insightful Experts don't realize how widespread their experience is, nor do they realize that they have the power to alter their situation by following the Third Eye Framework, and as a result they become discouraged about their ability to succeed. Understand that it *is* possible to change the dynamics of your interactions and to tackle the issues that frustrate you. In fact, beginning with the realization that you're not isolated, you can embark on a process that has the power to transform your entire professional life.

Sometimes we think ourselves into failure. We realize that we are not taking the actions that we must to succeed. On occasion, Insightful Experts tell themselves things like, "I can't do it," or "I'm just not able to make the changes needed," or "I'll never succeed." These thoughts are natural in a culture that does not openly value the thoughtful, quiet way of interacting that is associated with introversion.

You might expect that I will tell you to think positively, to know that you can, to build yourself up with affirmations—but I won't do that. By all means use such techniques if they help you (as they do many people), but some research shows that the more you focus on positive affirmation, the more you are reminded of your perceived shortcomings. I believe a more realistic approach is the one I introduce in this chapter.

Leveraging your strengths as an Insightful Expert does *not* mean changing your basic nature as an introvert, so rest assured on that count. You will be changing some behaviors on the margin that facilitate your career while remaining true to yourself. In fact, change can paradoxically support who you really are to start with. I think of this as analogous to learning manners. Think of how just saying "please" and "thank you" makes everything go so much smoother. These are little gestures, a few words, but what a difference there is between a request that includes them and one that doesn't! Most of us take such simple phrases for granted, but if we had not learned them in our younger years, they would be hard to learn as adults. When you undertake the Third Eye Framework, you are simply going back to basics and learning the techniques that will make your interactions with others in your professional life easier and more productive.

Some of the actions that you choose to enable your introversion to flourish may be hard at first. There are days when you might feel you've had your fill of trying to get along in an extrovert's world. You might occasionally feel down. You might be frustrated. Once in a while, you may feel stuck. It is important that you not let this become a persistent mind-set. Maybe you're already there, and you are reading this book as a way to change just such a mind-set. Well, there is a way through such feelings, and here it is.

Accept Thoughts, Change Behaviors

The approach[1] I recommend has a long history of success in managing human behavior, and I think it's especially applicable to the work that we Insightful Experts take on in developing our professional lives. Instead of simply repeating affirmations, try accepting your *thoughts* while changing your *behaviors*. Acknowledge the feelings that come from being an introvert in an extrovert's workplace, be they annoyance, anger, resentment, sadness, frustration, helplessness, hopelessness, resignation, or lack of energy. At the same time, however, heartily commit to changing some of the behaviors that hold you back—even though, of course, you will not change into something other than an introvert, because that's built in.

If you feel frustrated, don't fight being frustrated. Realize it, and be consciously aware that the feeling will eventually pass. Similarly, if you think, "I can't do this," realize that this is only a thought. It's not you. It's not permanent. The thought came, and later it will go.

Paradoxically, the more you try to suppress feelings and thoughts, the stronger they seem. To illustrate, try this exercise for a moment. First, close your eyes and imagine hearing a barking dog. Do you have it clearly in your mind? Okay, now for the next minute, do *not* think about a barking dog. Whatever you do, think about anything else or any other sound. You are forbidden to hear barks in your head, think of a barking dog, or think of the words "barking dog." All done? How did you do? What happened when you were asked *not* to think of a barking dog?

Of course, you probably thought of little else as you tried to push it out of your mind. That's exactly what happens when we try to push away any thought or emotion. Even if it goes away for a while, we can be certain that it will come back. That's the nature of the human mind. This insight can help you realize that it's useless to fight off your thoughts and emotions. It makes more (common) sense simply to let them be, and they will eventually pass. Trying to suppress or avoid them only makes them stronger.

Mindfulness practices can be very helpful as you work toward developing the habit of watching thoughts and emotions emerge without becoming ensnared in them. Thich Nhat Hanh, a well-known Buddhist monk nominated for the Nobel Peace Prize, has written a number of highly readable books on developing mindfulness in everyday life. Several of these are listed in the Notes for this chapter, along with some other resources for additional reading.[2]

A daily meditation practice can also be useful for developing mindful awareness. Such practices come from many traditions, including Buddhism, Hinduism, and Taoism. A personal favorite of mine is standing meditation from the Taoist Qi Gong tradition.

Try the following exercise as a way of finding a space for your feelings and allowing them to pass:

Begin by sitting comfortably in an upright position with your feet flat on the floor and your back straight. Set a kitchen timer or your watch for three minutes. Now close your eyes and simply pay attention to all the sounds around you. What do you hear? Listen to the sounds in your room. Listen to the sounds of your body, perhaps gurgles or the sound of your breath. Listen to the sounds beyond your room in the rest of your building. Then listen to the even more distant sounds outside. Do you hear traffic? Birds? Just sit and relax into the waves of sound that surround you.

You will likely find that the more you practice such exercises, the better you'll become at getting past the negative thoughts that your mind throws at you. Start with five minutes a day and work up to more time. Soon you'll develop a habit of mindfulness, and you'll recognize that your thoughts are only thoughts and not facts that prevent you from moving forward with your plan to optimize your career goals.

Once you have accepted that fears, emotions, and thoughts will come and go (and I'm not implying that this is a simple or quick process), you may also wish to focus more clearly on your values. Your values can help to keep you on course as you work toward allowing your introversion to lead you to success. Why are you making the effort to apply the Third Eye Framework, anyway? Beyond your obvious career goals, what is it that makes you want to optimize your profession? How does your career give meaning to your existence? We explore these questions in Chapter 10.

Milestones Along the Journey

Below are a few of the key ideas related to this chapter with a couple extra bullet points for you to fill in. I'd like to hear other ideas that may have resonated for you or were stimulated by what you read. Go to the website www.TheIntrovertsGuide.com to share with me those that have special meaning for *your* personal journey.

- Even understanding how change plays out, as you undertake any process that requires new ways of doing things, such as the Third Eye Framework, it's normal to feel some trepidation.

- It is common for an Insightful Expert to feel isolated. But you are far from alone.

- When you question your ability to accomplish the career goals that you set out for yourself, it is important to keep acting in ways that support them regardless of your feelings. The next chapter coming up (Chapter 10) will help with this by reminding you of your values.

- Practicing mindfulness techniques can help to cultivate a calm mind and a clear focus.

- _____

  _____

- _____

  _____

CHAPTER 10

Values = Meaning (and Motivation)

As you undertake the program outlined by the Third Eye Framework, it can be helpful to clarify for yourself the values that underlie the choices you are making in your professional life. Your values—your preferences for how you live your life—provide you with meaning that continually replenishes your motivation. Goals and objectives are *what* you plan to do or accomplish. Strategies are *how you plan to accomplish them*. At a more fundamental level, however, values are *how you want to live*. For example, do you want to exist in the shadow of extroverts, perhaps never fully exercising the full scope of your professional skills? What is it that you want your professional life to amount to? *What do you stand for?* If you know what your values are, they can help you decide what goals, objectives, and strategies are best suited for you. They are the foundation for everything else.

Most professionals choose their career because they want to lead a certain kind of life—often, though not always, one that benefits others in some way. When you identify the underlying drivers of your career choices, you can take advantage of the motivation that naturally emerges from the opportunity to actualize your deepest, most heartfelt desires. Being motivated is what will enable you to take the necessary actions to make the Third Eye Framework work for you.

Consider your preferences in each of the domains that your professional life encompasses. These are the spheres from which you draw, or could acquire, sustenance and satisfaction. Some of the common domains identified by Insightful Experts include relationship, professional, and personal values. Carefully consider what you want to stand for in each of these areas.

Relationship Values

- Relationships with your team, close partners, collaborators on key projects.
- Relationships with professional peers and colleagues, perhaps in other organizations and distant locations as well as those close by.
- Relationships with subordinates and protégés whom you may mentor.
- Relationships with your superiors, board of directors, etc.
- Relations with clients and key internal customers within your organization.

A way to better know your values is to consider differences in how relationships can be conducted. Common differences (which I call variables) include: the effectiveness of communication; the degree of mutual respect; uses of influence and power to accomplish tasks; conflict and its management; potential for growth and change between partners; leadership; extent of shared values and norms; personality differences; and differences in perceptions, attitudes, and motivators.

What is the state of each of your important relationships with respect to these variables? Most importantly, *How would you like it to be?* As you consider how you would like it to be, focus on what is within your control: your own behavior and attitudes. Remember, these are *your* values. It would be nice to be able to have others share them, but that's probably unrealistic, so it's better to stick with what you alone can control. With this perspective, the questions become: *How would I like to be in my professional relationships? What attitudes and behaviors are ones that I aspire to?*

Matt is an Insightful Expert who decided that he values integrity above all else in his relationships. This means that he feels compelled to be open and honest in his professional dealings. As a result, he may have to speak up more often. He's not comfortable with this, but it's something that helps him live consistently with his values. Matt also values being of service to his clients. He has decided that he wants to go out of his way to provide outstanding service, even if that means he has to provide services on a pro bono basis occasionally. Matt values keeping a business relationship with his direct reports that does not get too personal. Knowing this allows him to say "No thanks" when he gets invited to go out for a drink or to a personal event.

Professional Values

- Social responsibility; service to your profession and to society at large, and perhaps to a local community as well.
- Personal meaningfulness of the work itself; your mission and passion for practicing your profession.
- Education and professional development.
- Play; joy in your work, at work, with others at work.

Professional values are your preferences with respect to your career. What do you want to emerge from the many hours that you spend at your work? Is that happening? If you've never considered these issues, now is the time. How do you want to live your professional life? Consider each of the above-mentioned areas as well as any other issues that come to mind.

Personal Values

- Aspects of your physical and mental health that are affected by work, such as stress management, sleep, diet, exercise, time off, travel, exposure to new ideas.
- Your work's impact on your personal life, including family and friends.

Because work and life are intertwined, especially for professionals who have spent many years investing in their careers, you'll want to consider the personal areas that are affected by your work. For example, do you find that you experience work-related stress that affects your family? Is this what you want? What level of stress is acceptable to you? At this stage, you're not focused on *how* you can achieve these values for living your life a certain way. For now, you just want to become more acquainted with *what* it is that you truly value.

Here is an exercise that will help you clarify your relationship, professional, and personal values:

For each of the eleven domains on the worksheet below, write down what you most want to stand for. In your heart of hearts, where do you want to stand in that domain? This could be just a word, but more likely you will come up with a brief paragraph that describes the key dimensions of how you would like to be.

For example, consider the personal meaningfulness of the work you do. Do you wish to have a great passion for practicing your profession? If so, how would it manifest? Would it consist of pursuing new projects, ideas, endeavors? Developing new processes and theories? Going the extra mile for each and every client? Doing more than the required professional development? Reading in the field in your spare time? Making public speeches about your work or writing a book? Teaching? Doing pro bono work (which may overlap with the social responsibility domain)? Only you know the specifics of your specialty and its hold on your psyche. How do you want to be as a practitioner in this discipline? What behaviors epitomize your feelings for it?

For each of the domains, try to develop a similar list of ways that you want to be and what you want to stand for. Be an idealist! This exercise is intended to draw out your innermost valued ways of being in the professional world you have chosen. Don't worry what others might say were they to see your list. This exercise is not about your peers or anyone else; it's about you and you alone.

The next step is to prioritize your list of values. Select the most important value from each domain and rank it on a scale from 7 to 1 according to whether it is "very important" to you (7) or "not important at all" (1). For insight on where the greatest changes need to occur, take the following two steps as well. First, rate each domain according to your current achievement. Use a similar 7 to 1 scale, with 7 being "I'm doing this very well" and 1 being "I'm not making this happen at all." Then subtract each achievement score from the corresponding importance score. The resulting "Off Course" score shows you where your behavior needs to change in order to live your values more fully.

Higher "Off Course" scores illuminate areas where you are currently failing to maximize your potential to live a valued professional life. These gaps are the areas in which you will want to commit to action. As you develop goals for change, include these areas and emphasize them. Because our preferences are so important to us, they can motivate us to do great things!

Values Domain	Critical Value	Priority	Current Status	Off Course
RELATIONSHIP				
Relations with team				
Relations with peers				
Relations with subordinates				
Relations with superiors				
Relations with clients				
PROFESSIONAL				
Social responsibility				
Personal meaning				
Professional development				
Play and joy				
PERSONAL				
Health				
Family/Friends				

As if this values exercise hasn't raised your awareness enough, in the next chapter you'll learn more about the all-important value of self-awareness. This is a critical step that will help you reach your career goals.

Milestones Along the Journey

Below are a few of the key ideas related to this chapter with a couple extra bullet points for you to fill in. I'd like to hear other ideas that may have resonated for you or were stimulated by what you read. Go to the website www.TheIntrovertsGuide.com to share with me those that have special meaning for *your* personal journey.

- Your values are a key resource that will keep you motivated to achieve your goals in an extroverted business world.

- Values underlie goals, objectives, and strategies. They are abiding and when explicit, they can provide a razor focus to propel your actions and effort. Clarifying values is one of the first steps in raising your self-awareness, discussed in the next chapter.

- Personal, professional, and relationship values are among those that are important to your career.

- _____

  _____

- _____

  _____

CHAPTER 11

Raise Your Self-Awareness

Have you ever looked in a mirror to discover that your hair is sticking straight up in a strange new way that falls well short of the professional image you want? Just as the looking glass makes you aware of discrepancies so that you can maintain a certain physical appearance, people with higher levels of overall self-awareness tend to perform better professionally. Becoming more self-aware is an important first step for Insightful Experts seeking to attain higher levels of career success.

Self-awareness is an element of emotional intelligence (discussed in Chapter 14); it means that you see yourself as others do. It helps you know in what ways your introverted qualities could be hurting you rather than helping you in your interactions with others. For example, as you well know, sometimes our reservation is *interpreted* as a lack of energy or coldness when that's not the case at all. With the knowledge of how others see you, you can monitor the success of your efforts to leverage your introvert strengths such as your genuineness, your focus, your respect for others' space, or your astute insight to work-related situations and problems. Continued development of your self-awareness will enhance your professional performance by allowing you to counteract false impressions and to accurately shape others' perceptions.

Self-awareness is challenging because each of us, whether introverted or extroverted, has blind spots. Even if we do accurately perceive ourselves as others see us, it's easy to overlook or deny the impact of our behavior on our professional success, especially when things aren't going well. Attribution error causes us to tend to ascribe our failings to external factors, such as available time, resources, and the like.

As a pragmatist, I take two approaches to self-awareness. The first, which appeals to many, is data driven: What do the "facts" tell me about myself? The second, which appeals to others, is driven by feelings: What do my "feelings" tell me about myself? (Feelings can be viewed as facts also because they are simply emotions and thoughts to be paid attention to, but for purposes here, I'll keep them distinct.) Let's examine each of these as sources of self-awareness for Insightful Experts.

Just the Facts

Objective data about your professional interactions can come from a variety of sources. While it's true that most numbers are based on assumptions, that does not undermine their utility in most cases. Consider how many or how much you have of each of these (as they apply to your situation): clients, interesting projects, cases, professional invitations, peers who are allies, etc. These are *process* measures of your performance since they target your activities rather than final outcomes from your efforts. Absolute numbers often mean little, but when you compare your performance to that of your colleagues and peers, you can begin to see where you stand. So long as other underlying variables such as your specialty and the complexity of the work you perform, your geographic location, your company, and the market for your services are similar these numbers offer insight into how effectively you are advancing your career. Taking this a step further, you can consider *outcome* measures of your performance such as your income, promotions, how many of your cases or clients have had successful outcomes, or some other end result to which you aspire.

Comparing yourself to your professional peers can provide a useful benchmark but it can also drive you a little crazy if you fail to keep it in perspective. Always bear in mind that the most important criteria are your goals for yourself. Which of these measures are ones you aspire to, and if you do, what is the level of performance that *you want* for yourself?

These raw numbers don't reveal any detailed information about the possible effects of your introversion, but they do offer a baseline. You'll become more attuned to your performance, and you'll be able to measure how well the process of implementing the Third Eye Framework affects it.

Beyond numbers on outcome measures such as those above, consider hard data from other sources. Feedback from peer reviews, formal performance evaluations from your superiors, and multi-source feed-back[1] that includes data from subordinates are all valid sources to help you become more self-aware of how introversion may be influencing your professional life. Go to www.Rypple.com for an online tool that enables you to seek anonymous feedback from others in response to questions of your choosing. By the way, you can use this in a sort of pretest, post-test informal study to examine how the changes you make impact others' perceptions of your professional effectiveness.

Do you conduct formal assessments of client satisfaction? This is another excellent source of information to enhance your awareness of how you come across to others. Make sure you collect these data promptly and anonymously so that full candor is given. Often clients may be reluctant to provide feedback in other forms, especially if they are satisfied overall with your services. A written structured or semi-structured questionnaire can allow you to probe specific concerns in a way that facilitates concrete feedback. You can do this via a mailed questionnaire or an online service.[2] Use of a questionnaire confers the bonus benefit of demonstrating to clients that you are concerned with satisfaction and continuous improvement, just as a multi-source feedback survey done internally within your organization demonstrates these concerns and interest in your colleagues' feedback. Keep in mind that you can have both *internal* and *external* clients. Internal clients are those people or divisions within your organization for whom you provide some service. External clients are entities outside your company.

A major source of information that I administer on behalf of my clients is a series of self-assessment questionnaires.[3] I am careful to use only those that have been scientifically validated with established reliability and validity. It is important to differentiate these from the "feel good" instruments peddled by many consultants or published on various websites. Why go through the effort if you're not learning what you think you are learning about yourself? Depending on your situation, such assessments might address your cognitive style, conflict management skills, leadership and influence skills, emotional intelligence, or other key behaviors that are relevant to you. These deal with your behavioral propensities and competencies in organizations and can expand your self-awareness tremendously when you discuss their results with a qualified professional.[4] I also employ a series of exercises, much like some of those in this book (for example, the values exercise in the previous chapter), that expand into other areas of professional life.

Having gathered as many data as you can, compare the findings from various sources. So, for example, you could compare feedback about your performance from your self-examination with feedback from clients and from professional peers. While you aren't likely to find consensus on every facet, you might see convergence around at least some aspects of your interactions with others in the course of performing your job. It's a good idea to collect information not just from various sources but using more than one methodology. Oral reports, client/peer satisfaction questionnaires, and other documents such as performance evaluations are among the various ways of collecting data about yourself. If you are able to triangulate methodologies as well as sources, you can have greater confidence in the themes that emerge.

But I Feel Like—

In addition to facts, feelings can tell you a great deal about yourself. If you think this sounds too touchy-feely, think again. There is a great deal of scientific evidence that gut feelings are important. In Daniel Goleman's book *Working with Emotional Intelligence*, he tells the story of a lawyer with a neurological impairment who could explain all the rational pros and cons of a given decision but could not make the decision himself. The man ended up losing his job, his wife, and his home. The scientist who reported his case, Dr. Antonio Damasio, realized that it was the lawyer's lack of preferences, *feelings* really, that handicapped him.

Imagine a raging fire. Studies of people—such as firefighters—who make rapid decisions in the course of their daily work have found that such people are able to *instantly* assess the dimensions of a situation. Their assessment is based on their past experiences.[5] As soon as they find a similar situation in their extensive memory stores, they are able to fly into action. In such situations, there is no time for examining pros and cons for rational decision making, nor is there any need to do so. Instead, every piece of information from temperature to timing to smoke to sound—and more, no matter how minute—is considered simultaneously, and the appropriate response is evident. Yes, it's a gut decision, but it's one based on experience and fact.

Just because we cannot articulate the rationale behind a feeling, it is not necessarily invalid. All feelings are significant and some do indeed have a factual basis. Often we call such feelings *intuition*. I like to think of intuition as our brain making decisions for us in the background. Your mind is able to automatically assimilate all the facts and integrate them into a coherent whole. In a very real sense, our rational faculties can take a rest and let our brains do the work behind the scenes. For this to work, we must be aware of our feelings and, just as crucial, we must *trust* them. For example, the firefighter who responds in a certain way to fight a certain fire must trust his/her instant recognition of how to respond. It does no good to vacillate.

You can enhance your awareness of how your introversion affects your professional life by tuning into how situations make you feel. When are you uneasy? When are you confident? With *whom* are you uneasy? In what situations do you feel at your best? As you begin to pay more attention, you will find that this becomes easier. The skill of sensing your feelings and tapping your intuition will be invaluable as you undertake the process of working through the Third Eye Framework. It should enable you to change course quickly in the face of cautionary information or to proceed with confidence when you feel assured.

Any practice that helps you quiet your mind will also help you tap your feelings and develop your intuition and, by extension, your self-awareness. Various forms of meditation, including yoga, Qi Gong, Zen, transcendental, and so on, will assist with this. Similarly, the practice of mindfulness, as discussed in Chapter 9, can still the chatter of thoughts that obscure your ability to take in pure sensory data and access your feelings. In the words of Thich Nhat Hanh, mindfulness is "keeping one's consciousness alive to the present reality."[6] This practice anchors you in the moment, allowing you to open your senses for information that your mind can then process in the background. Try it for yourself for five minutes a day for two weeks, and see what happens.

Self-awareness is one of the most important elements of creating impetus in the Third Eye Framework. As an introvert, you often prefer not to engage at all with other people so you may not spend a lot of time considering how you are coming across to them. Alternatively, your deep introspection may cause you to ruminate on only one or two facets of your interactions, missing the bigger picture that is a truer representation of how you are being perceived by others. With facts and feelings you will become more self-aware, and that can help you realize your strengths and turn your introversion to your advantage. Another critical element is your self-confidence, and we'll turn our attention there in the next chapter.

Milestones Along the Journey

Below are a few of the key ideas related to this chapter with a couple extra bullet points for you to fill in. I'd like to hear other ideas that may have resonated for you or were stimulated by what you read. Go to the website www.TheIntrovertsGuide.com to share with me those that have special meaning for *your* personal journey.

- Heightened awareness of how you are perceived by others is a feedback mechanism, like a thermostat, that allows you to monitor the effects of your actions to build professional success and respond to deviations promptly.

- Both facts and feelings are important sources of self-awareness.

- _____

  _____

- _____

  _____

CHAPTER 12

From Experience Comes Confidence

Growing self-awareness and expanding self-confidence are impor-tant milestones on the path to create impetus for yourself. As you gain self-awareness and come to understand that the steps you are taking to advance your career as an Insightful Expert are the right ones, you will begin to access the confidence you need to move forward with your plan.

By acquiring knowledge of exactly how you are interacting with oth-ers, how that behavior is perceived, and what you need to do to move for-ward, you are preparing yourself to take action. Preparation itself boosts self-confidence. Recall how you felt when you were well prepared for a test in school—it's a good feeling! But that's just the beginning.

Studies of entrepreneurs reveal that many are "serial entrepreneurs," developing business after business until they find one that "clicks" in the marketplace. Their passion is innovation and starting new things, so they don't quit after one or two failures, including personal bankruptcies. Similarly, in order to gain the benefits of leveraging your strengths, you have to be willing to take actions that could be perceived as risky. For ex-ample, it was risky the first time my Insightful Expert client Jessica asked her boss for a new job description. Taking risks builds self-confidence, which enables you to continue to move forward.

Sometimes though, any action will do. Self-confidence often comes simply from just doing something. Taking action is self-reinforcing be-cause it helps you become more comfortable with new behaviors. And if the actions you take are rewarded, there is external reinforcement too. After all, we all love rewards! Imagine how Jessica felt when her boss was willing to present her proposed job description to the board of directors and they unanimously approved it.

The key to getting rewards is accumulating enough experience to know that the rewards will come. And there is only one way to do that—by doing. The more actions you take to build stronger relationships, the more experience you gain in the process of discovering that your Insightful Expert strengths such as being a good listener or a deliberative decision maker actually work *for* you, not against you. By failing to act, you deprive yourself of the opportunity to develop self-confidence, not to mention the long run benefits of becoming an introvert who flourishes in your career.

Your emerging self-confidence as you undertake the actions associated with the Third Eye Framework, beginning with raising your self-awareness, will soon begin to shift how you are seen by the people in your organization and professional context. You are creating impetus for optimizing your potential. As you do so, you will want to begin to pay more and more attention to individual relationships. The next few chapters take us there, beginning with how you open up to others.

Milestones Along the Journey

Below are a few of the key ideas related to this chapter with a couple extra bullet points for you to fill in. I'd like to hear other ideas that may have resonated for you or were stimulated by what you read. Go to the website www.TheIntrovertsGuide.com to share with me those that have special meaning for *your* personal journey.

- Now that you have a strategic career plan, you have clarified what it is you want (values and goals), and are on the way to becoming more self-aware, know that you will also gain confidence in the human elements of your career as you begin to interact with others in a slightly different way.

- Doing something leads to confidence that you *can* do something.

- Taking action to build relationships is self-reinforcing and, over time, will allow your introvert strengths to emerge and flourish.

- _____

  _____

- _____

  _____

Chapter 13

No Longer Hidden and Blind: Self-Disclosure as a Path to Connection

Insightful Experts frequently report feeling invisible, unheard, and misunderstood by those around them in their professional dealings. This is in spite of their intense engagement with issues, their strong task performance, their knowledge and equanimity, their diligence, and all of the other stellar traits that they bring to their professions. As you make the effort to seek greater career success, you begin to be seen, heard, and understood, and this creates momentum in a positive-feedback loop. Connecting with others in these ways is fostered by self-disclosure.

Self-disclosure is a communication process in which we reveal something about ourselves to others. Typically you might reveal information that others would not otherwise find out about you. Assuming that the facts are true, would you ever find yourself saying any of the following or similar statements to your colleagues?

- I'm not sure what I would do if that big project we're working on were to blow up.
- I am finding it hard to relate to some of the clients I've been meeting with lately.
- My goal is to make partner within three years.

- I've been under some personal stress that is affecting my energy level at work.
- I really enjoy working on this.

Introverts tend to disclose less than extroverts, yet research suggests that a whole host of benefits accrue to those who do self-disclose. Among the identified benefits of self-disclosure are the following:

- feeling better about yourself
- experiencing less psychological distress in stressful circum-stances
- being better liked
- discovering information about others
- developing positive and stronger relationships

These results from self-disclosure are significant outcomes that can benefit you professionally. The classic model of self-disclosure called the Johari Window was developed by Joseph Luft and Harry Ingham[1] and suggests how revealing information about yourself can help you grow and develop your personal and professional capabilities in an organiza-tion. The table below summarizes the model. It shows the different parts of you that exist simultaneously in relation to other people. When one part increases, another part decreases.

The Johari Window		
	Known to Self	**Not Known to Self**
Known to Others	Open Self	Blind Self
Not Known to Others	Hidden Self	Unknown Self

Your open self (top left quadrant) is what you know about yourself and what you share with others most routinely, although the amount you share will vary by how comfortable you are with any individual. This information could be anything from your age to your dreams and hopes. According to Luft, when you open up to yourself *and* others, communication is more effective.

Your blind self (top right quadrant) is the part of yourself that you don't know very well but that others can see. It may include your foibles or feelings and traits to which you're oblivious. To the extent that your blind self is *minimized*, you will enhance your interpersonal relationships. This is the self-awareness piece outlined in Chapter 11, where a wide range of actions you can take to expand your knowledge of yourself were explained.

Your hidden self (bottom left quadrant) is made up of your secrets, things you know about yourself but choose not to share. Many individuals wisely disclose *selectively*, depending on the situation and with whom they're speaking, while others habitually over-disclose or under-disclose. *Introverts often under-disclose*, starving relationships of mutual disclosure much as a fire is starved by lack of fuel.

Your unknown self (bottom right quadrant) is an unconscious self that consists of things unknown both to you and to those around you. It is usually seen only when you learn new truths about yourself, such as in psychotherapy.

As you can see, the Johari window is about knowing yourself (i.e., self-awareness) and then using that insight to enhance your communications and relations with others. In this way, your expanding self-awareness (Chapter 11) logically precedes this step. *The former helps you grow and develop your character and demeanor as a professional. The latter helps you develop the interpersonal relationships and network you need to do well in your career.*

If you fail to disclose yourself in interpersonal relations in your professional life, you miss out on the support you stand to gain from those around you. Support can range from friendship to new client referrals to information that helps you do better work, and more. Self-disclosure is a first step to making genuine connections with other people. A subsequent step is intentionally influencing others though reciprocal exchanges, coming up in Chapter 16.

For many Insightful Experts, self-disclosure is not something that comes naturally. We crave privacy. We often experience the chatter of small talk and inquiries about our activities as intrusions. We want just to get to the task and do our jobs. We have fewer friendships than extroverts because we like depth—but in extremely small doses. *Self-disclosure is precisely so important because it is so difficult for us.*

How to Disclose More About Yourself

How should you get started? Begin with self-reflection about how much you currently disclose and where you fall on the continuum from over-disclosure (lots of extroverts here!) to under-disclosure (introverts, please step forward!). As you do this, you may discover that you disclose differently to different individuals and in different situations. This is normal and actually quite functional, because it shows that you have the social ability to discriminate with judgment. It is *selective disclosure*. But the real test is whether your overall levels are under or over what would be best for your career. Spend some time considering these issues and get feedback from others, such as a mentor or qualified professional.

Continuum of Self-Disclosure

Over-Disclosure   Selective Disclosure   Under-Disclosure

After you have determined whether you need to disclose more or less in certain relationships, start by identifying one colleague as your guinea pig. This should be someone with whom you'd like to develop a strong relationship, but not someone who is extremely important to your future, such as a boss or mentor. Very gradually, begin to shift how much you disclose. Rely on feedback from the other party to determine whether to proceed or back off. See what happens to the relationship after six months. I suspect you'll find that it's better.

As you undertake the process of expanding your disclosure, be careful what you reveal to others, especially early on. It's usually best to steer clear of details about your private life outside work, aside from neutral topics such as your interest in sports or hobbies. Begin by discussing your work projects, what you're learning from your current experiences with clients or projects, your thoughts about trends in your field, and so forth.

You are slowly revealing more about yourself with each exchange. You may find that, as an introvert, you need only begin the conversation and that your conversation partner will take over from there, especially if they are an extrovert. Each little bit that you reveal of yourself adds up over time so, no matter how small, what you say counts.

As the relationship evolves, you can gradually expand the range of your revelations. But always know in advance how much you are willing to reveal and do not feel obligated to share more than you're comfortable revealing. Be willing to just smile enigmatically, like the Mona Lisa, and say something like, "That's a conversation for another day."

Consider this story about professional colleagues who failed to self-disclose to one another:

Dr. Rachel Naomi Remen, in her thought-provoking book Kitchen Table Wisdom, recounts the story of two physicians who separately visited her counseling practice. Bound by confidentiality ethics, she of course could not reveal to either of them that his practice partner was also seeking counseling. Both were in despair—with their careers, with the sorrow of their patients, with the way that medicine is practiced today. Both lived in fear that their colleagues would discover their emotions and deem them "unprofessional."

These colleagues' lack of self-disclosure may have made their professional lives easier in some respects. Many of us would argue that they simply showed good judgment in not revealing what their professional culture might condemn. And yet, if each had known of the other's despair, they could have supported one another. There is little doubt in my mind that a more authentic way of being would likely have had benefits for both men as they struggled to find meaning in their careers. Fear held them back. It is possible that a pragmatic approach aimed at selective self-disclosure—as I have prescribed here for you—might have yielded great benefit at little cost, since it allows for stopping whenever feedback indicates.

Just as self-disclosure can help you begin to forge authentic relationships with the people in your professional life, you can create impetus for achieving your goals by developing and practicing emotional intelligence, as discussed in the next chapter.

Milestones Along the Journey

Below are a few of the key ideas related to this chapter with a couple extra bullet points for you to fill in. I'd like to hear other ideas that may have resonated for you or were stimulated by what you read. Go to the website www.TheIntrovertsGuide.com to share with me those that have special meaning for *your* personal journey.

- Because we are so private, we introverts tend to under-disclose information about ourselves to others.

- Self-disclosure in your communication with others helps to develop their trust in you and leads to genuine connection.

- Beginning to self-disclose just slightly more will help you begin to develop more honest relations with others. This is a step toward building your network.

- _____

  _____

- _____

  _____

CHAPTER 14

Emotional Intelligence:
The Insightful Expert's Secret Tool

The term *emotional intelligence* emerged some years ago and quickly became a management buzzword. Is it having the right emotions at work? Getting along with everyone? Liking the right people? Well, no. Psychologist John Mayer and his colleagues, pioneers in developing the concept, call it "the ability to carry out accurate reasoning about emotions and the ability to use emotions and emotional knowledge to enhance thought."[1]

Emotional intelligence can be viewed as a type of social intelligence, akin to IQ (intellectual quotient). Rather than helping us perform cognitive tasks involving thinking, emotional intelligence helps us perform emotional tasks instead.[2] Our emotions provide us with important social cues and information about situations and people. They help us understand how others behave around us. For example, my sadness can provide my colleagues with information that I need support, if they are sensitive to that cue.

Emotional intelligence includes the ability to:

1. accurately *perceive* our own and others' emotions;
2. *use* our emotions to help us *understand situations*;
3. *comprehend* what emotions are conveying and the content of emotional language; and
4. *manage* our own emotions effectively.[3]

People with greater emotional intelligence are not only more sensitive to others and enjoy better relationships in general, they also experience stronger working relationships in their professional lives. Amazingly, these capabilities are *four times more likely* to determine professional status and success than is IQ.[4] Some researchers have suggested that emotional intelligence provides a foundation for the social and interpersonal skills that are fundamental to professional success.[5] Emotional "competency" seems to become increasingly relevant and important in senior leadership positions. Author Daniel Goleman believes that analytical thinking is less important in a leader than the ability to influence others and his or her achievement motivation, characteristics viewed as emotional competencies.[6] What's more, he says this holds true *"even among scientists and those in technical professions"* (emphasis added).

An important element of the Third Eye Framework is developing self-awareness, previously discussed (see Chapter 11). Your self-awareness includes knowledge of your performance and your personal characteristics as well as knowledge of the emotional skills you possess in your quotient of emotional intelligence.

You may be asking yourself, "Can I develop my emotional intelligence at all if it's not something that comes naturally to me?" Absolutely! A systematic program of change and learning leads to an increase in emotional intelligence.[7] Emotional intelligence expert Richard Boyatzis reports that the most successful efforts include features such as heightened self-awareness and ongoing continuous improvement, incorporating both experimentation and practice of new behaviors. I recommend working with a qualified professional to develop your emotional intelligence.

A study of a long-term development program for physicians, lawyers, engineers, and professors revealed that self-confidence was a major outcome of the learning process, especially as a result of relationships with others who joined in a common venture of change.[8] Recall the connection between experience and self-confidence? This implies not only that you should work to develop your emotional intelligence, but also that you will gain by support from other introverts online, at retreats or workshops such as those that I run, or in small support groups with like-minded colleagues. You should also seek out executive development programs offered by your employer *if* they are "safe" situations where any social missteps you might make will not be reported back to your superiors. Investigate first.

Emotional intelligence is relevant to Insightful Experts because you have a tendency to live in your inner world, sometimes selectively attending to it rather than the social world around you. (It is similarly relevant to extroverts because they can be oblivious to others simply because they are too busy talking, but extroverts are not our concern here.) The purpose of developing your emotional intelligence is to help you expand your social skills repertoire so that you can more effectively build professional relationships one at a time. Because you have the capability to readily tune into subtleties and to be quietly effective, you will succeed at this!

How do you decide where to focus your professional relationship-building efforts? In the next chapter you will learn how to start thinking of others as strategic stakeholders in your success.

Milestones Along the Journey

Below are a few of the key ideas related to this chapter with a couple extra bullet points for you to fill in. I'd like to hear other ideas that may have resonated for you or were stimulated by what you read. Go to the website www.TheIntrovertsGuide.com to share with me those that have special meaning for *your* personal journey.

- Emotional intelligence can be developed.

- Emotional intelligence is highly correlated with professional success.

- Emotional intelligence is an important element of the Third Eye Framework because it helps you develop good interpersonal relations to complement your technical expertise.

- _____

   _____

- _____

   _____

CHAPTER 15

Get to Specifics: Identify and Target Your Stakeholders

Underlying the need for Insightful Experts to create impetus prior to tackling the inner layers of the Third Eye Framework is the simple fact that a professional career doesn't happen in a vacuum. Instead, your career plays out within a specific and unique human context that is relevant to your success. Understanding your stakeholders can help you prioritize and target your efforts.

Your context is your organization—including colleagues, employees, and superiors—and other people with whom you deal professionally on a routine basis. For most professionals, this means your clients (whom you may also call patients or customers, depending on your industry) and others. It may include other professionals with whom you compete for clients, your professional peers, mentors, the general public, media representatives, government (including regulators), and others. These constitute a community of relationships, sometimes interconnected, within which you practice your profession. As you seek to leverage your introverted assets more fully, you ignore this web of relations and human expectations at your peril.

Consciously or not, people make judgments about your professional capabilities and ultimately determine, either directly (e.g., superiors) or indirectly (e.g., clients), whether you achieve your aspirations or merely tread water. The stakeholder concept is a way to explicitly address this reality and build it into your success plan. The word "stakeholder" is so widely used today that it is taken for granted. In fact, though, it has a precise meaning that, once understood and acted upon, makes it a useful tool in your quest to actualize your career aspirations. Stakeholders include anyone who *affects or is affected by* your success. As you'll see, many of the individuals within your professional context no doubt fall into one or the other of these categories.

Your clients are of utmost importance for the obvious reason that they will judge you by your interactions with them and vote with their feet—which is to say that they will choose another service provider if you disappoint them and an attractive alternative is available. But other stakeholders also are sensitive to how you get along with or come across to them. If they fail to see your quiet competence and the many strengths that your introversion offers (e.g., focus, hard work, introspection, reliability, professional demeanor, etc.), then you will be at a disadvantage. It is important that you know and make sure that how you are judged is how you *want* to be perceived.

Your organization may be large or small. Some Insightful Experts are solo practitioners, in which case you will have external (i.e., outside your organization) stakeholders (including clients) to keep in mind as you seek to leverage your strengths. Other Insightful Experts work in larger partnerships or companies. In this case, you must consider partners, colleagues, and often employees and superiors or bosses. In larger organizations you may interact across departments or divisions, and your actions can affect not only your personal success but also that of your team or division. Thus, as you can imagine, your professional context—the number of stakeholders you interact with on a routine or even infrequent basis—can be complex. It's not hard to see how these people could alter your career path and have an impact on your ability to fulfill your professional goals.

You may wonder why you should be concerned about people who are affected by what you do but cannot exert a direct impact on your success. I recommend that you include such individuals among your stakeholders because, as a professional, you are more than likely not just in a career for its monetary rewards. Instead you want to have a meaningful life, and you want to put your time at work to "good use," as you define that for yourself. This often means helping others in some way, whether by inventing or applying a new technology, saving lives, building energy-efficient structures, providing accurate and reliable information, or some other highly personal aspiration. Because this is true for many if not most Insightful Experts, considering *all* your stakeholders is a useful way of ensuring that you are doing things the way you want to—according to your values, within your community of professional relationships—even if your effect on some stakeholders far overshadows any reciprocal influence they might have on your career.

By conducting a survey of your stakeholders, you will identify who is important to your career and how they are important. As you move through the process outlined in the Third Eye Framework, this information will enable you to target your efforts so that you can prioritize which relationships are most important and which are most urgently in need of your attention. These may or may not be the same.

As a result of surveying *all* your stakeholders, you also will better understand the potential ramifications of changes in how you are perceived within a social *network* rather than just within the dyad of you and a single other stakeholder. Opinions can change quickly within social networks as a result of communication by influential members and the shared understandings that groups can quickly develop. So-called trendsetters can accelerate your progress if you focus on them. After a comprehensive survey, you will also be better able to see where roadblocks with one person may be offset by opportunities to develop a stronger relationship with someone else.

Below is a simplified sample stakeholder survey, represented by a diagram. The direction of the arrows indicates the possible effects of one party *on* the other's attainment of goals.

In this typical example, Susan's career outcomes are affected by DS, a potential mentor who works in another company; IW, a colleague who works on several project teams with Susan; JM, an important client; BW, Susan's longtime assistant on whom she depends; TJ, Susan's practice/business partner; WT, her former boss who continues to give her advice and provides recommendations for her; ZR, the vice president of Susan's division; and ST, a member of the board of directors who does not affect Susan directly but who can influence ZR and DS, who do affect Susan directly. Susan also can see that she has a direct influence on others with whom she has professional interactions: JM, her client; BW, her assistant; her partner, TJ, who also has a reciprocal influence relationship with BW; and ZR, the vice president.

The stakeholder survey allows Susan to identify where she needs to begin developing stronger relationships and who, because they have a

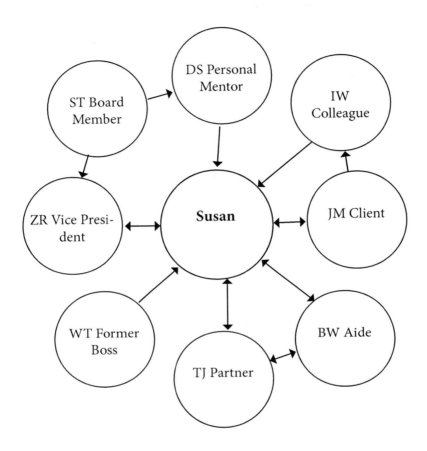

Sample Stakeholder Survey

mutual stake in her success, might be of the most assistance to her as she seeks to optimize her career. She can also discern second-order relationships among key members of her network that might otherwise be overlooked.

Take the time now to work through the following exercise to develop your preliminary understanding of your own stakeholders and how they are important to your career. Go to the website www.TheIntrovertsGuide. com to download forms to accompany this exercise.

Stakeholder Survey Exercise

Step 1: Identify each of your stakeholders by name and consider how they can affect your success in your career and, conversely, how you affect their ability to achieve their own goals. As you do this, rank your stakeholders in terms of their importance to you.

Step 2: Draw a diagram with lines between yourself and each stakeholder and between stakeholders where appropriate. Decide which direction the arrows go.

Step 3: This visual diagram will help you to see the entire network of relationships that are relevant to your career outcomes. You can also identify which relationships need immediate attention and which can be delayed.

Step 4: Expand your analysis by developing two diagrams: one for inside your organization and one that focuses on external stakeholders, such as professionals in other firms with whom you interact on a regular basis. Alternatively, you may wish to draw one big diagram that includes all your stakeholders.

Now that you have a handle on your stakeholders, you are ready for the *final and most critical* phase of creating impetus. In the next chapter you begin to put all the information gathering, analysis, and planning that you've undertaken so far into your everyday activities. With your foot against the pier, you will push off into the charted sea and begin to exercise your power and influence as the Insightful Expert that you are.

Milestones Along the Journey

Below are a few of the key ideas related to this chapter with a couple extra bullet points for you to fill in. I'd like to hear other ideas that may have resonated for you or were stimulated by what you read. Go to the website www.TheIntrovertsGuide.com to share with me those that have special meaning for *your* personal journey.

- Stakeholders are anyone who either can affect or is affected by your professional success.

- Understanding your stakeholders enables you to target your professional career building efforts where you will gain the biggest payoffs.

- A stakeholder map can tell you who is and/or should be in your network and with whom you should forge a strong relationship, discussed in the next chapter.

- _____

  _____

- _____

  _____

CHAPTER 16

Learn to Exercise Your Power and Influence Others

On January 28, 1986, the United States space shuttle Challenger launched with seven astronauts aboard, including high school teacher Christa McAuliffe. Its booster rockets exploded shortly thereafter, blowing the shuttle to bits. Studies of the accident revealed that while engineers on the project were aware of problems with the vital O-ring seals on the rockets, officials of the National Aeronautics and Space Administration (NASA) overrode their objections and went ahead with it anyway. In 2003, the destruction of the space shuttle Columbia on its return was also deemed to have been due to organizational dynamics as much as any technical fault. Again, engineers' concerns were overridden by management, and again, seven astronauts died.[1]

The human dynamics behind both space shuttle catastrophes are ones that are common in many organizations. Simply put, professionals with technical expertise, many of whom are Insightful Experts, are discounted by others. Such accidents shine a glaring spotlight on the potential for disaster that exists when expert professionals lack power to influence decisions.

As you seek to create momentum for your career within your professional practice or organization, it is *imperative* that you begin to pay attention to political dynamics, to understand power and your own resources, and to learn how to influence others. I have saved the most important step to create impetus for last, because it is much easier to execute if you have done the preparation beforehand: planning, clarifying your values, becoming more self-aware and self confident, learning to self-disclose, identifying stakeholders, and so forth. *But make no mistake—it is the number one most important activity to give you momentum to achieve your career goals.*

Political skills will help you attain a more meaningful professional life by enabling you to accomplish what you value. They help you get things done. At the same time, these skills will allow you to build the relationships that lead to career success. Advancement in a profession is highly dependent on connections with mentors, colleagues, superiors in your organization, and others in your professional network.

Attention to power and influence is part of the initial, impetus-creating phase of the Third Eye Framework because how you are perceived and valued by others around you at work is a long-term endeavor. Like the caterpillar that becomes a butterfly—albeit more slowly—you undergo a metamorphosis as you learn new ways of interacting in your workplace and other professional settings. Not only must you learn *how* to do this and then *do* it, you must give others time to react to your changes before you can reap the benefits. The sooner you begin, the better.

You're Not "into" Politics

Some Insightful Experts think, "I'm not the political type. I hate office politics and never want to go down that road." Chances are, however, that this attitude is based on old stereotypes about getting and using power and influence that are based on strong-arm tactics. When many people think of power, they think of formal authority—the ability to *order* someone else to do something—or the ability to *coerce* and force another to do one's bidding no matter how capricious the task. Influence is frequently seen as political manipulation based on deception and aimed solely at meeting the selfish needs of the one doing the influencing.

Such views of power and influence are based in win-lose, zero-sum thinking. But when power is viewed simply as an ability to get things done, and when influence is understood as the beneficial exercise of one's capabilities, the concepts are re-framed in *win-win* terms. In this more benign view, the application of power leads to transactions that benefit *all* the parties involved. Coercion and/or deception are neither required nor recommended.

Sometimes merely contemplating the exercise of power can induce pangs of fear in an introvert. Such feelings might arise from your need to think things through before speaking, your distaste for energy-draining interactions or conflict, or your simple need for solitude to get your work done without having to deal with others. Fear can also be aroused when you begin to take steps to become all that you truly can be, with all your Insightful Expert brilliance and competence out front for all to see. After all, Insightful Experts often just want to blend chameleon-like into the tapestry of their organization's daily workings. Exercising power, or even acknowledging that you have power, can be scary if you're the kind of introvert who has been happy to be reclusive and anonymous. It is your professionalism, though, that calls you to act. You must be powerful and brilliant to achieve optimal results for your stakeholders (including clients) and to create the most meaning from what you do for a living. The psychologist Abraham Maslow called this ultimate fulfillment "self-actualization." In many professional circumstances, you can't serve your profession, much less your ambition, by retiring into a cubicle (although I, for one, can certainly identify with that desire!).

In a sense, understanding and using power is the largest part of what you may have to do to leverage your strengths as an introvert. My advice is simple: take the risk and be brilliant and powerful.

You are about to learn what power is from this different perspective and how you can make it a part of your repertoire of professional skills. You will discover that it can help you facilitate all your relationships and interactions at work.

The Nature of Power

In a company, organization, or other professional setting, power is simply potential. It is capacity, capability, and ability. You can have it but not use it, just as a battery doesn't light a flashlight until the button is pushed to turn it on. Power is latent until it's actually exercised as influence over someone or something. If exercised, power can make things happen that might not otherwise happen. It can accomplish things, but *only* if it's exercised. Right now, at this moment, you possess power that you may not even know you have.

Let's examine this more closely. Sources of power in organizational settings tend to fall into two main categories: (1) power that results from your *personal* qualities or characteristics; and (2) power that results from your *position* in your organization.[2] Within each of these broad categories are several subcategories, the most significant of which are summarized below.

Power Based on Personal Characteristics

- A key source of any individual's ability to accomplish things with other people is naturally that individual's likability. Likability is sometimes called *referent* power or attractiveness. (See the end of this chapter for some tips on How to Be Liked.)

- Knowledge and ability is another way that an individual can successfully get things done. This is sometimes called *expert* power.

- Another way that individuals can get things done is through sheer persistence and *effort*. These personal qualities differ from mere likability.

- One's history is also a source of power. Think about people whom you have known well. They develop a *reputation* that gives them credibility (or lack of it).

Power Based on Role and Position

- The type of power that we all have firsthand experience with, in others if not in ourselves, is the ability to get things done that derives from the *authority* vested in one's position. Only a physician can sign a death certificate, even if everyone else in the room knows someone has expired. "The boss" always has some degree of position power by virtue of her role. This is known as formal authority.

- A variant of formal authority is the power to reward or sanction others, which are known as *reward* power and *coercive* power, respectively. By use of "the carrot or the stick," we can induce other people to do things they might not otherwise do.

- One's position confers other types of power too. For example, if someone has freedom and *autonomy* by virtue of their job or role, they can get things done that others with less freedom cannot. Having a highly *visible* role, such as president, also often confers power.

Once you recognize these diverse sources of power at play in a typical organization, you can begin to see how things get done when power is exercised. One of the first insights you should have is that formal authority only works so long as others respect that authority. Think of the teenager who flaunts the 11 P.M. curfew. The demand inherent in the curfew itself doesn't mean it will be obeyed; rather, obedience is induced by the penalty (coercive power) for *not* doing what is asked, by the parent's track record (reputation) for noticing curfew violations, by the parent's interpersonal relationship with the child (referent power), and by the parent's past persistence (effort power) in enforcing penalties. Some of these same inducements cause professionals in organizations to do what powerful others require.

None of these sources of power need require Machiavellian tactics of deception and selfish intrigue. All are perfectly legitimate and aboveboard ways of getting things done in a professional setting. If you want to be most effective in your career, you must be willing to go beyond the cultural stereotypes that equate power with authority and attach negative connotations to its use.

Your first step can be to identify the sources of power *you* already hold. I use a scientifically validated assessment instrument with my clients to do this, but a good informal place to start is simply to examine the above list of power sources, thinking about your role and your personal characteristics. Because power is always in relation to others—i.e., *context-specific*—you must also think about the context for your current role. Begin by examining the Stakeholder Survey exercise you completed in Chapter 15. Expand your diagram as necessary to add additional people with whom you interact professionally. Jot down notes for yourself. As you consider the Stakeholder Survey, in which relationships do you have some power to accomplish goals and tasks that you value? What do you believe are your power sources in each instance? (Visit my website www.TheIntrovertsGuide.com to download the exercise worksheet to organize and record this analysis.)

As you assess the constellation of relationships in your Stakeholder Survey, you are also assessing your functional network. It is important to evaluate which others you depend on and which others depend on you, i.e., your interdependencies. Think about those with whom you collaborate, requiring their compliance and willingness to work with you on issues, projects, and tasks. Consider subordinates, superiors, and your equals in other professional roles. Who can hinder you from doing your work well and being successful? Conversely, whose work might be compromised by your actions?

You will apply this analysis of your Stakeholder Survey when you put your power to work through the influence process.

Growing a Network at Work

By completing your Stakeholder Survey and exploring your workplace interpersonal network,[3] you will begin to evaluate where you have developed strong trust and positive feelings with others that can lead to your ability to influence them. Linda Hill, an expert on power relations and career development, states that trust will emerge when you are perceived to be competent and when you are perceived to be of good character—i.e., when you know what to do and when you want to do what is right.[4] She notes that you will be more credible to the extent that you are seen as both trustworthy *and* able to get things done.

Neither character nor competence alone suffices. You might be trustworthy, but if you can't get things done, you won't be able to help others get their jobs done. And you might get a lot accomplished, but if you can't be trusted, people will shy away from you as a result of your Machiavellian use of power. To sum it up:

Trustworthiness + Accomplishment = Relationships.

You can see that a strong network must emerge from others' perceptions of your credibility. As introverts, however, you and I both know that you are faced with all the stereotypes and misunderstandings that extroverts tend to attach to us: We're unfriendly, cold, uncaring, lacking in enthusiasm, not on the ball, and so forth. There is no escaping that management of perceptions is part of network building, but by building your relationships on *accomplishments*, you can bypass or at least minimize these stereotypes. If you leverage your power resources to get things done, *and* do the right things, *and* do what you can to make other people shine, you will be perceived positively, and no sleight of hand or exhausting public relations will be needed.

Getting the right things done so that others can shine is integral to the concept of influence that I will discuss next.

Influence: Power in Action

Being able to leverage power into actual accomplishment means that you must be willing to engage with individuals at work and put significant effort into figuring out their needs and the needs of the organization that they (and presumably you) care about. The more unlike you someone is, the more difficult this will be for you, so be prepared for that. Different professional backgrounds, personalities, work experiences, divisional loyalties, etc. all create potential barriers to understanding. With time, however, you can overcome these. Learning to exercise power is part of creating impetus for the very reason that it takes time to build influential relations with others. You are establishing a track record that can later help you be effective in structuring your interfaces and developing stronger overall relationships at work. (And perhaps you are just starting today if you don't like the track record you currently have.)

The process of influencing others activates your latent power to change the world and get things done. You may be a good listener (a latent power based on a personal characteristic), but if you fail to take the time to listen to your colleague talk about the problems she faces, you have virtually no chance of getting her to realize (remember those perceptions?) how good a listener you are and appreciate your support enough to help you accomplish your goals. Your power means little if it is not activated and translated into influence. It's like money under your mattress, neither earning interest nor buying necessities.

Influence is applying your power to alter others' attitudes, beliefs, preferences, or behavior. You build influence with others most effectively when you adhere to the Law of Reciprocity, a concept popularized by influence experts and professors Alan Cohen and David Bradford.[5] The Law of Reciprocity is the simple yet powerful idea that people prefer to pay you back for what you do for them—and of course, they also like it when you repay them for favors done for you. In politics (the government as opposed to the professional variety), this is known as logrolling, as in "you scratch my back and I'll scratch yours."[6] Mutual exchange is simple and simultaneously brilliant because it is so embedded in human nature. Most people derive genuine pleasure from helping others.

How then to tap into your influence? Simply figure out what people need or want that you can provide, and give it to them! Whether or not you've ever taken a marketing class, you may recognize this as "Marketing 101." It's not difficult, but it does require thought and effort. Here are the steps to take:

> ***Step 1:*** *Start with your Stakeholder Survey to identify the people who are most important to your career. Beginning with a high-priority relationship, put yourself in the other party's shoes—get inside his head and work life. Figure out what she wants or needs by examining her challenges, both personal and professional. It might be as simple as someone to share her troubles with over lunch once a month. It might be your knowledge of specific clients or procedures. It might be another couple of grand in his annual budget. You get the idea.*

> ***Step 2:*** *Find a match between what that individual needs or wants and one of your sources of power, either from your role in the organization or from your personal characteristics.*

> ***Step 3:*** *Then give it to him or her in the course of your interactions. Voila! You are on the road to building a reciprocal relationship, and at the same time, beginning the process of developing your influence with that person.*

I call the things you give to others to build influence *exchanges*. It's important to become more aware of what you have available to use as exchanges. I list examples on the next page. Add to the list according to your situation.

Identify the exchanges you can use to build influence with each high-priority individual in your Stakeholder Survey. Write these on your list. Your next step will be to implement your approach. To do this, pick two or three people from the list and work for the next month on making the exchanges you've identified. At the end of that time, reassess. How did it go? What needs to change? Be aware that results won't happen overnight, especially if you are engaging in new behavior patterns. Be patient and stick with it. Gradually work your way to the rest of your list of key stakeholders, revising your strategy as needed.

Sample Exchanges from the Power of Personal Characteristics:	Sample Exchanges from the Power of Role and Position:
Access to your network	Access to other people
Affiliation	Autonomy
Attention	Budgetary allocation
Collegiality	Clarity of expectations
Commitment to follow-through	Cooperativeness
Cooperativeness	Human resources
Expertise	Inclusion in decisions
Help when needed	Increased/decreased client interaction
Humor	Information
Integrity and trustworthiness	Meaningful work
Listening	Motivating goals
Mentoring	New job title
Moral support, encouragement	Opportunity for growth
Personal space and privacy	Performance feedback
Pleasant demeanor	Physical resources (e.g., private office)
Positive work environment	Professional development opportunity
Praise, recognition	Project assignments
Quiet	Promotion
Respect	Recommendations to others
Technical assistance	Responsibility
Trust	Salary/incentive funding
	Technical assistance
	Time off
	Visibility

How Reciprocity Works[7]

The Law of Reciprocity functions so well because it helps any community, including professional colleagues, work together to share resources and divide labor. It is believed to exist in nearly all, if not all, cultures. As children, we are taught to share with others and to repay favors—so clearly our learning about expectations for mutual exchanges goes very deep.

Someone doesn't have to like you for the Law of Reciprocity to function (although you can use likeability as an exchange). A study of people who received a gift revealed that they reciprocated by later buying something from the gift giver when it was offered, regardless of whether they liked him or not. This means that the favors that you perform for others in your day to day work activities will lead to payoffs. You need not worry about whether your personality is inviting. So, if you can't or don't want to rely on your referent power, turn to your expertise and do something for someone else—help them solve a problem that they face.

Reciprocity obligations are stimulated even when you perform a favor for someone that they haven't requested. So when you give something, the other party will feel obligated to return the favor. This means that even if you have never used this approach in the past, you can begin at any time to develop your relationships today, from scratch!

If mutual exchanges are to be perceived as fair, it is important that exchanges are roughly equivalent in value. So, for example, if you provide two hours worth of help to someone on a project, it would be unwise to expect that they would dedicate two days to helping you in the future. While someone might do so simply because the power of reciprocity expectations is so strong, they would resent it. In the long run, you would not do yourself any favors (no pun intended) and, let's face it, the reason for applying the Law of Reciprocity here is not so much to get help as it is to build a long term relationship based on familiarity and trust.

Activation of the Law of Reciprocity should be based on honest intentions to do something or make a concession to another person. If you simply use it to get others to do what you want, they will judge you unkindly as someone who is untrustworthy. Your influence will expand only to the extent that you act in good faith.

Power in the Long Run

The best way to build your power and influence over the long haul in your professional career is to focus on building your expertise. As an Insightful Expert, it is something you can offer as an exchange many times over. This is why professions such as medicine, which require long training and apprenticeships, are so highly respected in comparison with those that can be mastered within a few months. Seek out learning opportunities early in your career and whenever you are in new situations. As you learn and prove your abilities, you will simultaneously be exposed to new people who will begin to comprise your network.

With the increased expertise that results from taking on challenges, you will demonstrate performance results for your organization and team. This builds your reputation and record of accomplishment. As your reputation builds, you will gain more challenging assignments along with an expanding network. You will become more visible and important within your organization. All of these factors lead to even higher levels of expertise, positive outcomes from that expertise, and a positive reputation.[8] Your expanded network also gives you the opportunity to become liked and to develop other sources of personal power and influence beyond just expertise.

Margaret Thatcher, British Prime Minister during the 1980s, is a prominent example of someone who was able to capitalize on both position and personal sources of power to gain influence, often against the odds. A woman from a modest background at a time when only men were dominant in government, she thrived early in her career through the adept use of personal attributes. She worked harder than anyone else, learning important facts about legislative issues and campaigning with dogged determination. Later in her political career, she was able to use the positions she attained through hard work to gain visibility and to build a strong network with key figures in British politics.

Ashley was a scientist for a manufacturing firm. An Insightful Expert, she wanted to make more money and take on new challenges. But she was stuck and could not seem to achieve the promotion she so desired. She hated the interpersonal exchanges with other scientists and the need to be polished when giving presentations to management. But Ashley was astute and also realized that her company valued technical performance above all else. So Ashley decided to put more effort into product innovation, using her specialized training to get results in the laboratory. She put in many long hours and was eventually successful in achieving an innovation that would save the company millions of dollars each year in the production process. Finally, her expertise was rewarded with the performance evaluation and promotion that she wanted.

In this way, your power from a personal characteristic—expertise—can lead to positional or role power as you are given higher levels of responsibility and visibility. As an introvert, you can develop a network and strong relationships with your stakeholders in this fashion. An extrovert might employ personal charm and fast talk to get by, but you are better served by focusing on what you do best. When you think about your expertise, begin by thinking about your strengths that derive from your introversion, then later think about the specifics of your professional training and experience—those skills that are unrelated to introversion per se. Remember that your introversion gives you the ability to pay careful attention to the task at hand, to work independently without close oversight, thoughtfulness, a calm demeanor, and many more qualities that are valuable professional abilities.

As you continue to seek challenges and do well with them, you will enjoy the invaluable outcomes of increased levels of competence and expertise. A side effect of your growth will be increased access to exchanges. With greater position power, you will be able to add exchanges based on your position to the ones that you already possess on the basis of your *personal* characteristics, including your high level of expertise.

Marshalling your power and influence is likely to be the single most important activity that you undertake. By building power and influencing others, you set the stage for all the other things you will do to become more effective as an Insightful Expert—outlined in the next two layers of the Third Eye framework. Remember that power need not be based on extroversion or Machiavellian tactics. If you make the effort to build your stature in the ways outlined here, you will be better prepared for the specific events that tend to trip up introverts, such as leading others, meetings, communications, networking, and so forth, discussed in subsequent sections of this book.

At the same time, you will build social capital that will afford you more opportunities to work in solitude where possible and maintain your energy reserves. And that's a huge reward for those of us who are introverts!

With efforts in place to expand your power base and build your influence, you have now successfully set up your professional milieu for what is to come. You are creating the necessary impetus for the other changes that you choose to make as an Insightful Expert. Creation of impetus is a long-term strategy that is now in motion for you. In the next part of the book, you will learn how to structure your interactions in ways that benefit *you* more than the extroverts around you.

How to Be Liked

Although it may not matter much to you if others like you, it will help your career if you are liked or – at least not disliked! Your ability to be liked by others is called your *referent power*. It is one reason why extroverts are so successful. They strike up casual conversations with ease and typically develop familiarity and trust more quickly than introverts. Psychologist Robert Cialdini identified reasons why we like someone. While these, by far, are not the only ways to be liked, can you make any of them work for you?

- *Good looks* lead to a halo effect that causes others to judge us favorably in other areas—such as our intelligence, integrity, hard work, and so forth. Because it's unconscious, many people even deny the influence of physical attractiveness. Nevertheless, studies of elections, hiring, and the judicial system all support its existence. More attractive people end up with more favorable outcomes.

- *Familiarity* also builds commitment to an individual. The more we are around someone, the more we tend to like her. If you are hidden in an office, where many introverts choose to spend their time, then it's likely that you will not be liked as well as the extrovert who is hanging around the water fountain or the lunch room. It's that simple. I recommend use of the Law of Reciprocity to build relationships in part because it makes and keeps you visible. A related way to build familiarity, perhaps more attractive to introverts, is by using social media. By making regular updates to your online presence/site, you stay visible and gradually expand others' knowledge of you and your activities, including your accomplishments.

- Our *similarities* with others also lead to liking. These could range from our looks to our political beliefs. While I do not recommend that you conjure up similarities where none exist, you may want to make an effort to know more about your pivotal stakeholders. If you identify similar traits or likes, gradually and carefully engage in more self-disclosure (discussed in Chapter 13). When you are so reserved that no one knows you, then it's impossible to take full advantage of this reason for someone liking you. A small way to make this work for you is to pay attention to how you dress in professional settings. Make sure you fit in.

- Giving *compliments* is another way to build positive feelings toward you. Praise has been shown time and again as a way to gain someone's affection. Like your usage of the Law of Reciprocity, I recommend that if you choose to employ this, that you do it with integrity. Be genuine.

Milestones Along the Journey

Below are a few of the key ideas related to this chapter with a couple extra bullet points for you to fill in. I'd like to hear other ideas that may have resonated for you or were stimulated by what you read. Go to the website www.TheIntrovertsGuide.com to share with me those that have special meaning for *your* personal journey.

- Using power with integrity is a win-win strategy to accomplish career goals.

- An Insightful Expert's best source of power and influence is usually his or her professional expertise.

- Learning to exercise power and influence others is the single most important activity to build impetus for other positive career changes. As you do so, you can simultaneously begin to Structure Your Interfaces, coming up in Part III. These are complementary activities.

- _____

  _____

- _____

  _____

CHAPTER 17

From Impetus to Interfaces

After you have created impetus by setting into motion a well-thought-out plan to build sustainable relationships with the most important people in your professional milieu, it will be time to learn how to manage day-to-day interactions to your advantage *as an introvert*.

When you view a satellite image of the earth, you see shapes of blue and green. Only when you zoom in can you see that the green is broken into varying shades, including brown. As you zoom further, you discern trees, houses, and cars on streets.

Like the objects in the view from space, an introvert and an extrovert look very similar from a distance. Closer up, they still look alike if we view only an individual in isolation. But if we move in closer and view them as they *interact* with other people, we begin to see that—at least some of the time (and it would be more often if they had their way)—introverts don't behave at all like extroverts. Introverts tend to talk less, show less animation, respond more slowly, keep more distance, and spend more time alone.

It is in the specifics of interpersonal contact that introversion is most visibly set apart from extroversion. Unfortunately, these are the interfaces in which extroverts often form their opinions about Insightful Experts, and those opinions are frequently negative.

One of the primary reasons for this outcome is that it's human nature to be fearful of what is different. This reaction takes place in the primitive parts of our brains predating cognition, so its effects are quite potent. In ancient societies it made us wary of potential conquerors, thus conferring an adaptive advantage. In response, we seek to quell our fear or uncertainty by treating those who are different as an out-group, adopting an "us-versus-them" attitude, and we sometimes justify our original recoil by deciding that the others are inferior to ourselves. In business and professional settings in the United States, this natural tendency is bolstered by a culture that values an *alpha*, take-charge personality. The result, as you and I know perhaps too well, is that introversion frequently is viewed as a serious defect in professional settings.

Compounding this is that introverts tend not to be at their best performing in social interactions, especially as the number of participants grows. Often Insightful Experts simply don't want to expend the energy to be more gregarious than called for by their natural inclination, which is for solitude. Introverts also present themselves differently from extroverts, sometimes appearing uncomfortable in interactions.

The most effective way to combat the discomfort of professional interactions and the corresponding inaccurate judgments sometimes made is to rely on the strengths of introversion. This turns the situation on its head and takes you from a position of weakness to a position of strength. By taking control, you are *proactive* in establishing your professional reputation for yourself rather than defending it against the assumptions others make about you.

You have considerable strengths. The nature of Insightful Experts is to be introspective and thoughtful. You do well in one-on-one and smaller group environments, especially when you are prepared. Among your assets generally is also the ability to consider alternatives rationally and plan ahead. Structuring your interfaces to capitalize on these and other positive characteristics that you possess allows you to more effectively manage your interactions with others and to leave them with a more accurate (and positive) impression of your capability.

One of the reasons why structuring interactions to better suit your predispositions works so well is that it enables you to project the confidence and self-assurance that the professional world expects. You project confidence not by faking it—playing the role of extrovert— but from your core. You genuinely *feel* more confident. Some research shows that introverts and extroverts can be virtually indistinguishable when the introverts are in situations that are very comfortable for them. *Structuring your interfaces is the process of creating such strong situations for yourself.* Self-assurance emerges naturally from relying on your introverted strengths as an Insightful Expert.

The Three R's

Just three activities, done well, can help you structure your interfaces effectively. I call these the *three R's*, but they're not reading, writing, and arithmetic. They are:

- **Research**
- **Rules**
- **Rehearsal**

Research. Research is what you do in advance of your interactions. As an Insightful Expert, research will come naturally to you! By doing your homework, you will be better able to make appropriate verbal contributions and to exert your influence to modify the unwritten rules of the game when that's possible.

Rules. Rules are the unwritten norms that guide the way that business normally is done. As you begin to better understand your introversion and what works best for you as an Insightful Expert, you can take actions to make the interface with others accommodate your needs. The self-awareness work that you undertake in the first layer of the Third Eye Framework prepares you for this, as does the introductory reading in Part I of this guide that explains how introverts are different from extroverts.

Rehearsal. Rehearsal is what you do to prepare and get ready for specific events. Because Insightful Experts are so busy thinking of so many different scenarios, we don't do as well on our feet as we might like. We can stumble over words and be unprepared to reach conclusions quickly. By rehearsing for professional situations, we create more comfort for ourselves and mitigate the effects of these tendencies. Perhaps we'll never be as quick as extroverts, but we can be effective nonetheless.

Over the next several chapters in Part III, I explain each of these so that you can begin to apply them right away in your workplace and in your professional dealings with others. When combined with the effort you make to create impetus for yourself by establishing long-term, authentic relationships, structuring interfaces can give you an edge to get to your career objectives successfully.

The natural place to start is with the research that you can do prior to an interaction to make it work to your advantage. That is coming up in the next chapter.

Milestones Along the Journey

Below are a few of the key ideas related to this chapter with a couple extra bullet points for you to fill in. I'd like to hear other ideas that may have resonated for you or were stimulated by what you read. Go to the website www.TheIntrovertsGuide.com to share with me those that have special meaning for *your* personal journey.

- With the impetus created by developing a plan, becoming more self-aware, and beginning to build strong relationships, you are ready to focus on setting the terms for your interactions with others.

- The introverted strengths of reflection, thoughtfulness and careful planning lay the groundwork for structuring interfaces with others to maximal advantage.

- The new 3 R's are Research, Rules, and Rehearsal. These enable an introvert to structure situations to better accommodate his/her strengths.

- _____

  _____

- _____

  _____

PART III

Structure Your Interfaces

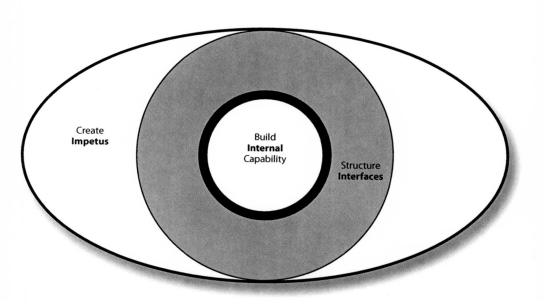

CHAPTER 18

Do Your Research

Now we move inward to explore the principles of the middle layer in the Third Eye Framework: Structure Your Interfaces. Introduced and outlined in Chapter 17, the important strategy of structuring your interfaces rests on three critical activities: doing your *Research*, deciding on the *Rules* for interactions with others, and *Rehearsing* what you will say in high stakes situations.

The three R's are designed to create stronger social situations for you so that your Insightful Expert competencies can come to the forefront. By making your professional interactions more comfortable for yourself, you enable others to see how much you have to offer, giving your career a boost as you emerge from the shadows of being unseen and unheard much of the time. We begin by focusing on the data gathering phase of your homework—doing your research.

The first step in effective preparation for professional interactions with others is doing the research necessary to identify the other party or parties and his or her predispositions. Just as you would not give a speech intended for your professional peers to a classroom of second graders, you won't get far by saying and doing the same things regardless of whom you are addressing in the professional world. People are different in their training, professional backgrounds and experiences, cognitive styles, divisional loyalties, likes and dislikes, and so forth. Targeting your messages is simply good sense, and you can't target without first knowing who is there and what their differences look like.

Who Will Be There?

First, identify with whom you'll be interacting. A one-on-one meeting, such as with your assistant, is easy, but for a larger group such as a project team, take the time to find out exactly who has been invited and who is expected to show up. Group dynamics can change drastically if even one person is absent or shows up unexpectedly.

Pamela is a young researcher who was up for a performance review at her university. There was no reason for anyone to believe that her review would not go smoothly. She is a good scientist, careful in her work, bright, and gets along well with others. She's respectful and pleasant. But things went awry when her project leader suddenly announced an out-of-town commitment the day the review team was to meet. The meeting went ahead as scheduled since no one, least of all Pamela, suspected that the project leader's absence would make any difference, given that she was so highly perceived and genuinely qualified. But go wrong it did. One of the reviewers asked Pamela a question she couldn't answer because she misunderstood what he was asking. Others tried to restate what they thought the question was, but Pamela was flustered. Each time she tried to answer what she mistakenly thought they were asking, their disapproval grew. Her project leader could and would have prompted her, but he was absent. By the end of the meeting, the members of the review team had reached an informal consensus among themselves that Pamela was not performing up to par—on the basis of her misunderstanding and inability to answer just one crucial question. Her project leader learned the outcome to his dismay, but the damage had been done. Pamela failed the review and waited six months before another review, at which everyone was present. That time she passed with flying colors.

You can see how critical even one member of a group can be. If you are attending a meeting, find out who will be there. If it's a presentation to a board, make sure you know which board members are likely to attend. If it's a professional conference, explore in advance who will attend. In any situation where you must meet with more than one individual, it will behoove you to identify everyone.

What Are Their Personal Agendas and Biases?

Second, after you know who will be there, you must do the harder work of finding out their biases, or what are commonly called "agendas." What are their goals? Why? By spending some time thinking about the differences among individuals, you will gain substantial insights into the dynamics of groups and workplace politics. Because you are an introvert, you must prepare yourself in advance. Were you an extrovert, except perhaps a very shy extrovert, you would find it easier to respond on your feet and either address or deflect an issue. But your strength is not there; it is in focusing beforehand to carefully plan your approach.

To predict biases you may not know about, consider these variables:

- *Education and training:* This can include everything from an individual's field of concentration (medicine, civil engineering, pediatric nursing, etc.) to where he or she went to graduate school, since different professional schools emphasize differing paradigms. Consider specialties, sub-specialties, and mentors.

- *Background and history:* Think about how people ended up where they currently are. Have their careers been long or short, and have they stayed in one company or partnership or moved among multiple professional settings? Have their backgrounds been monolithic or diverse? How might such differences shape their various perspectives?

- *Loyalties:* Some experts view organizations simply as conglomerates of groups who all have competing goals. If these goals are not pulled together in some fashion and anchored to an organization-wide goal, an organization is likely to disintegrate from the conflicts over scarce resources. On a smaller scale, this can happen in your meetings with project teams, partners, board members, and employees. While your concern is not to resolve and avert conflicts unless you are the meeting leader, as an introvert, your concern must be to present yourself effectively. And if you don't know where the landmines (i.e., individual biases and goals) are, you'll find it hard to do this.

- *Responsibilities:* While loyalties may be less tangible, responsibilities tend to be clearer. What formal roles do parties to an interaction fill? What must they do to perform their roles well? How are they evaluated? To whom do they report?

- *Individual differences:* Individual differences include personal values, strengths, predispositions, cognitive styles, religious and ethnic backgrounds, social status, and so on. Each of these variables can affect how people respond and interact with one another.

What is the Formal Purpose of the Interaction?

A third step in your research is identifying the formal or main agenda. This will of course vary according to the purpose of the interaction. A chance meeting with a coworker in the hallway of course has no explicit agenda. A networking event typically has an implied agenda on the part of its participants—to meet new people and to build relationships that may lead to advantageous business outcomes.

Formal meetings typically will have more explicit agendas, written or not. It is important for you, an Insightful Expert, to find out in advance as much as you can about what will be discussed. In this way you can prepare yourself adequately prior to the interaction. Know the topics, and if need be, research their history so that your contributions can be informed. Remember that one of your goals is to present yourself in a positive light. This isn't self-promotion; it's unveiling your authentic professional expertise with the full recognition that, as an introvert, you may not think well on your feet.

If a meeting involves a broad array of individuals, you can also research informal agendas by talking with invited attendees prior to the event. Does this mean that you must spend your time seeking out everyone and making conversation prior to a meeting? I can imagine that that's not your favorite thing to do, and it's not what I mean. Instead, you may only need to seek out one person who tends to be in the know. You'll know who if you spend any time thinking about it.

If you're thinking that this sounds like a lot of work prior to an interaction, you're right—it can be. But since you don't want to act like an extrovert, it's to your advantage to do the homework you need to present yourself well as an introvert. And once you get the hang of it, these basic research steps will rarely take long.

After you've done your study of the interaction beforehand, you can begin the next stage of structuring your interfaces and deciding what rules would work best for *you*, the Insightful Expert.

Milestones Along the Journey

Below are a few of the key ideas related to this chapter with a couple extra bullet points for you to fill in. I'd like to hear other ideas that may have resonated for you or were stimulated by what you read. Go to the website www.TheIntrovertsGuide.com to share with me those that have special meaning for *your* personal journey.

- Doing your homework before an event is crucial to being prepared for it as an Insightful Expert. It is the first step in pushing back against professional norms that suit extroverts, who are good on their feet.

- Personal differences among individuals can mean that they each carry unconscious biases that affect the dynamics of their relationship.

- Having done your homework prior to an interaction, you are positioned to push-back against the unwritten rules that structure professional interactions, coming up next in Chapter 19.

- _____

_____

- _____

_____

CHAPTER 19

Decide on the Rules

Imagine a baseball game with no rules. Players might circle the diamond clockwise or counterclockwise. When the ball is in play, players on base might pass each other running in opposite directions. The strike zone could be anywhere, and woe to the batter who misses that below-the-knees 90 mph fastball. Bats need not be regulation size and weight. In fact, a player might use a 2 x 4 or a club to hit the ball. (So easy even a caveman could do it!) Ball? No set size. One pitcher chooses a softball, while another selects a golf ball. The game could be called at four innings or fourteen, depending on the whim of the players.

Without rules, a baseball game would be radically different from the game we know—and not only different but unpredictable—day to day and team to team. Put yourself in the shoes of a baseball player and consider how this uncertainty might affect your game. A few individuals might thrive, but most of us would be thrown off our games (pun intended).

It's been said that mastering a skill takes 10,000 hours of practice.[1] A professional ball player is a professional because he has acquired mastery of his craft over many years of practice according to a stable set of rules. He knows the strike zone. He knows the infield. He knows the feel of his favorite ash bat. He knows how to time his bat to hit a ball coming toward him at high speed. Take away these constants, based on long acquaintance with the structure of the game, and the professional player is no longer an expert. He may have fundamental skills, but the changing landscape renders them useless much of the time.

Structure constrains how people interact. It establishes necessary boundaries. The "rules of the game" may be intentionally altered from time to time, but otherwise they provide a stable structure within which interactions take place. At a micro, or personal, level in organizations there are rules of the game for getting along with others. These rules favor extroverted behavior, such as talking loudly, an assertive stance, quick answers, banter, warm exchanges, ready disagreement with others, visible enthusiasm, not admitting failings, and so forth. Linguistic style expert Deborah Tannen notes that strong self-confidence, challenging others, talking up your achievements, bluntness rather than indirectness, taking solo credit, and not asking questions all serve to increase your stature because they are standard expectations.[2]

Because extroversion is the dominant "language" of business in the United States, the fact that this language sets up rules for behavior that potentially can be modified is not always understood or even readily visible to Insightful Experts. You may know that something is wrong because you don't fit well into the prevailing professional business culture, but you don't know why. If you do recognize how the "game" works, you may not know how to go about changing it to your benefit.

In most Western culture, the rules of the game call for a particular communication style and certain structural characteristics of interactions. After you have proven yourself and developed a positive reputation, you will be given more leeway to vary from these norms. (The outer layer of the Third Eye Framework, Create Impetus, consists of action steps that are designed to get you to this place more quickly.) Until that time, you may be able to deviate from a couple of extroverted expectations—for example, perhaps getting others to accept that you will be saying less rather than more—but, by and large, you will be expected to conform unless you personally take proactive action to change the rules of the game.[3] Coming up, you will learn more about where to intervene and how to modify them to your advantage as an Insightful Expert.

Part IV of this book includes several chapters discussing communication skills. These may help you redress any communication weaknesses your self-assessment turns up, but they are no substitute for paying attention to how you structure your interfaces at the outset.

The Rules of Engagement

Many rules or structural norms associated with professional inter-actions are amenable to modification. Because they have the potential to be altered, I call them *variables*. These variables are set up now to accommodate extroversion. But you can seek to modify them to accom-modate your introversion. As you review the following list of interaction variables, take note of your own preferences and strengths within profes-sional interactions. The interaction variables are also summarized in a table at the end of this chapter.

Meetings. Meetings, the most basic of interactions among people, can take place one-on-one (i.e., in a dyad) between two people, in small groups, or in larger groups. Many introverts naturally prefer dyads and small groups to larger groups, and it is easier for an introvert to be heard and recognized in a smaller group.

Communication. Communications can take place either verbally or in writing. Some introverts prefer written communication because it gives them time to think about what they will say. Another advantage of writ-ten communication (including e-mail) is that it gives you a record of what was discussed, what was decided, and supporting arguments for later reference and continuity. On the other hand, written communica-tion can be open to misinterpretation. Verbal misunderstandings can be checked and cleared up quickly.

Verbal communications can be one-way (a lecture or a state of the union address, for example), two-way (one-on-one dialogue), or all-way. The latter is a structured or free-form interplay among more than two persons—a scheduled or impromptu group meeting with or without an agenda. Written communications can be formal or informal in tone and structure. Preferences may vary by the organizational culture, the profes-sion, or the individual to whom the communication is addressed.

Interactions. Professional interactions with clients, peers, superiors, or subordinates can be either spontaneous or planned. Some introverts prefer planned interactions, since these afford an opportunity to think through in advance what will be said and done and to consider various alternative situations that may arise. While extroverts have an easier time reacting spontaneously and finding something—anything—to say, this can often be difficult for introverts.

Time. The time dimension of interactions can be either limited or open-ended. An open-ended interaction might be working next to someone in a nearby cubicle or desk. A time-limited interaction might be a meeting that is scheduled with a predetermined ending time. With an introvert's need for solitude to recharge the energy that is drained by social interaction, an Insightful Expert will often prefer interactions that are limited in duration.

Props. Props can make the difference between an interaction that works for introverts and one that doesn't. Props are any physical object that allows you to perform more effectively. At its most basic, a prop could be a desk that offers space between you and the other parties and creates a more formal atmosphere for an interaction. A laptop computer is another type of prop that can allow you to take notes during a meeting, which will divert attention from the fact that you may not be saying much. A note pad and pen function similarly. Do you need notes to remember what to say? Bringing them can help you keep your poise and ensure that the few things you do say are memorable. A well structured PowerPoint® presentation can help an Insightful Expert look cool throughout a formal speech. In almost all situations an extrovert, who can speak extemporaneously at length, will do well with or without props, but an introvert will usually benefit from appropriate props. Can you think of other props that would benefit you?

Location. Because we are private, most introverts prefer private interactions to public ones. By private, I mean ones conducted behind closed doors or at least without onlookers or eavesdroppers. Extroverts tend to be more oblivious to their surroundings, since they typically don't experience the same need for personal space.

Facilitation. Whether or not input is sought from many participants in a systematic fashion can be an important variable for an introvert. Where there is no conscious effort to involve everyone, introverts will probably be underrepresented in the decision-making process. Extroverts will naturally speak up and take as much time as they need, even rambling off topic or into the trivial. Because meetings and events are often time-limited and the attention span of some participants is low, the result can be almost total neglect of introverts. Strong facilitation that consciously seeks input from all participants will benefit introverts; weak or nonexistent facilitation that allows speakers to engage at will typically places introverts at a disadvantage.

Meetings in which the real or metaphorical microphone is passed around the circle to solicit everyone's contributions provide greater equity to introverts, even if you dread your turn in the spotlight. So-called "popcorn style" discussions, in which contributions emerge randomly from a group, tend to disadvantage introverts and give extroverts an advantage for getting their ideas heard. Regardless of the meeting style, a strong facilitator will ensure that everyone's input is given time and consideration.

Culture. The culture of an organization—whether a large firm, a professional practice, a nonprofit, or a small business—is another structural variable that affects how interactions among professionals take place. In an authoritative patriarchal culture, decisions flow downward, information flows upward, and conformity is highly valued. A collaborative culture fosters multidirectional communications across divisions or departments and up the organizational chart, and decisions tend to be democratic in nature. Differences are expected and valued.

Which of these will benefit introverts? In many cases, it will be the one that is collaborative. In an authoritative culture, only the loudest and most forceful will have their opinions heard, so extroversion is highly valued. Introversion, emanating from a feminine archetypal view of the world, is viewed as a weakness in an authoritative culture. The opposite is true in a well-managed collaborative culture, in which quiet dissent is heard and accepted. In a collaborative culture, introverts can flourish. This is not to say that you may not find collaboration uncomfortable because it does involve a lot of communication and willingness to manage conflict. But if you follow the long run strategy of creating impetus for yourself, building strong relationships with others based on your expertise and personal traits, you are likely to find that collaboration works better for you than an authoritative culture where only the most articulate and outgoing are heard.

Event Set-Up: Plan Interactions to Suit Yourself

By considering the interaction variables above, you can begin to take actions to construct your interactions to play to your strengths. Do your critical interactions include day-to-day workplace communications and performing tasks with others? Teams and projects? Supervising and leading others? Performing services for clients? Marketing and sales activities? Meetings with board members or your boss? Formal presentations? Whatever the interaction, consider how you can alter these variables to re-configure it to *your* advantage as an Insightful Expert.

Begin by considering the day-to-day activities revolving around your workspace. Most introverts value personal space and privacy because we feel drained by constant social expectations and conversation. How can you carve that out for yourself? If private offices don't exist in your work-place, how can you create the cubicle seclusion you need? Recall how, in Chapter 7, Helen rearranged her office so that she could keep her door open to show collegiality but at the same time keep herself from being visible from the hallway when she was working at her desk. This gave her the solitude she needed to work.

After considering your physical space, consider how you can struc-ture communications to play to your strengths. Can more of them be in writing, if writing is a strength of yours? Can you make more of your meetings in your private space with only one other party, in a dyad? Perhaps you can invite someone to lunch to talk off-site. Think about your situation and what you might be able to do.

Using these principles, Bryan, a teacher, learned to facilitate classroom dis-cussions like a pro, enabling him to use Socratic method to create learn-ing rather than carry around all the answers in his head. He frequently breaks students into pairs and small groups to work on exercises so that he can work with them rather the entire class as a whole. When he presents lectures, he keeps them to a defined time period of twenty minutes and prepares detailed word for word notes for himself in advance. He also uses PowerPoint slides to structure his presentations to the class. He never tries to entertain but instead relies on carefully structured exercises to engage students' attention.

A designer, Morgaine relies on her website to support the marketing she has to do for her business. She provides many examples of her work at different price points and includes the options available to customers. She uses her laptop as a necessary sales prop when she meets with customers. In this way, she can show rather than tell what she does when she is face to face with them, having prepared the website in the solitude that suits her best.

Joshua has embraced electronic meetings as a way to avoid the discomfort he feels in large face to face interactions. It allows him to use the props he needs and a structured facilitation style. Not only can he get the job done, it makes the meetings more convenient for attendees and he gets better participation.

The more strategic you can be in modifying variables to establish new rules for yourself, the better you can perform in your interactions. This process of examining your interfaces and deciding how to alter them to your advantage may take some time. Approach it in four steps, summarized below:

1. *Identify your strengths, based on your degree of introversion, your other personality characteristics, and your analysis of the structural variables discussed above and shown in the table below.*

2. *Identify the interactions that are key to your professional success in light of your achievement goals. These may be team projects, supervising others, getting along with colleagues or a boss, creative collaborations, etc. The important thing is that you clearly define which interactions are current priorities.*

3. *Now put the two together. Given your strengths, carefully consider how the high-priority interactions could be better structured to play to your strengths, not someone else's.*

4. *Begin to make the changes. Don't try to do it all at once. Start with one interaction and work on it. Then try another. Keep modifying what you do to find what works both for you and for those in your organization with whom you have to interact.*

Expect some resistance, but don't bow to all of it. Know that you will be able to change some things but not all. Take to heart the serenity prayer attributed to Reinhold Niebuhr: "Grant me serenity to accept the things I cannot change, courage to change the things I can, and wisdom to know the difference." Over time, the people with whom you interact will begin to see you differently, and things will get easier.

The last step in structuring interfaces is to practice before you go "live." In the next chapter we'll talk about rehearsing.

Interaction Variables		
Variable	**Some Available Options**	
Meeting Size	Dyad	Larger Group
Communication	Written	Oral
Oral Communication	One-Way	Two-Way or All-Way
Written Communication	Formal	Informal
Interaction Timing	Planned	Spontaneous
Time-frame	Limited	Open Ended
Location	Private	Public
Facilitation	Strong	Weak
Props	Present	Absent
Culture	Collaborative	Authoritative

Milestones Along the Journey

Below are a few of the key ideas related to this chapter with a couple extra bullet points for you to fill in. I'd like to hear other ideas that may have resonated for you or were stimulated by what you read. Go to the website www.TheIntrovertsGuide.com to share with me those that have special meaning for *your* personal journey.

- The rules of the game provide boundaries that structure interactions among people. In most cases in the business world, these are set by extroverts and benefit extroverts.

- Variables that may be amenable to configure interactions so that they are more suitable for introverts include group size, communication, timing, location, facilitation, props, and cultural norms.

- By seeking to modify variables of interactions, you enable your introverted strengths to flourish rather than struggle to fit your predispositions into extroverted contexts.

- _____

  _____

- _____

  _____

CHAPTER 20

Rehearse

The final step in structuring your interfaces is to rehearse your part. It sounds contrived, doesn't it? But it can be essential for many Insightful Experts and in reality is quite practical. This step requires you to review the information you gathered during your research phase and consider what you will say when you enter into interactions with others, regardless of how well you managed to set the rules for the interaction. This step is often necessary because introverts sometimes struggle with spontaneous exchanges. Their minds are so focused on the details and nuances of the communication that they cannot formulate replies quickly. Introverts need time to think. By rehearsing, you can rely on your strengths of diplomacy, careful deliberation, and thoughtful diligence.

Like a good actor or actress, you will want to consider how you will come across to others and work on polishing your demeanor and communication skills if they are not up to par. But the content of your contributions—your "lines," to use the theater analogy—is equally as important, if not more so, so focus on both. You can't rehearse without first thinking through what you want to say. That should be your first step, just as you might prepare a series of index cards prior to a giving a speech.

Any interface with others in your professional life that occurs routinely or that you can predict is open to rehearsal. This ranges from what you might say to a colleague each morning as a greeting, to managing your subordinates, to meetings, and more. You can even do a "what if" and formulate and practice alternative responses that you might make depending on the real-time conversation.

As any good attorney who heads into a courtroom knows, how you come across influences how you are perceived and whether you make your case successfully. Without a plan for what you will say in a given situation, you run the risk of being distracted by events and what others say. The result is that you can easily forget the important conversation points that you wanted to make. This is especially likely if you are prone to social anxiety; the nervousness you feel can lead to memory lapses. The more you rehearse in advance, just like a president before a State of the Union address, the greater will be the likelihood that you will recall facts and gradations in meaning to deliver your statements with confidence. Your rehearsal should encompass both the verbal and nonverbal elements of the interaction. Help with verbal and nonverbal communication skills is found in Part IV, Build Your Internal Capability.

Christopher is a high-profile global consultant who rehearses out loud prior to telephone conversations that he believes may be difficult. Another Insightful Expert, Ruth, writes out line by line what she will say prior to talking on the phone or when facing a situation where conflict may emerge.

Make the Right First Impression

Making a good initial impression is especially relevant when you are meeting someone for the first time such as at a job interview, starting a new position, a networking event, or a presentation to a professional group. It's also a concern when you first begin to spend time with others such as on a new project team or in another working relationship. Research suggests that a major reason why first impressions mean so much is that people rarely deviate from them. Lasting opinions are formed in an instant!

Although extroverts are naturally expressive in a way that is sanctioned by Western culture, the natural reserve of Insightful Experts is often viewed with less favor. Plus, it leaves more room for interpretation. Because you are less expressive, you run the risk of having someone form an inaccurate first impression. Your lack of facial, vocal, and/or gestural expression can lead others to view you as cold, distant, unprepared, lazy, lacking energy, lacking initiative, unengaged, unpleasant, or worse!

It's time to set the record straight. As you embark on a process of building impetus for yourself by developing credible, strong professional relationships, it pays to work on making the best possible first impression. Here are some ways that are founded on your introverted assets to do so.[1]

Begin by paying attention to your looks. Yes, that's right—your looks. You need not be beautiful or handsome but you do need to be clean, tidy, and well-groomed if you want people to form a positive impression. A good haircut, trimmed and clean fingernails and spotless good quality clothing are essential.

Make eye contact. This is one of the first things that people notice and, if you are shy, you may find it especially hard to do. Often shy people don't make direct eye contact when they are addressing someone they don't know well. But your eyes, sometimes called the mirror to the soul, link you to another human in a profound way. In your profession, they establish that you are safe, trustworthy, and competent. Look directly into another's eyes as you speak and as you listen. It is a sign of disrespect to fail to look at someone else when they are speaking. In meetings, no matter how bored you may feel, be sure to maintain eye contact with others around the table. On the other hand, be careful not to go overboard with eye contact so that it becomes staring. It's a fine line but with practice, you will learn it. Finally, if you are speaking to a group, try to make eye contact with each of the members of your audience at one point or another.

Be calm and collected. As a professional, it is to your advantage to appear deliberate and self-assured at first glance. I believe it can even afford you leeway later on when you need time to gather your thoughts in your typical Insightful Expert fashion. Disorganization and multitasking don't work well for this. Practice walking into a room with confidence and grace. Keep practicing—rehearsal builds habits that persist and ultimately pay off.

Milestones Along the Journey

Below are a few of the key ideas related to this chapter with a couple extra bullet points for you to fill in. I'd like to hear other ideas that may have resonated for you or were stimulated by what you read. Go to the

website www.TheIntrovertsGuide.com to share with me those that have special meaning for *your* personal journey.

- Rehearsal is not just for actors. It can help you manage the impression that you make on others so that it is a more accurate reflection of your true assets.

- First impressions are lasting impressions.

- Rehearsing enhances your position as an Insightful Expert by making you better prepared to respond and engage in verbal conversations with ease. It helps to compensate for your need to sort through your thoughts that sometimes leads to stumbling or hesitation over words.

- _____

  _____

- _____

  _____

CHAPTER 21

From Interfaces to Internal Capability

Congratulations! You've made it through the first two segments of the Third Eye Framework, and are well on your way to letting your introversion truly be your distinctive competence rather than your bane. In Part III of this book, I have explained how you can structure your interfaces to suit *your* strengths as an Insightful Expert. This has included the 3 R's: research, rules, and rehearsal. These initiatives can take place while you continue to follow the long-term strategy of creating impetus for yourself that you learned how to do in Part II. You created impetus with sustainable, authentic relationships, and now you've structured your professional interfaces to accommodate your introversion. With these two sets of activities underway, you're prepared to move to the inner core of the Third Eye Framework and focus on building your internal capabilities!

The innermost core of the Third Eye Framework is about developing the personal *skills* you may need to follow through with these career-changing initiatives. Some Insightful Experts, especially if they are at an advanced stage of their careers, have developed these capabilities the hard way through trial and error. Many others, though, have not.

Make no mistake: these skills are not about becoming more extroverted in how you interact with others. Rather, they are about learning how to smooth the edges of your interactions, how to become more strategic in how you get along with others, and to confront issues—that scare or bore you—with pragmatism instead of avoidance.

Begin by referring to the strategic career plan which I recommended that you develop for yourself (see Chapter 7). If you have done the work of becoming more self-aware, assessed your strengths and weaknesses relative to the career challenges confronting you, and taken steps to build influence with others *and* to structure your interfaces as outlined in Part III, you understand your professional capabilities for the human expertise dimension of your career. It is wise to take advantage of your strengths as you pursue your goals. In addition, it serves you well to remediate your weaknesses. A weakness may be something that you struggle with or simply an issue that you are not sure how to master.

There are a number of such issues that many Insightful Experts find challenging in the human expertise dimension of their careers. An overview of those covered in Part IV is coming up. Refer to your plan and select only those to work on that apply to you and best serve your goals. *Not all may apply to you.* Of those that do, choose the order in which you wish to address them on the basis of their importance and urgency for your career situation. An issue high on both counts would be one that I recommend you choose to start with. Unlike the steps in the first two phases of the Third Eye Framework, creating impetus and structuring interfaces, there is no set order for building your internal capability. But after you decide which areas you will tackle first, second, and so on, incorporate them into your plan by setting specific objectives for yourself to benchmark your progress. This will help you stay focused on what's most important and it will give you the satisfaction of seeing your progress as you accomplish what you set out to do!

Manage Your Energy. Most Insightful Experts in jobs that require interaction with others struggle with maintaining their energy. The heightened sensitivity of introverts to external stimuli means that we are easily tired by teamwork, client dialogue, or fast-paced action.

Networking Made Simple. This is a chief stumbling block for many Insightful Experts. But once you understand what a network is, I think you will find that its ominousness dissolves. By learning to exert your influence, you have already begun to build your network.

How to Participate in Teams and Lead Them Effectively. Teams are ubiquitous in professional settings but they can be designed to suit extroverts at the expense of introverted ways of being. There are some simple strategies though that can be employed to make them work better for you.

Communication Basics. There are a variety of dimensions to communication. Because introverts would rather retreat, we don't always pay enough attention to how others perceive our attempts at communication. A first step is to understand the communication biases to which many people fall prey. After that, both verbal and nonverbal aspects of communication should be refined to best achieve professional success.

Listening is Communication. Introverts tend to be good listeners. We are almost always processing what we hear, making sense of it. But even we can use a refresher because listening is so critical to professional work.

Communication Reciprocity. One of the areas that Insightful Experts can overlook is the need to reciprocate communication with others. We are so immersed in our inner worlds that we simply forget. It is a capability accessible to all but its importance is not always understood. Failure to reciprocate leads to misperceptions of your professionalism that can hinder career advancement.

Assertive Interactions. Because introverts are not facile with words, it's easy to let those who are well-spoken (read: extrovert) override our preferences. But for you to make your greatest impact as a professional, you must be heard. Sometimes that means taking control and exerting your technical know-how as *the* right way to get things done. Becoming more assertive is a valuable skill.

Communicate to Connect. Much of what you learn in the Third Eye Framework is about connecting with others. That's what human expertise (as opposed to your technical expertise) is all about. By connecting with others, you are able to build strong relationships that benefit your career. There are some special techniques that you can employ to make this easier.

Social Anxiety: Nothing to Shy Away From. Finally, some Insightful Experts truly are shy *and* suffer from social anxiety. If this is you, you will want to know what I have to say about how you can master this challenge.

Nurturing your internal capability is acquiring the ability to act on your weaknesses and to confront the issues related to your introversion that have plagued you. Expect that you will continue to develop this aspect of your human expertise throughout your career. It underlies and bolsters your efforts in the first two phases of the Third Eye program. With this final step in hand, you are positioned to achieve the goals you set out for yourself in your strategic plan, relying on your introverted strengths!

Milestones Along the Journey

Below are a few of the key ideas related to this chapter with a couple extra bullet points for you to fill in. I'd like to hear other ideas that may have resonated for you or were stimulated by what you read. Go to the website www.TheIntrovertsGuide.com to share with me those that have special meaning for *your* personal journey.

- Building your internal capability is the third and final element of the Third Eye Framework.

- Unlike the sequential steps in the two outer layers of the model, you choose which elements to focus on in this inner layer. It is about your needs based on your growing self-awareness, your strategic plan from Chapter 7, and your experience.

- Building your internal capability has to do with either developing your skills or learning and deciding how to confront certain issues you may face, such as working on teams.

- _____

  _____

- _____

  _____

PART IV

Build Your Internal Capability

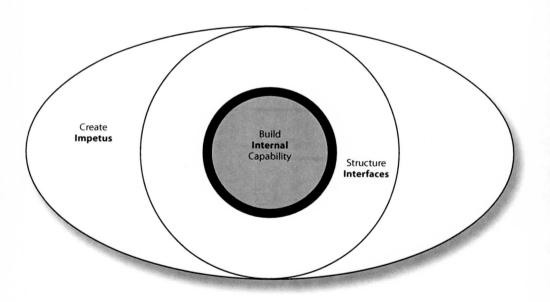

CHAPTER 22

Manage Your Energy

Energy is one of the distinguishing features that separates introversion from extroversion. I recall a day-long interview after which I felt like mush. And still—I faced a dinner with potential colleagues to cap it off! I was—quite simply—exhausted. I imagine that you have had similar experiences. Depletion of energy is one of the most difficult and pervasive issues reported by introverts who spend a lot of time around people. The drive to be alone and recharge was noted by psychologist Carl Jung in his first identification of introversion as a distinct personality feature. It is central to what makes you different from an extrovert.

Chances are that you have to work with others to practice your profession, meaning that you almost certainly face this issue. Long days at the office no doubt tire you out, and a networking event or an intense meeting with an employee or a team of colleagues tires you out even more.

You can't banish your natural tendency to be fatigued by social interactions, but many of the actions you take in the Third Eye Framework will help you. By working through the stages of creating impetus and structuring your interfaces, you have already (without intending to) done much to manage your energy. For example, by structuring meetings to better suit yourself rather than the extroverts around you, you also make the meetings less tiring. And by building influence with others over the long haul, you may alter how they perceive your need to take time away to regain your equilibrium; when your relationships are based on lasting respect, your need for space may be seen as a benevolent quirk. And that's not so bad—some of the great geniuses in history, such as Einstein, were considered a bit quirky.

But there is little doubt that, as an Insightful Expert, you will find yourself exhausted at times from professional interactions. One fellow that I know, George, reserves a late-afternoon hour in each day of a conference to flop in his room prior to evening cocktail gatherings and dinners so that he can be civil and amiable after a long day of energy-depleting conversations. Here are some other strategies for conserving and rebuilding your energy.

Pace yourself. Be strategic in how you schedule your time, both on a daily basis and for special events such as conferences. Don't take on too much. Remember that *less is more* for an introvert. This also means that you should avoid letting others schedule your time without clear guidelines from you on what is acceptable or not. You may not be able to see as *many* clients as someone else, but if your life is better, does it make a huge difference? Is it quality or quantity of output that matters most? You can't have both all the time. Let your awareness of yourself and your needs be your guide.

Alternate activity with downtime. Make every effort to build in breaks. Go for a walk around the building, run an errand away from the group, or go to your office, hotel room, or some private space. Be relentless in seeking out these times for yourself. One professional, Jill, spends her lunch break at the lunch counter in an out-of-the-way way shopping center so that she can recharge alone, since she's unlikely to run into any colleagues in that setting.

Rest. Yes, rest. When you get time alone, close your eyes for a few minutes and relax. Daydream. Whatever you do during this time, make it *not* about work. If you're lucky and have both uninterrupted time and a private space, take a nap. Anything that helps clear your head and recharge your body will help. Maybe it's taking a walk outside or sitting in the sun.

Seek privacy. Make every effort to get a private office or workspace. If you can, work in a home office one day each week, or get a day a week away from the front lines of your work. You will work hard during that time away, and you will get more done and feel better. The more you follow through on creating impetus for yourself by developing your credibility and influence with others in your workplace, the more likely it becomes that you are granted these luxuries. Over time, these kinds of synergies in the program that you are undertaking will offer greater gains.

Focus and be mindful. Chapter 9, "Mustering the Courage to Take Action," discusses mindfulness and offers an introductory exercise for enhancing it. By focusing on your breath and observing your body and what your senses are telling you, you can relax amid stressful interactions and busyness. Cultivate the habit of being more present each moment. This has had huge payoffs for me. Try it.

Here's what not to do: Don't feel awkward or apologetic for needing to implement these strategies for conserving your energy. Introverts comprise half the population, and we have every right to work in a way that enables us to be most productive. Of course, it helps to be diplomatic and sometimes discreet. (It also helps to be the boss, but alas, not everyone can be!) I urge you to be tenacious. This is your life and your career. Don't contort yourself into an extrovert's model for how the workplace is supposed to work. And don't expect that they will understand; your needs are so different that it's simply not likely.

With these simple strategies you will begin to claim your right to a more rationally paced work life. To get started, sit down and do some planning. Think about your job and figure out what you can do on a daily, weekly, and monthly basis to create space to recharge, following some of the guidance here. Start with one or two items and build up to bigger changes. Plan in the same way for upcoming networking events and conferences. By thinking in advance about what may tire you out and what you will do to recharge, you will grant yourself a much greater chance of following through and rejuvenating your energy, and then you'll be ready to take on the next big thing that comes along. It's your right.

Milestones Along the Journey

Below are a few of the key ideas related to this chapter with a couple extra bullet points for you to fill in. I'd like to hear other ideas that may have resonated for you or were stimulated by what you read. Go to the website www.TheIntrovertsGuide.com to share with me those that have special meaning for *your* personal journey.

- It is natural for introverts to experience fatigue after professional interactions.

- By implementing the steps in the Third Eye Framework, you are also setting the conditions to manage your energy more effectively. You are focusing on leveraging your strengths rather than forcing yourself into a mold meant for extroverts. When you can be yourself, you may experience less energy drain.

- _____

    _____

- _____

    _____

CHAPTER 23

Networking Made Simple

A dislike of networking is nearly universal among Insightful Experts. It goes against our nature to make small talk with strangers—or, for that matter, to make *any* talk that seems to offer little or no immediate payoff. We'd much rather stay in our offices than either attend an event with the express intent of networking or make telephone calls with no purpose that's obviously connected to getting our work done.[1]

You might be surprised to learn that even many extroverts dislike networking. It has been estimated that about three-quarters of all people dislike attending a party with strangers, so you're hardly alone. I suspect that doesn't make you feel any better about it, though—it certainly doesn't help me much—and I see no reason to try to convince you that you should *like* networking. You don't have to like it, but it helps to know some of an introvert's best strategies for doing it. You may find that you *need* to network to get ahead in your career, which is why you're reading this book in the first place.

Networking is usually used as a synonym for schmoozing, which means chatting idly or with the express purpose of self-promotion.[2] In reality, however, constructing your network means much more than that, and schmoozing is the least attractive form of networking for Insightful Experts. So I want to begin by explaining what constitutes a network and what it's based upon. Then I'll tell you how to build one. After that, I'll briefly discuss networking events, aka schmoozing.

Networks: What They Are and How They Work

Networks can be vital to your career. A network has three major benefits, according to networking experts Brian Uzzi and Shannon Dunlap.[3] It can help you (1) gather more political clout; (2) gain access to diverse sources of expertise; and (3) learn information that is not publicly available. Ties with others can lead to projects and other opportunities that build your professional expertise and reputation, giving you political power. Others' expertise that diverges from your own can help you be more effective in your professional endeavors; your perspective is broadened by your network. Private information gained from your network can give you a competitive advantage to position your practice, learn new techniques, or seek attractive professional opportunities.

In Parts II and III of this book you learned how to prepare for the events and interactions that you face by creating impetus and structuring your interfaces. These concepts lay an introvert's foundation for networking as well as for routine workplace interactions, such as meetings and day-to-day operations.

Trust. Begin to explore your network by thinking about your stakeholders (see Chapter 15). As you have already learned, trust is central to building influence. Not coincidentally, trust is also at the center of networking. Here the emphasis is not necessarily on becoming influential but rather on simply developing strong connections with others. As with your network inside your workplace, in order to network successfully with those outside your organization, think about the trust that others have in you. What is it based upon? Why do they trust you?

Trust is a belief that another person will behave in ways that show good intentions toward us. It tends to be reciprocal and self-sustaining in nature—the more we trust others, the more they in turn will trust us. We build trust by demonstrating our good intentions. In Chapter 16 you learned that trust emerges from perceptions of your competence and good character. Fernando Bartolome, an expert on trust at work, expands on this by identifying six primary ways to develop and sustain trust:[4]

1. Communicate openly.
2. Support others with help, advice, etc.
3. Respect others by listening to them and delegating to them.
4. Be fair and give credit to others.

5. Be predictable. Keep promises.
6. Be competent in your profession.

These ways of developing trust reflect many of the topics we have already covered or soon will. The activities that you engaged in to create impetus for yourself, such as learning to self disclose (Chapter 13) and swapping valued exchanges with others (Chapter 16), as well as your initiatives to build your internal capability in upcoming chapters, such as remembering to listen (Chapter 26) and reciprocate (Chapter 27), are explained in other parts of this guide. Earning trust is a process that you undertake over time. It doesn't happen overnight. By following the above guidelines, you will develop trusting relations with your professional colleagues and clients. In time, the result will be a larger network of associates.

Brokers. According to Uzzi and Dunlap's research, however, not all members of your network are equal. Some can extend your reach farther and more quickly than others. These people are the so-called information brokers who can connect you with many other diverse people.

The best way to identify the brokers in your network, so that you can think about where you met them and perhaps replicate that success, is to systematically analyze your network. Refer to the Stakeholder Survey you undertook in Chapter 15 or simply draw a line down the middle of a blank sheet of tablet paper. In the left column make a list of your contacts, and in the right column identify how you met them. In this fashion you'll learn who is helping you meet others.

If you're meeting most of your network on your own, you may suffer from a lack of diversity that lessens its benefit. If you meet people through others, your network is likely to be more diverse and consequently more effective. If one or more individuals have introduced you to multiple other connections, these are your information brokers. Pay special attention to nurturing your relationships with them.

Building Your Network

What's the best way to build a network? Put simply, seek out activities, professional or personal, that are passions for you. Knowing that you're good at the things you feel passionate about reduces the stress of these social situations. What is it that you really enjoy? Perhaps it's cycling or the local historical society. By joining and helping to run a group and its events, you'll quickly meet others who share your passion and who also have a broad network of contacts that will be dissimilar to your own. This diversity of contacts is critical; it expands your network's range and makes it more useful.

Involvement in any activity or group gives you the opportunity to develop reciprocal trust among other participants. It's not usually enough just to show up. Involvement means taking on tasks of the group, such as volunteering to help with events or lending your talents in some way to accomplish a goal. Find ways to contribute that you will be comfortable with and able to perform well. Back-office work is ideal for Insightful Experts. You can bake pies for a church fund-raiser in the solitude of your own kitchen. You can do data entry for a political campaign rather than knocking on doors. All organizations need help with website development, maintenance, and updating. Show your paintings in an art association or enter competitions in a ski club. In a book club, read the book and show up with just one comment. Whatever the group does, look for ways that you can get your feet wet alongside others.

You may be thinking that joining a group is the last thing you want to do, but take it as a challenge to find one that works for you. Smaller is usually better. Experiment. The rule of thumb for building relationships is to show up at least seven times.[5] If you do this, you will become familiar to others and be seen as an insider. Once you're an insider, you'll find that you enjoy it more. If you don't enjoy a group after giving it this kind of chance, exit it and find another. Don't fall prey to escalating commitment—i.e., doggedly sticking to an unproductive course simply because you've already invested time and effort in it. Learn to cut your losses and try again someplace else, just as a thrown rider gets back on her horse. Keep trying, and sooner or later you will find a group that suits you.

Remember that this is not a "quick fix" short-term process. It takes time and energy, and it takes a willingness to fail a few times until you find people and groups that are just right for you and make you feel at home.

Participating in Networking Events

In Part III of this book you learned how to structure your interfaces with others in order to take advantage of the unique attributes of introversion. The structuring of interfaces is based on the three R's:

- Research
- Rules
- Rehearse

These three activities lie at the heart of successful networking event management, just as they help Insightful Experts do well in other interactions. Let's examine each one as it relates to networking.

Do Your Research. It pays to know who will be attending an event where you have an opportunity to meet others who can advance your professional endeavors and your career. If you can, find out in advance the list of attendees. For example, a professional conference publishes its program ahead of time. This gives you a long list of presenters and moderators. There's a good chance that these individuals will show up at a social event, luncheon, or coffee break during the conference. Keynote speakers, officers, and conference organizers are also likely to make an appearance.

With a list of possible attendees, you can begin to narrow down your approach to the event. Select just a few individuals from the list whom you would like to meet for professional reasons. One is enough, but if Murphy's Law functions, your first choice won't show up that day. I suggest having a couple more possibilities in your back pocket.

Do you know what the person looks like? In addition to scanning nametags on site, the best way to pinpoint who you want to talk to is to know in advance what he or she looks like. Go to Google™ search, type in the name, and search images. If that doesn't work or is confusing, go to his or her company website and look for a photo there. With photo in hand or in your memory, you'll know who to look for. If you can't find a photo, you'll be reduced to scanning nametags, but that's better than nothing.

Insightful Expert Elizabeth followed this strategy to locate an editor when she attended an annual professional conference. By looking him up in advance, she was able to zero in at the evening's social gathering and strike up a conversation to find out if her article was suitable for his publication. She got to know him personally and later was successful in publishing her article.

Another option you can pursue if the person you want to meet is a presenter at the event or conference is to attend her session prior to the networking function. You will then recognize her in the later networking event, or you might meet her at the presentation and be able to circumvent the networking event altogether!

Now consider what you might want to learn from this person and, just as important, what you want him to know about you. Think carefully about this. Is there a question you want to ask? Could you ask for advice on a project, client, or patient? Do you want him to help with an introduction to someone else? By clarifying what you want, you will avoid inane conversation that leaves you frustrated and wishing you'd never made the approach. There is sometimes nothing worse than a missed opportunity.

Consider whether you have anything in common that might spur conversation or interest, such as a shared hometown or studying under a certain professor (though perhaps at different times and in different universities). A professional specialty in common is ideal, since it opens the door to a tremendous shared body of knowledge. Is there an emerging trend in your field that you can discuss?

Identify as many questions as you can that do not have yes or no answers. Ask, "what do you think about—" or "how—" or "why—" rather than "is it—" or "does it—" or "are you—." Your goal is to stimulate the other person to talk so that you can listen. It's no secret that people like to talk about themselves. More to the point, research shows that your target will evaluate you more favorably if she does more talking while you do more listening. Develop a possible sequence of questions for each of your potential conversation targets.

If you have no idea who will be attending an event, develop a list of general questions you might ask anyone in a professional setting. Here are a few examples:

- What do you think of the event so far?
- What do you do? Can you tell me more about that?
- What brings you to this event today?
- What did you think of so and so's presentation/talk?
- What do you think was the most valuable aspect of the slide presentation that speaker X presented? Why? How does it relate to your own experience?

As you think of questions, simultaneously think about how you yourself might answer them. That way, you'll be prepared if the person is interested in you. Consider what else you want to say to make yourself known and to accomplish your objectives for the event, and write out different ways of saying these things. Find the one that sounds least awkward and most authentic to your own way of saying things. Write it down.

Finally, you will need an "elevator speech," the 30-second blurb that describes what you do. Most likely you will want two versions: one for the layperson and one for a fellow professional in your field. The story goes that this should be something you can recite on an elevator ride to give someone an idea of your skills and professional expertise. Sometimes it helps to make the blurb interesting rather than bland, so that it sticks longer in someone's memory. Instead of saying, "I'm a teacher," you might want to say, "I help young people learn GPS skills so that they can become world travelers in the 21st century—I teach geography to middle-schoolers." You don't want to appear overly cutesy, and you don't want people to have to guess, so play with a number of alternatives and choose one that resonates for you. It can be helpful to try them out with a trusted colleague.

Make notes on the outcomes of all your research and preparation endeavors. You may be so energized during the actual encounter that everything you wanted to say flies out of your head. Though you won't be able to refer to your notes when you meet someone, if you go over them a few times in advance, your planned statements are more likely to be available to you in short term memory for recall.

Decide on Rules. Are you still skeptical that this can work for you, an introvert? Seeking an amenable context can help. During the research portion of your preparation, you decided what you will say. Now do your best to structure where you will say it, if that option is available to you. If you remember to play to your strengths as an introvert, you will quickly figure out how to do this.

Do you do well in large groups? Most introverts don't, though you may be the exception. Assuming that you don't, look for a person who is standing alone, perhaps looking awkward, perhaps not. Talking to this person will warm up your social skills. In five minutes, find out as much as you can from her and also tell her about yourself, then move on. One of the biggest mistakes people make at networking events is to stay planted in one spot. It's easy to break away by making the excuse of getting a snack or just saying, "It was wonderful to meet you. I set a goal for myself to meet several people here, so I need to move on now, but it's been such pleasure and I hope we can talk again." Of course, you will exchange business cards as well.

If you spot the key person you are hoping to meet, you will have to find a way to get closer, even if he or she is in a group. Go stand on the edge of the gathering. Listen and smile. Say hello to someone. Eventually the group will move around, with some folks leaving and others joining, and you may then find an opportunity to get closer to your target. In this case, staying somewhat planted though flexible is good, since you are close to your goal. Use the power of body language to make eye contact with the person. The goal here is not to interrupt an ongoing conversation, but to get his or her attention long enough that your face will be remembered later.

Setting the rules of the game is all about finding what works best for you. Don't feel compelled to mingle for mingling's sake, something you probably hate to do anyway. Focus on your goals and how to accomplish them using your strengths as an introvert. Don't try to do more than that.

Rehearse. Your final step, mentioned briefly above, is to make notes for yourself of who you might run into and want to talk to, what you might say, and how you might respond. Put your notes on index cards and go over them until you know them. If possible, rehearse with strangers (e.g., waiting in line at a restaurant or working out at the gym), colleagues, or your significant other. By rehearsing *out loud*, you will hear nuances that you wouldn't otherwise pick up. You can then revise conversation starters and replies until you find the tone that is authentic for you. The strangers and colleagues with whom you rehearse don't need to know you're rehearsing—and no, you're not being manipulative, you're simply being polite. Who knows, your rehearsals may forge new connections with colleagues.

Finally, don't try to act like an extrovert. If you find one or two people at an event with whom you can develop a genuine connection, you will have succeeded.

Network Upkeep

Long after a networking event or even *sans* an event, a key part of networking is maintaining the contacts you worked so hard to develop. Send a simple follow-up phone call, e-mail, or handwritten note to each person with whom you had an extended conversation. Keep it simple by acknowledging that you met them and perhaps suggesting a future connection, such as lunch. It's also helpful to share professional resources. Your goal is simply to be remembered in a positive light.

Make it a point to go back over your key contacts, looking at those who may be information brokers for you, and contact them periodically. It's likely that you will never be an effusive communicator, like an extrovert, but you can stay in touch and usually that's all that's needed. Some people set up a tickler file to do this, ensuring that they don't forget anyone. Remember that you are building trust. Seek ways to help others, even if that help is only suggesting a colleague with whom your contact can talk shop, and ask for help in return. People are generally flattered by requests for advice or some other easy way to help and will remember you for it. Reciprocal exchanges build trust and stronger relationships. As your network grows, you will become more powerful, access information that is not yet publicly known, and gain the benefits of your network's diverse expertise.

Now that you've built your network, let's explore how you will get along with the team in your workplace or the one you participate in while building your external network in some other organization.

Milestones Along the Journey

Below are a few of the key ideas related to this chapter with a couple extra bullet points for you to fill in. I'd like to hear other ideas that may have resonated for you or were stimulated by what you read. Go to the website www.TheIntrovertsGuide.com to share with me those that have special meaning for *your* personal journey.

- Building a network is based on the same principles as the power and influence strategies that you learned in Chapter 16. These two processes work together toward the same end.

- Trust is at the heart of building a strong network.

- Analyzing your stakeholders can help you identify the all-important *brokers* in your network.

- Seeking out passions, at work or away, can help an introvert build a beneficial network.

- _____

  _____

- _____

  _____

CHAPTER 24

How to Participate in Teams and Lead Them Effectively

If you're a typical Insightful Expert, much of your time is spent in teams[1] and small groups. These may be made up of coworkers who interact daily or ad hoc groups formed around a specific issue. Even solo practitioners face teamwork in professional associations and on volunteer boards. An important part of your career success as an introvert depends on how well you navigate, present yourself, and lead in the teams with which you're involved. As an Insightful Expert, you bring many assets to the teams in which you participate. You may not say a lot but you bring the level of in-depth thoughtfulness that every team needs to do its best. Your attention to detail and reflective ability to see the implications of various perspectives are invaluable.

Decision-Making for Introverts

In the second half of this chapter you'll learn about the best ways to facilitate team discussions. But even before you lead a team, you will be a member of one. Being an introvert, you cannot outdo extroverts in the extent to which you fill the airwaves with talk. So it's up to you to gain an edge in other ways that make you a full participant and allow you to be seen as the competent team member you are. Understanding the decision-making process and making sure you are heard is vital.

It is when decisions are made that Insightful Experts are most apt to be left out or, worse yet, their contributions not recalled. Two related factors are especially relevant to how team decisions are made: (1) what *information* the team pays attention to (as opposed to information that is presented but not heeded and information that is known to one or more participants but not shared), and (2) what *decision rule* is used. Even when operating with the same information, two teams may reach very different decisions if they get there using different decision rules. The most common methods of reaching decisions (i.e., decision rules) are by *voting*, by *authoritarian dictate without consultation*, by *authoritarian dictate with consultation*, by *logrolling*, and by *consensus*.

Aim for Consensus. Other methods of decision-making are quite often easier, but evidence shows that deliberate consensus building leads small teams to higher levels of performance than taking consensus for granted or using another decision rule. An introvert runs the risk of being unseen and unheard in nearly any team, but your chances of being heard are better when consensus decision-making is employed, and if you want to advance in your career, you would do well to take advantage of the opportunity this mode of decision-making offers.

Consensus-building allows a team to fulfill its mission by making the best use of its members' contributions. Almost all teams employ consensus-building to some extent, but that extent varies widely. Done well and often, consensus-building enables a team to take full advantage of the expertise of its diverse members. And when faced with difficult or complex decisions, the more diversity of expertise and opinion a team has to draw on, the better. In contrast, other decision rules tend to shut down rather than encourage informed dialogue.

Evidence of the value of consensus as a decision rule comes from research conducted by social psychologist Jay Hall. He first recorded the answers reached by *individual* team members working on a complex problem-solving task. Then their *team* was charged with solving the same problem. Almost always, the team outperformed its highest scoring member, a result labeled *synergy*.

Only if the team members communicated effectively could they surpass the highest individual score. To work, such communication must include good *listening* skills, clearly *articulated explanations*, and *balanced input* from introverts and extroverts. Also essential is a shared commitment to democratic principles—with paramount concern for the best possible outcome for the team as a whole rather than any individual member.

Contrast this outcome with your experiences in teams in which the most talkative people were most heard in the decision-making process. When extroverts dominate, the team result suffers. *Synergy is only possible when introverts are full participants.*

Seek Synergy. There are just a few steps that a team need follow to achieve synergy and take advantage of all its members' expertise. The accompanying list presents basic guidelines for achieving consensus. These are simple steps that guide the information seeking and decision process. When you participate on a team, you may want to try to get these steps adopted. When you lead a team, make sure all the members carefully review these, discuss them as a team, and commit to them. It will also be your job to mediate the discussion to ensure that everyone gets heard.

When I teach team building, I advise extroverts that they have an obligation to draw out and hear from the introverts on their team, and I remind introverts that they have a mandate to speak out. As an Insightful Expert, you must take personal responsibility for contributing to your team for your own career success as well as your team's. I learned this the hard way while participating on a team in graduate school. Even though my individual result on the task was high, the team's outcome was not as good because I deferred to an extroverted team member who appeared to be more knowledgeable. (Well, why not—he sure *sounded* like he knew what he was talking about!) We did not achieve synergy because I failed to make my voice heard. Then and there, I decided that, introverted or not, I was never going to let that happen again. And you shouldn't either.

As a full participant with valuable information and insights, you also build your professional credibility and influence with other team members, continuing the process of building career momentum for yourself. What's more, your full participation on your team will also lead to greater *cohesiveness* among team members. Cohesiveness is the degree to which team members are attracted to each other and are motivated to stay in the group. It's a sign of a healthy group![2] In moderation, cohesiveness is associated with increased effectiveness of the team. Guess what that does for you, the Insightful Expert? Yes. It raises your stature and credibility to be associated with a winning team. Another win-win outcome.

One of the things I help Insightful Experts with in my consulting practice is learning how to engage and contribute more fully to their work teams. We consider the specific individuals on the team, the issues the Insightful Expert faces, and what strategies will lead to their being heard when decisions are made.

Guidelines for Reaching Consensus[3]

1. Pay attention to how people react to your statements. Don't argue in support of your suggestions.

2. When you encounter a stalemate, look for another alternative to the two being discussed. Never assume that there will be winning and losing ideas (or members). Always seek a win-win.

3. Don't try too hard to reach agreement, especially if it means changing your mind just for harmony's sake. Give way only to logic and reason. Use logic and reason rather than emotion to make your points.

4. Stay clear of simple conflict-minimizing decision methods such as assigning numerical ratings that are averaged, flipping a coin, voting with majority rule, or logrolling (garnering support on one issue in exchange for your support on another).

5. Seek out differences of opinion. They ensure that you are getting all the good ideas on the table for discussion. Disagreements help a team because they offer a spectrum of opinion and information.

Facilitating Team Discussions

For an Insightful Expert, effective participation on teams means having the ability to take charge and lead when necessary. While this often is not an introvert's preferred role, a good facilitator helps to structure the interactions among team members to accomplish a team's mission. If you have leadership aspirations, one of the best ways to develop your leadership skills is to facilitate team meetings. If you are already a leader and you are drafted into meeting facilitation due to your role as a manager or supervisor, some simple guidelines for the facilitation will help you succeed.

As a team facilitator, your role is to manage the meeting process and the work of the group. This means that you must focus on how people get along, the decision rules, and the group's overall climate. If you are also the formal leader of the team, you will of course also be responsible for setting the agenda and the content of the discussion and its outcomes.

Establishing an agenda in advance and distributing it prior to a meeting is probably the most effective meeting-management tool at your disposal. The facilitation role thereafter is concerned mostly with surfacing information by asking questions, summarizing, synthesizing concepts that are expressed, questioning assumptions, and so forth in order to move the meeting along toward its conclusion at the scheduled time.

This role comes naturally to an introvert, since it involves good listening skills and thoughtful introspection on the progress of the discussion. These are some of your most powerful strengths. It may occasionally require you to take charge more forcefully if an extrovert takes control of the process, but the manner in which you do this should be consistent with your nature as an introvert. Rather than "talk over" someone else, for example, you will do better to use a silent stare to draw everyone's attention back to the task at hand. Facilitation is not "command and control," which is why it can be so well suited to an introvert's temperament. Think of it as gentle yet firm nudging, like a sheepdog herding sheep. The key is to let members set their own guidelines, then gently but assertively hold them to those. This is especially helpful to rein in extroverts who by nature, and often without conscious intent, want to take over. Guidelines that teams develop may include topics such as listening, maintaining confidentiality, avoiding sarcasm and arguments, handling conflicts respectfully, and managing the time to ensure that the agenda gets covered.

As team facilitator, you will want to use open-ended questions rather than simple closed questions begging yes or no responses. Open-ended questions often begin with words such as "how" or "why" that probe for more information. In contrast, questions that begin with "does" or "can" tend to evoke single-word answers. An example of an open-ended question is, "How do we know when the client's needs are met?" In addition to such fact-seeking questions, you may also ask questions that test team members' opinions or beliefs. An example is, "What do you think of the client needs assessment form that we used last year?"

It's useful to frequently check the assumptions and perceptions of team members about what is being discussed, seeking to involve as many points of view as possible. You may also paraphrase what has been said by putting it into different words.

In order for consensus decision-making to function, a good facilitator must ensure that team members participate actively in the discussion. One of the best ways to do this is to create a climate that is friendly and open. Humor is a good way to break the ice and get people to relax and open up. Just because your topic is serious doesn't mean you can't see the humor in situations. It is also valuable to get members to share or think about what they stand to gain from the work of the team. Recording and sharing this at the outset puts the value of the work in their minds, and they will be more invested in the meeting.

It's important to be aware and attuned to nonverbal communication. As mentioned previously, eye contact can be used to signal disapproval. It should also be used liberally to include everyone. By making eye contact, you let people know that you hear them, respect them, and want their input. Making eye contact can even encourage another introvert or a shy member to speak up.

When you believe that you are not getting adequate participation from direct dialogue, consider using a technique that evokes anonymous or semi-anonymous input from the group. Brainstorm a topic by having people write ideas on slips of paper that are then compiled, shared, and discussed. You may also wish to put members into smaller groupings. Two people often talk more freely and can report back to the main group with their conclusions on a topic.

You will find, with practice, that you can facilitate team meetings, if not with ease, then at least without pain! Your work on this will give you increased visibility and stature among your colleagues and employees.

The next chapter is a communication primer that will help you figure out where your skills need polishing.

Milestones Along the Journey

Below are a few of the key ideas related to this chapter with a couple extra bullet points for you to fill in. I'd like to hear other ideas that may have resonated for you or were stimulated by what you read. Go to the website www.TheIntrovertsGuide.com to share with me those that have special meaning for *your* personal journey.

- Teams are vital to the functioning of many professionals. But they can easily be dominated by extroverts, undermining your own ability to make meaningful contributions, much less advance your career.

- Synergy is only possible when introverts are full participants on teams.

- Consensus decision making leads to higher levels of team performance, in part because it provides a process for introverts to be heard.

- Strong facilitation is needed to ensure that introverts are fully represented in team processes.

- _____

  _____

- _____

  _____

CHAPTER 25

Communication Basics

You may think that you already know how to communicate, and no doubt you do. What you may fail to understand, however, are the unwritten rules of communication that favor extroverts over introverts. Failing to understand these rules can lead to miscommunication and, more importantly, misjudgments of your capabilities and value to your profession and organization. Understanding the rules will enable you to capitalize on your strengths and avoid an introvert's common pitfalls. Good communication allows you to overcome the perceptual biases and implicit judgments that are applied to Insightful Experts.

Communication Channels and Processes

Communication occurs when information is transmitted between two or more people and they hold a common perception of its meaning. The purpose of professional communication can be to get others to do something either by motivating them or giving them feedback, or to express emotions, or simply to communicate information and knowledge.

A generic communication process is shown in the diagram that follows. At its most basic, a sender transmits a message to a receiver. Channels for communicating the message include oral (or face to face), written, and electronic. A face-to-face method incorporates body language along with a verbal component. In this process, the message that is sent may not be the message that is received, since both sender and receiver may imbue the actual words (or other characteristics) of the message with diverse meanings. However, feedback from the receiver is useful in identifying a potential discrepancy or so-called miscommunication. Listening skills, as discussed in Chapter 26, are an important part of the process.

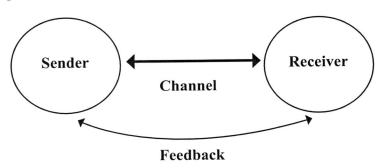

The Communication Process

Perceptual Biases

Even though introverts comprise roughly half the population, they are the quieter half and face enormous pressure in professional life to be more like extroverts. For this reason, perceptual biases that devalue introverts can be devastating to your career. How can you ensure that others see you accurately? The number one weapon in your arsenal is your ability to communicate with others. By communicating, you can overcome biases and learn to present yourself in ways that allow your significant technical abilities and professional knowledge to sway opinion.

Have you ever been in a situation where you were misjudged by someone and felt wronged? For example, you may have had a teacher who assumed you were lazy when you just didn't understand the material. Or you may have had someone draw erroneous conclusions about you because you are naturally quiet and don't like large groups. How did you feel when those events happened? Not too happy, I suspect. We almost always harbor a sense of injustice when we are wrongly judged (though we choose whether or not to hang onto these feelings). Unfortunately, such misjudgments are quite common.

Perception is the mental process by which people make sense of situations or others. Impressions are formed on the basis of a limited number of facts, and they may differ dramatically from objective reality. Nonetheless, we all use perceptions, and as a consequence we are all subject to perceptual biases. It is likely that your experience in the examples above is due to a perceptual bias on the part of the other party.

As introverts in the professional world, Insightful Experts are subject to several common perceptual biases:

Selective perception. People perceive selectively when one distinctive characteristic draws their attention to the exclusion of others. This occurs because we can't possibly be familiar with all the information available in our environments, so we make decisions based on what we do know. Often what we see is biased by what we know. It's an instance of the well-known adage, "If all you have is a hammer, every problem looks like a nail." Selective perception often arises from the backgrounds, histories, and attitudes we bring to a situation.

For example, a talkative extrovert will draw conclusions about you based on her propensity to talk. Your lack of the same propensity may lead her to assume you have nothing to say, and it doesn't matter that her conclusion is the farthest thing from the actual truth. Her perception of you becomes her reality. I'm sure you can think of other examples of selective perception from your own or others' life experiences.

Stereotyping. Stereotyping is a perceptual bias based on the group one belongs to or hangs out with. Racial, ethnic, and gender stereotypes are common in our society. We often hear generalizations such as, "Workers over 50 can't learn new things," or, "Introverts have poor social skills." The perception about the group as a whole may be dead wrong, as in the two examples here, and it may be doubly wrong in its application to you as a member of the group. Stereotyping makes two assumptions: (1) that all members of a group are the same; and (2) that we can pinpoint attributes of a group and all its members. Both assumptions are incorrect.

Halo Effect. A halo-effect perceptual bias occurs when someone draws a general conclusion about another based on a single attribute, such as one's appearance. This is similar to stereotyping but is not necessarily based on your inclusion in a class of people; it simply highlights a single characteristic that you possess. An example might be that, as an introvert, you have made it known to colleagues that you hate networking events. From this information, others may conclude that you dislike all interactions with large groups of people, whether or not that's true. In a positive vein, if you are attractive, others may assume that you are also smart. (And sometimes a perceptual bias happens to be accurate!)

Self-Fulfilling Prophecy. A self-fulfilling prophecy is the outcome of any perceptual bias that leads the victim of the bias to act consistently with the expectation. In short, we live up to (or down to) what others expect of us. Therefore, if our boss concludes that, as an introvert, we cannot make effective sales presentations to new clients, we will tend to do more poorly in those presentations than we might have done without the burden of that expectation. This phenomenon happens because the biased perceiver behaves differently toward the pigeonholed person, who then responds in a way that is consistent with the expectation. Self-fulfilling prophecies can lead people to excel or fail, depending on the expectation set for them.

Fundamental Attribution Error. The fundamental attribution error is a perceptual bias wherein we attribute our own successes to what we ourselves have accomplished to achieve them. At the same time, we tend to attribute another's successes more often to external factors, such as luck, rather than their own efforts. With failures, we make the opposite attributions. When others fail, we blame their lack of effort (e.g., she didn't work hard enough), but when we fail, we attribute it to external factors (e.g., the economy was in a slide).

Fundamental attribution errors are common. Your performance evaluations and those you make of others are subject to this bias. You need to communicate effectively, both as a sender and a listener, to overcome it. It is possible that negative cultural stereotypes about introversion could cause others to attribute your failings to your quiet demeanor, need for solitude, and so forth (internal characteristics) rather than outside factors.

Primacy and Recency. You may wish to pay particular attention to primacy and recency effects on how others pay attention to verbal information. *Primacy* is what comes first. Thus, in any situation, your initial statement will get a lot of attention. *Recency* is what others have heard most recently—in other words, the last thing you said. Typically your first statement should reflect the main point you want to make, and your last sentence should reiterate that point and often, in business, suggest how any recommendation you've made might be implemented. Between the first and the last things you say, you'll want to offer a concise rationale and perhaps an example that supports your premise.

Here's how an oral statement might evolve in this fashion:

1. Main point: "It makes the most sense to switch our strategy to go with Vendor X."

2. Rationale: "We have debated this for some time and covered most of the issues that might come up with switching. It seems like now is the time to take action."

3. Evidence: "In fact, we've reviewed the data that show Vendor X saving our company over 20 thousand dollars last year."

4. Final point: "What do you think about going ahead with a new strategy of switching to X by formulating some new guidelines for our purchasing department?"

By constructing in advance what you will say in this fashion, you structure the communication interface for yourself and build on your strengths as an Insightful Expert. After you've decided what to say, practice your statements aloud to give yourself confidence and enable you to hear how natural you sound. Once you have done this several times, you may revise and then re-practice. In the end, you are likely to be more satisfied with the results of this structured process than with the responses to important statements composed ad hoc.

Primacy and recency also apply to nonverbal communications, so your body language at the beginning and end of your communications is especially important to how you may be perceived.

Face-to-Face Communications

The unwritten rules of communication that favor extroverts often hold their most powerful sway in oral communications. Yet even in oral communications, the words that are said play only a minor role:

Words = 7 percent of message
Nonverbal voice quality = 38 percent
Nonverbal body language = 55 percent

Very little of the message we send is carried by the verbal content of our speech. The verbal component is simply the words we say. In contrast, the nonverbal component provides the preponderance of the message—through intonation, facial expression, and other physical variables such as personal space, gestures, and posture.

Contradiction between a message sender's verbal expression and his or her body language undermine the credibility of a verbal message and can lead to discomfort and mistrust. Actions always speak louder than words, and a mismatch will lead to mistrust of your words. A simple example of this is a non-smiling, limp, cold handshake accompanied by a monotone, "I'm so glad to meet you." Contrast this with the firm, warm handshake of someone who leans forward with a big smile and says with enthusiasm, "I'm so glad to meet you!" The words are the same, but in the first case, you're likely to doubt the sincerity of the words because the nonverbal elements don't support them.

Extroverts are often more comfortable speaking, so they are *much* less likely to be caught in the trap of this perceived mismatch. Introverts, on the other hand, need to be aware of it because many of us would rather not be talking in the first place. That preference and discomfort comes through loud and clear and leads to uncomfortable body language that is open to misinterpretation.

Unwritten rules seem to apply to face-to-face communications in professional settings in the United States. Such rules are culture-specific, so the rules may or may not be the same if you happen to live in another country. Some of these rules are as follows:

Verbal Rules. The primary unwritten verbal rule is to say more rather than less in most situations. This does not mean you should go overboard, but it is expected that you will be able to talk socially as well as fully articulate concepts and ideas in the course of your work. Extroverts tend to be good at both of these because they draw energy from conversing. They are able to speak extemporaneously and will say whatever comes to mind, whether or not it is especially relevant to what is at hand.

In addition to saying more, what you say makes a difference. Apologies, sharing credit (e.g., saying "we" rather than "I"), asking questions, and modesty are shunned in business.[1] As an Insightful Expert, you can work toward building self-confidence and eliminating habits that diminish your stature, but it is unlikely that you will ever have the verbal facility of an extrovert. After all, your strengths lie in your thought processes and careful attention to professional issues and concepts rather than in how you say things. It is natural for you to speak more slowly, pausing between phrases, and to speak in a more measured—and parsimonious—way. It is also natural for you to make fewer self promoting statements to build your reputation because your attention is inward focused *on* your thoughts rather than in outward projections *of* those thoughts. Even knowing its potential importance, you may view verbal self-promotion as a waste of time and energy!

To counter misperceptions and underestimates of your competence based on your verbal contributions, your greatest asset is the personal credibility that you build through the application of your professional expertise and that you nurture within individual relationships that you have forged one by one. You will do well to put most of your efforts there rather than trying overly hard to squeeze yourself into saying the right things with finesse—an extrovert's strength rather than your own.

Nonverbal Rules. Because the nonverbal is so dominant in communication, there are many nonverbal expectations. Just a few of the key ones for introverts are discussed here.

Eyes. In the United States, eye contact is essential in business communications. A direct gaze tells others that you respect them and are paying attention. Looking away, looking down, or shifting your eyes back and forth diminishes credibility and can lead to your dismissal as someone who is unimportant or, in the case of shifting eyes, not to be trusted. Introverts and shy people often find it difficult to maintain a direct gaze. At the same time, your gaze should not be reptilian—i.e., it should not be staring and unblinking. What is expected is that you occasionally glance away from the other's eyes and then quickly back again to maintain contact.

Hands. In the United States, a firm handshake signifies trustworthiness. This does not mean a gripping, painful hand lock anymore than it means a limp-wristed cold-fish offering. On meeting someone, a smile is also appropriate. In other situations, it is expected that your hands will remain relatively still. Fidgeting or tapping is a sign of nervousness or boredom and will be judged negatively.

Body. How you position your body when you talk to others is important, whether sitting or standing. In general, an erect, assertive stance is desirable. It sends signals that you are in control of yourself and confident. Lean toward others to capture their attention and when the intensity of a conversation rises. It demonstrates interest and engagement.

Nodding your head up and down occasionally while you listen is also expected in the United States. This may be accompanied by quiet vocalizations, such as "yes" or "uhhuh."

Crossing your arms or legs can be misinterpreted as disinterest, deviousness, or defensiveness. In professional interactions, you want to be seen as open and interested rather than withdrawn, so it is best to keep your arms and legs uncrossed in most situations.

It is also important that you maintain dynamic posture. This means simply that you should show movement rather than rigid stasis in your face and body. Static positions suggest that you are withdrawn, cold, and lack energy. In business, energy is prized because it is interpreted to mean that you are industrious and a hard worker.

Voice. Your voice is also part of your body language. The expected norms of business culture include a moderate volume that is neither too loud nor too soft, moderately paced speech, a tone that is well modulated in the middle range, and clear, articulate enunciation. An overly soft voice, mumbling, shrillness, excessively slow pace, and poor articulation are undesirable.

In addition to the factors discussed above and summarized in the list that follows, there are many related variables associated with nonverbal communication that are worthy of your attention. For example, the distance that you stand from others is important. How people use personal space is called *proxemics;* levels of intimacy dictate the comfort of physical closeness. Normal distance for personal interactions is about 18 to 48 inches, but normal social distance, most comfortable in many business settings, ranges from 4 to 12 feet. As an introvert, your preference is likely to be for a greater distance than an extrovert might prefer. Because this may make you appear cold and withdrawn, you may wish to compensate by making it clear in the content of your speech that you are engaged and personable.

Paying attention to these unwritten rules of oral communication lets you see the impression that you make on others in a whole new light. The best way to begin working on your demeanor in oral communications might be to find someone to videotape your interactions for a period of time, but that's seldom possible. Another way to gain insight is to ask a trusted person to observe your interactions and give you feedback. In either case, you will begin to see when you are communicating consistently with the unwritten rules and when you are violating them.

Some of the unwritten rules for verbal and nonverbal communication in professional settings are summarized below:

Verbal
Say more rather than less

Nonverbal

Make eye contact
Maintain a direct gaze
Offer a firm handshake
Avoid fidgeting
Lean toward your listeners when intensity rises
Maintain an erect, assertive stance
Listen actively by nodding
Move, don't freeze
Keep your vocal volume moderate
Pace your speaking moderately
Keep your voice well modulated and in the middle range
Practice clear, articulate speech

How to Project Confidence

One of the most effective things you can do to counteract the stereotype that you are not "on the ball" is to learn to speak with confidence. Because you are not as facile with oral communication, you may fall prey to common mistakes of ineffective speech. Examples are shown on the next page, with a brief explanation of what you can do instead.

Examples of Ineffective Speech	What to Do Instead
I was really, really pleased! Your report is way over the top. Wow!	Avoid overstatements because they reduce the power of what you intend to emphasize.
I didn't get to the end of your report, but...	Avoid statements that disqualify your main point. They suggest that you feel uncertain.
Hot damn! ***###!!!	Stay clear of slang and swearing because they suggest that you lack class.
It's *umm* time for us to *ah* meet again with the *er* Jones family clients.	Don't hesitate. It makes you sound tentative and unsure of yourself.
I'm not an expert, but...	Project confidence by not telling others when you feel inadequate. Self-criticism and false modesty serve only to reduce your stature in their eyes.
The forecast demonstrates that business will be up next year, don't you agree?	Avoid ending your statement with a question asking for the other's agreement. It suggests that you are uncertain.
I'm the new administrator of this project. (vocal uptick at end, as if questioning)	Avoid ending a declarative sentence with a vocal uptick. It is an affectation that sounds as if you lack confidence in what you are saying. If you are truly asking a question, then ask it directly.

Based on DeVito, 2008.[2]

Written and Electronic Communication

Introverts tend to shine in written communications. Letters and telephone calls are traditional communication channels. E-mail and teleconferencing are less traditional electronic methods that have come to dominate business communication. Skype™ and video-conferencing are now common as well. Most letters are now sent via e-mail, but e-mails need not be formal letters.

Writing may come easier to some introverts because it allows the sender time to compose and choose one's words more carefully than does oral communication. It also affords the receiver time to process information and emotional content before he/she replies. This time available to compose and to read means that written communications, including e-mail, may play to your strengths as an introvert. E-mail provides a valuable record of discussion points, data, background, context, etc. In an environment where discussion threads might be picked up again after a week, a month, or even longer, e-mail archives provide a way of re-familiarizing yourself with an issue that you're just not going to have if the prior discussion was oral. Some of the disadvantages of e-mail are discussed below. Extroverts may prefer oral communications since they do not need the extra time to process what they say and usually can speak with ease without prior contemplation. This doesn't mean, of course, that what they have to say always has great value; it simply means that they can talk spontaneously.

Telephone calls are a form of oral communication that lacks the face-to-face element of body language to signify intent and convey information along with words. A phone call does incorporate vocal intonations, however. Many introverts have to learn how to speak well over the telephone, and it helps to script as much as possible in advance.

It is characteristic of an introvert to make longer pauses during a telephone conversation than an extrovert typically makes or is comfortable with. These pauses give an introvert time to process information, and at times they may also reflect shyness. If you have a script for transitions and closings, the pauses will be less noticeable, and others will learn that this is simply your speaking style. A transitions script might be something like, "Now that we've covered that, let's talk about this," followed by an introductory statement of the next topic. Problems may arise if others talk over any pauses due to their impatience. In that case, you would be wise to develop some assertiveness techniques, as discussed in Chapter 28.

Teleconferencing holds many of the same pitfalls for introverts as do dyadic telephone conversations, seemingly magnified by the multiple people on the other end of the telephone. Scripting as much as possible is essential.

Skyping™ and video-conferencing can be even less friendly to introverts. They carry the weight of oral face-to-face communications because added information is conveyed by facial expressions and body language, along with voice, and these tend to be an extrovert's strengths. For this reason, these forms of communication require significant preparation to develop face-to-face skills and scripting where possible. On the other hand, electronic video-based communication may allow you to have notes at hand that are out of camera range.

Making Choices

As an Insightful Expert, it is to your advantage to use the form of communication that best matches your strengths as much as you possibly can. Introverts frequently choose written communication (e.g., e-mail) over oral communication of any sort. This a useful way of taking advantage of your strong suits *unless* (and this is important) you are dealing with people or situations for whom or in which written communication is simply not acceptable. For example, you may work closely with someone who has a clear preference for face-to-face oral exchanges and will not bother to read anything in writing. You must think carefully about your audience when deciding what channel of communication to use.

Although written communication comes naturally, it is easy for e-mail to lead to miscommunication because the words you say provide such a small portion of the message (see the prior discussion of non-verbal communication). While you want communication that fits your style, if it harms your ability to be seen accurately as a competent professional, you should rethink its use. Be strategic and aware of the effects of e-mail on its intended recipient. The disadvantages of e-mail include: (1) it is often simply inadequate for dealing with new, complex, or ambiguous settings; (2) it does a poor job of conveying the emotional tone of what is said; (3) it diminishes diplomacy, leading to hurt feelings and misinterpretation.[3]

Of equal importance is what e-mail fails to do for your career strategy: it does not facilitate the personal relationships built on your credibility and authentic presence that you are working to build. Overuse of e-mail could undermine other efforts you make to create impetus and structure your interfaces. So when you use e-mail, be aware of its possible downsides and employ it with care.

In the next chapter, we continue to explore the topic of good communication—with a focus on listening.

Milestones Along the Journey

Below are a few of the key ideas related to this chapter with a couple extra bullet points for you to fill in. I'd like to hear other ideas that may have resonated for you or were stimulated by what you read. Go to the website www.TheIntrovertsGuide.com to share with me those that have special meaning for *your* personal journey.

- The unwritten rules of business communication disadvantage an introvert if you do not consciously make an effort to compensate for them.

- Perceptual biases lead others to misunderstand introversion. By being aware of them, you may successfully counteract their potentially negative effects.

- Communication is multifaceted. The actual words that you employ are the least important factor in how others interpret what you say.

- _____

  _____

- _____

  _____

CHAPTER 26

Listening is Communication

One-half of the responsibility for successful communication rests with the recipient of the message. Imagine being blindfolded on a busy street corner. If your partner clearly and audibly says, "It's not okay to go," but what you hear is, "It's okay to go," you may step out in front of a bus, and the fault will lie with how well you listened and paid attention to what was said.

Introverts are not necessarily poor listeners. In fact, we're more likely to be better listeners than extroverts, simply because we talk less. But we may be just as likely as anyone else to filter what we hear through our perceptions (or misperceptions!), and we can fall prey to the same mistakes all people can make when listening to others. What's more, because we live in our inner worlds, we introverts may be less adept at *appearing* to listen. Especially if you don't talk a lot, it's important to be perceived as a good listener to win points as an introvert. It can be a valuable professional asset.

Perception Checking

Verifying that your perceptions are accurate is one of the most valuable listening skills you can develop. Perceptions are subjective. Instead of trying to read minds or assuming you know what people are thinking or what their intentions are, simply learn to ask. This can be especially beneficial around extroverts, who tend to say things before thinking them through. As we know, extroverts often think *as* they speak, not before, so their statements are often open to various interpretations. Perception checking gets you to a place of mutual understanding, which is the goal of communication.

Begin perception checking by making an observation. What have you heard? Clarify and ask questions as needed. "Do you mean that we are not doing what we should be doing with the Smith account? Tell me more." You may go further by seeking feedback, as in, "I'm trying to fathom this situation. Am I correct that you feel _____ about it?" Paraphrasing is similar in that it involves putting in your own words what you think someone just said, as in, "What I heard was _____." or, "Do you mean _____?"

These perception-checking techniques help you gain stature among others because they show that you respect and care about what they have to say. This caring can build a strong relationship that is reciprocal in nature. Verifying your perceptions will also surface assumptions that are implicit, thus helping to prevent miscommunication. Clearly comprehending what others say boosts your credibility.

Body Listening

Active listening involves your whole body. Use eye contact to listen and look for nuances of the speaker's expression. Lean forward, change position to screen out distractions, nod, and signal verbally that you hear by saying, for example, "Yes, I understand." Pay attention to nonverbal cues such as tension in the shoulders, a frown, or worried eyes. Wait until someone is finished speaking before jumping in. It is important not to interrupt or talk over someone else. If interrupting is routine in your work culture, you should try to get others to acknowledge it and abandon the habit.

It's also important to pay singular attention to the speaker. Don't multitask by using your computer, glancing at your cell phone, or attending to another digital device. Be sincere in your attempt to communicate with others effectively.

None of the listening techniques mentioned here requires you to act like an extrovert. These habits are sometimes taken for granted, but they make a big difference in how you are perceived. Remember that you are combating stereotypes of introversion to build your reputation in a world where you are starting in second place. How you listen is central to perceptions of your professional competence and consequently to your career potential.

Beyond listening but related to it is responsiveness in communication. Because introverts are happy being alone, they sometimes forget to participate in give-and-take as much as others might like. In the next chapter, you'll learn more about this.

Milestones Along the Journey

Below are a few of the key ideas related to this chapter with a couple extra bullet points for you to fill in. I'd like to hear other ideas that may have resonated for you or were stimulated by what you read. Go to the website www.TheIntrovertsGuide.com to share with me those that have special meaning for *your* personal journey.

- Listening is a natural strength that you have. You can get even better results by honing your listening skills.

- Verifying perceptions is an important listening skill that assists in building trust and strong relationships.

- Body language can be used to good advantage in listening.

- _____

  _____

- _____

  _____

CHAPTER 27

Communication Reciprocity

Most Insightful Experts have a compelling inner life that keeps them occupied and satisfied most of the time. It's simply the way you are, and that's okay. Sometimes, however, it can cause you to fall short in your interpersonal communications. For example, your staff member, Fred, might genuinely need some feedback on how he's doing his job, but you may be busy working on a project and have little interest in speaking with him. Preoccupation with your own affairs can end up harming him by undermining his motivation and future performance. Unbeknownst to you, your silence creates ambiguity and makes his job harder as he tries to guess what you want from him.

To better appreciate this, imagine yourself in the position of seeking factual or subjective information or feedback that never comes. Imagine, for example, that you're driving down the highway with a coworker who knows the route, but when you ask which exit is coming up next—i.e., when you seek factual information—your coworker says nothing. You're likely to be frustrated. Similarly, if you ask which exit your coworker recommends that you take—i.e., if you seek subjective information—and she refuses to give an opinion, you are likely to find her lack of engagement even more frustrating.

Reciprocity of communication has been neglected in both examples. Conversation is impossible without reciprocity, or give and take. Both verbal and nonverbal communications are severely hampered. For all practical purposes, interpersonal communication flounders when one or both parties are less than fully engaged.

This is not solely a problem for introverts, of course. Extroverts fail at communication when they say too much, go off topic, or dominate so that no real dialogue is possible. As introverts, however, we are more likely to make the opposite error—we are likely not to say enough rather than to say too much.

Introverts have diverse reasons for their reticence. Some introverts are so focused on their inner worlds that they are oblivious to the need to respond to others. Some are so inner-focused that they are emotionally insensitive to others, failing to detect the frustration and emotional impact caused by their inaccessibility. Other introverts who are shy fear speaking out. Crippling social anxiety may keep them silent. They may want to talk, to partner with others and dialogue, but feel trapped by their discomfort at speaking out. Still other introverts may believe, falsely, that they simply are not important enough to weigh in on certain topics or with certain groups or individuals. While low self-esteem is not the sole province of introverts (not by a long shot!), it can poison reciprocal communication when an individual shuts down because of it. For these and other reasons, introverts often fail to say what needs to be said.

It is important to be aware of this introvert tendency so that you can guard against it. Conversation—authentic, effective communication—relies on reciprocity. The need for clear professional communications is reason enough to pay attention to reciprocation, but remember too that silence can be interpreted (or misinterpreted, as the case may be) as not caring. Whether or not you genuinely care about what you're hearing is not the point here. Treating others with respect is a hallmark of professionalism, and it is to *your* benefit to reply to e-mails from colleagues and clients, to give feedback to your direct reports when sought, to speak when spoken to (at minimum), to answer questions, to reply to invitations (yea or nay), to express gratitude, to return phone calls, etc.

On the other hand, there is no need to let others take advantage of your willingness to be open and forthright. Often you must set boundaries in your interactions with other professionals. Next we'll look at assertive interactions.

Milestones Along the Journey

Below are a few of the key ideas related to this chapter with a couple extra bullet points for you to fill in. I'd like to hear other ideas that may have resonated for you or were stimulated by what you read. Go to the website www.TheIntrovertsGuide.com to share with me those that have special meaning for *your* personal journey.

- Effective communication depends on reciprocal exchanges.

- Reciprocity is sometimes a weakness for an introvert. It is important for Insightful Experts to make the extra effort that may be required to respond to others' communication attempts.

- Good reciprocal exchanges help others to know you better and they position you as a reliable professional.

- _____

  _____

- _____

  _____

CHAPTER 28

Assertive Interactions

One of the difficulties some Insightful Experts encounter in their professional interactions is dealing with conflict and being more assertive. In part, this is because introverts have such rich, engaging inner worlds; it is a natural tendency to avoid interactions with people. But when conflict is involved, this predisposition is compounded by a well-justified reluctance to engage in a verbal exchange where extroverts hold the edge. Extroverts are fast thinkers and talkers. Quite simply, it is hard for an introvert to keep up. Your many strengths come out best when you are in solitude, with sufficient time to think.

As you develop your internal capabilities, this issue can emerge as one that holds you back from your professional goals. In this chapter, I explain how you can approach conflict, what it means to be assertive, and how to employ some readily applied assertiveness techniques.

Conflict arises when a person (or group) perceives that his (or its) desires may be thwarted by the actions of another. Conflict is valuable in most groups and organizations because it promotes the airing of differences. Too much harmony leads to stasis, inhibiting innovation and creativity. A healthy level of conflict allows new ideas to surface and ultimately flourish. On the other hand, too much conflict can cause coworkers to spend most of their time locked in bitter disputes that never get resolved and that keep people from being productive.

As an introvert, you may respond to conflict in ways that harm your career mobility and professional growth. I usually use the empirically based Thomas-Kilmann conflict model to assess how clients approach conflicts at work. By identifying how you currently deal with conflict, you can learn to adapt your responses in the future.

According to the Thomas-Kilmann framework,[1] which is based on extensive research on professionals, your approach to conflict is a function of your assertiveness and your cooperativeness. If you are highly assertive but uncooperative, you will *compete*, or force your own way on others. If you are highly assertive but cooperative, you will more frequently *collaborate* to solve problems together.

If you are unassertive and also uncooperative, you will tend to *avoid* conflict whenever and however you can. If you lack assertiveness and are highly cooperative, you will tend to yield and *accommodate* instead. If you're moderately assertive and moderately cooperative, you'll often reach a *compromise*, splitting the difference on an issue.

While each of these ways of managing conflict is useful in certain situations, it's important to recognize that being unassertive is desirable only when the issue is trivial or unimportant to you and you can safely accommodate what the other person or group wants. In order to carry the day or collaborate on important issues, or to compromise on moderately important issues, you must exercise assertiveness skills.

The Meaning of Assertiveness

Being assertive is not the same as being aggressive, but it's not being passive, either. To better understand assertiveness, think of it as occupying a place near, but not on, the continuum between passive and aggressive, as shown below.

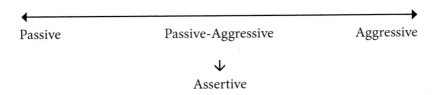

At the passive end of the continuum, you tend to go along with whatever is proposed. Your voice may be soft, your words hesitant, and you may slouch or look down, with submissive body language.

The aggressive end of the continuum forms a sharp contrast. Exuding confidence, you may speak quickly and loudly. You may attack and interrupt others. Your body language will be intimidating as you stare boldly, plant your hands on your hips, or shake your finger in someone's face.

Between these extremes, a passive-aggressive style appears passive but is really aggressive, as will be explained shortly, and it undermines your colleagues' trust in you. The better alternative is assertive communication, which not only occupies a middle ground between passive and aggressive but moves you off the continuum altogether. Assertive communication is direct and punctuated with real listening and respect for others. You will be confident but empathetic, open and honest. Your tone will be even, your body language neither weak nor "in your face." You will make eye contact without shifting away or staring. Your arms and legs will be uncrossed, and you will be relaxed but alert.

If you rely routinely on one extreme or the other, or if you use a passive-aggressive style, you'll tend to run into problems. If you are passive in every situation, you will fail to express your thoughts and ideas, especially if they diverge from others' desires. In the workplace, you may come to be viewed as someone who has little to contribute. Your professional reputation will suffer accordingly, and you are likely to fail to achieve your career goals.

If you are continually aggressive, you will be viewed as a bully who always has to have your own way. This also will have professional consequences. You will alienate clients and colleagues alike.

A passive-aggressive approach combines the two extreme styles. It appears passive but is aggressive. It's usually used by someone uncomfortable expressing anger and resentment. It can emerge as sarcasm, a facial expression that belies the cooperative words spoken, or disconnect between words of compliance and subsequent actions. Joking sometimes masks aggression in this way. You may seem passive in body language, voice, and word choice, but you will be uncooperative when it comes to what you do. That is, you may verbally agree and go along with what a colleague proposes but then go away and do what you want regardless. Sometimes this can even be sabotage as a way of getting even with the other party.

This communication approach can appear attractive to some introverts because it allows them to avoid conflict and thus minimize interactions with people—it can take time to discuss and work through disagreements. However, a passive-aggressive style is a huge mistake if you want to develop your credibility and move ahead in your professional career. It does not take people long to figure out that you say one thing and do another. They will not trust you nor advocate on your behalf. This is true for both clients and other professionals, including your subordinates. Genuine connections are dependent on the trust that can only be undermined by passive-aggressive communication.

Using an assertive communication style, you can stand up for your convictions and ideas while remaining polite and respectful to others. This helps you compromise and collaborate effectively when conflicts arise, and it also builds your professional stature for two reasons. First, by being respectful to others you enable them to save face and retain their reputations. You're seen as a team player, and you're trusted. Second, by standing on your convictions you contribute positively to professional projects and thus build your reputation as a professional with valuable expertise. Both personal trust and reliance on your expertise are central to the aim of building a successful career as an introvert.

Let's examine a situation from the perspective of each style. Rachel's assistant, Zachary, has just revealed that he inadvertently shredded the client's file that she needs for her important meeting today.

Aggressive Rachel: I can't believe how incompetent you are! What could you possibly have been thinking? (Said loudly, with a look of disgust.)

Passive Rachel: If you have time, would it be too much trouble to check the file cabinet again to see if there's a back up copy anywhere? (Said softly, without direct eye contact.)

Passive-Aggressive Rachel: Well, we can't all be perfect. (Said gently, with slight smile. After Zachary leaves the room, Rachel pulls his personnel file from her desk drawer and angrily scrawls a nasty assessment.)

Assertive Rachel: I feel frustrated at this turn of events. I would appreciate your help please in checking immediately to see if we have a backup file somewhere. (Said in an even tone, with relaxed posture.)

One of the ways (though not the only way) to learn to be more assertive is to begin statements with "I" rather than "You" followed by your feeling about the situation. The feeling must come from within, such as Rachel's feeling of frustration; it is your own and not caused by someone else. This can be followed by a request for a specific behavior from the other party. Rachel asked for help in looking for a backup. Assertive statements are direct without being demanding or submissive. In Chapter 29, you will read about a related approach to assertiveness through the use of nonviolent communication techniques.

Here's an exercise to help you better understand the different communication styles. Guess which of the following are passive, passive-aggressive, aggressive, or assertive statements. Answers are at the end of the chapter:

- There's no way that you're right.
- Oh yes, I see. I think that we should do it that way, too.
- What you've said makes sense to me. I don't know if I can do it, though, because—.
- I'm not sure, but it seems to me that—.
- That's crazy. How could that possibly work?

Assertiveness Techniques

Expressing feelings is one way mentioned above to become more assertive. But that may not be appropriate in all situations. A number of powerful assertiveness techniques have been recommended by psychologist Manuel Smith as a result of his extensive study of communication.[2] The following techniques are from his bestselling and timeless book, *When I Say No, I Feel Guilty*.

Persistence. Often, as an Insightful Expert, you will find yourself in situations where others insist that you do what they want, ignoring your own needs and desires. Since calling them out directly is likely to escalate the situation into open conflict or simply lead to denials, it's helpful to have a verbal strategy for holding your ground without giving in. By learning to speak like a "broken record" (this was coined in pre-MP3 and CD days), we calmly and repeatedly stick to our position until the other person or group backs off. For example, consider the following exchange:

> *You:* The payment due for today's consultation is $125.
> *Client:* I don't know if I can pay this today. I forgot to bring my checkbook, and I don't remember you telling in advance how much it was going to be.
> *You:* I'm sorry you forgot your checkbook, but the payment due for today's consultation is $125.
> *Client:* You didn't charge me that last week.

You: Last week's session was different from today's. The payment due for today's consultation is $125.

Client: I need to be going now. My ride is waiting.

You: I see. We'll get you out in just a minute. The payment due for today's consultation is $125.

Client: Is it all right if you just charge me for this and send a bill?

You: I should be able to arrange that for you, since we do that routinely. We'll send you a bill for $125.

Compromising. By being persistent, you retain your dignity even if the other party doesn't give in. The result is that you will feel more confident and better about yourself than if you had quickly succumbed. With your self-respect intact, it is perfectly acceptable to reach out to another with a "workable compromise." In the example above, it might be, "The payment due for today's consultation is $125, but since you clearly don't have it, can you pay $25 today and I'll bill you for $100?" In this case, you're not passive; you're reasonable, and you're seeking to get along, all of which keeps you appearing professional and in control of the situation.

Dealing with Critics. Professionals deal with criticism routinely, often beginning in college or graduate school. Frequently, the criticism is poorly delivered, leading to unnecessarily hurt feelings. But even worse than hurt feelings, some Insightful Experts allow themselves to be manipulated by criticism in an attempt to get along with others. Here are three guidelines for dealing with critics: (1) never deny it; (2) never return it; and (3) never allow yourself the luxury of getting defensive about it. Instead, verbally deflect it.

"Fogging" is one method of verbal deflection. To employ it, first agree—if you can—with the truth or possible truth in someone's statement. Suppose, for example, that a team member or coworker says to you, "Was it you who wrote the project report last month? I'm curious, because the report was not only a week late but also—in my opinion—full of holes and should be reworked." Your initial response might be simply, "Yes, I did finish the project report last month." You can also agree in principle with a fair or objectively true criticism, as in, "You're right, Don. It is important to have the reports done by the 15th." But you need not and should not agree with manipulative or unfair criticism—in this case, that your report was shoddily done and late and ought to be redone.

Although you do well to admit to fair criticism and make suitable amends, you may not want to lose face in those occasional professional settings where simply to admit a failure, no matter how minor, would be deemed unprofessional. In such instances you can employ what's called a "negative assertion." You might, for example, respond to the criticism of your report with, "You're right. My report was late and I failed to consider that important issue that came up this morning." In this way you take responsibility but stick to the facts without being self-deprecating. Taking responsibility doesn't mean falling on your sword.

"Negative inquiry" is another technique for dealing with critics. Let's say you are criticized for writing only five rather than ten pages in your monthly report. You can reply by saying, "I always do five-page reports. So what?" or you can say, "I don't understand. Can you tell me what is important about the length of the report?" The first statement will put the other party on the defensive, while the second statement focuses attention where it belongs—on the rationale behind the critique of your performance. By showing that you are puzzled but not upset, you induce your interlocutor to reconsider the critique. Your response shows that you are not passively agreeing with the criticism, but you are thinking about it and are concerned with what is best for the organization or the client.

Self-Disclosure. Self-disclosure and its benefits are discussed in Chapter 13 as part of your strategy to create impetus for yourself. Self-disclosure is vital to networking, the bane of many introverts. Not surprisingly, it can also be useful for developing your assertiveness with others. In fact, self-disclosure is itself an assertive behavior. If you fail to reveal your thoughts, convictions, values, tendencies, or interests, you don't give others an opportunity to engage with you in a genuine professional relationship.

This doesn't mean you have to reveal everything about yourself—not that that's likely for most Insightful Experts—but a failure to reveal anything at all will block the two-way flow of communications between you and a colleague, diminishing trust. Sometimes, when conflict brews, revealing your personal concerns can open up a dialogue that might otherwise never happen. The revelation might be as innocuous as, "I agree with you, but I'm not certain how to proceed," or "I don't think I agree, but I'm having trouble putting into words how I really think about the proposal."

Connecting Assertively

In some assertiveness self-help books you will find a discussion of rights that everyone has, such as the right to say no without justification.

Because we Insightful Experts sometimes lack confidence and question our rights in an extroverted professional world, it's helpful to acknowledge that we are equals in our workplace interpersonal relations. The imposter phenomenon can lead you to think you're not worthy of having your needs met. At the same time, beware of informing others of your rights. It's likely to only deter effective communication and conflict resolution. Sometimes the best things are left unsaid.

In the next chapter I'll discuss how to connect with others, a process that helps shine a spotlight on the need to be heard, to be competent, to have self-respect, and more. Everyone possesses these needs—these rights—without attaching an imperative to them. By making objective observations, becoming aware of human emotions and universal human needs, and establishing connections to get those needs met, you can learn to communicate in an assertive way that works without provoking defensiveness from anyone. You and the people you deal with professionally—including extroverts–more often than not share the same needs. With this insight forefront, you will instantly recognize your common stake in resolving conflicts constructively.

Answers to the exercise on page 205:

- There's no way that you're right. *Aggressive*
- Oh yes, I see. I think that we should do it that way, too. *Passive-Aggressive or Passive*
- What you've said makes sense to me. I don't know if I can do it, though, because—. *Assertive*
- I'm not sure, but it seems to me that—. *Passive Aggressive or Passive*
- That's crazy. How could that possibly work? *Aggressive*

Note: Words alone can't distinguish a passive from a passive-aggressive response. The former will be followed by compliance, while the latter typically will be followed by some action (or failure to act) that is not true compliance.

Milestones Along the Journey

Below are a few of the key ideas related to this chapter with a couple extra bullet points for you to fill in. I'd like to hear other ideas that may have resonated for you or were stimulated by what you read. Go to the website www.TheIntrovertsGuide.com to share with me those that have special meaning for *your* personal journey.

- Healthy conflict promotes the airing of differences.

- Assertive communication allows you to display your professional expertise and consequently build your reputation. It can be a key element of your strategic plan for professional success.

- Persistence is a valuable assertiveness technique.

- _____

  _____

- _____

  _____

CHAPTER 29

Communicate to Connect

How we communicate with others can determine how we get along with them, which can affect career success. Some ways of communicating are more helpful than others in building beneficial relationships. If, for example, Hannah's colleague says, "You're slow," she may react defensively. What she hears sounds like a judgment even if the statement was well-intentioned. If the colleague says instead, "It took you two weeks to get that project started. Did you run into some issues that were frustrating?" Hannah is likely to respond in a more positive way. In this case, the colleague is being specific about the time it took—a fact—and he asks an empathetic question that shows interest and concern.

Nonviolent communication enables movement toward greater connectedness with others, and it is especially useful as a path through conflict. Refusing to make judgments and assumptions and focusing instead on universal human needs (acceptance, challenge, self-respect, integrity, etc.), this approach can be especially useful for bridging the style differences between introverts and extroverts. It opens the door to connecting with extroverts simply as fellow humans who possess far more in common with you than the few characteristics that set you apart.

Psychologist Marshall Rosenberg has developed a process for nonviolent communication that is taught worldwide (see www.cnvc.org). In addition to the fundamental premise that all humans possess the same basic needs, nonviolent communication holds that we are all compassionate beings. If we can learn to be conscious of our feelings and make connecting with others a priority, we can learn how to listen and at the same time take responsibility for getting our own needs met. The nonviolent communication process helps us do that.

As conceived by Rosenberg, the basic nonviolent communication process has four parts. First, we observe something and state what we see without judgment or assumption. Second, we state honestly what we feel about what we have just seen. Feelings are not the same as thoughts and are sometimes difficult to access if we're used to hiding them. Third, we state the needs—universal human needs—that underlie our feelings. Finally, we request a concrete action that might establish a connection between the two parties to the communication or help both meet their needs.

If you're like many professionals, you're probably cringing to read that I'm recommending Rosenberg's approach—that you go so far as to state your feelings at work. Let me be clear—*by feelings I do not mean the kinds of feelings that you might express to friends or loved ones in a setting unrelated to work.* Bringing those up at work can be a good way to get yourself into plenty of hot water, as my mother used to say. Rather than intense emotions (e.g., love, hate), focus on those that are milder—such as irritation, frustration, satisfaction, pride, or gladness. Used judiciously and with care, these can be appropriate expressions in professional settings and should provide the benefits of this technique to you. Whatever feelings you choose to express, be tactful. Never misuse this approach to blame or point fingers. Stay focused on how you feel, knowing that emotions happen independently within you and no one can ever *make* you feel one way or another.

> *Heather and Michael are developing a new website together, but Heather is frustrated with the speed at which Michael is getting his part done.*
>
> *Heather's observation: "Michael, we agreed that the deadline for this section was yesterday, but I haven't received anything from you."*
>
> *Heather's honest statement of feelings: "I'm frustrated that I haven't gotten it so that I can add my portion to it."*
>
> *Heather's acknowledgement of universal human needs: "Michael, I suspect that we both want to be seen as competent professionals; I know that I do, which is why I'm feeling so frustrated with this."*

Heather's request: "Michael, would you be willing to give your section to me tomorrow morning?"

In nonviolent communication, we seek to be more aware of our own feelings and needs as we listen to what others are saying to us. At the same time, we try to be empathetic to the feelings and needs that are being expressed. We try to avoid taking things personally and assuming that we're under attack—responses that only hinder the communication process.

Nonviolent communication skills can carry Insightful Experts beyond the stereotypes about introverts that exist in professional settings. Rather than feeling isolated because you're misunderstood, you can learn to express yourself more fully and develop stronger connections with the extroverts and introverts around you.

Milestones Along the Journey

Below are a few of the key ideas related to this chapter with a couple extra bullet points for you to fill in. I'd like to hear other ideas that may have resonated for you or were stimulated by what you read. Go to the website www.TheIntrovertsGuide.com to share with me those that have special meaning for *your* personal journey.

- Nonviolent communication techniques can help defuse conflict and lead to greater connection with others, building your long term credibility.

- Objective, factual observations and tactfully honest statements of work-focused feelings can forge productive workplace interactions.

- _____

  _____

- _____

  _____

CHAPTER 30

Social Anxiety:
Nothing to Shy Away From

W hat would happen if you were hiking in the woods and came face to face with a bear? If you're like most people, your eyes would widen and your heartbeat would race. You might crouch a bit and look around for an escape. You might run.

We are all familiar with this so-called "fight-or-flight" response, which is simply Mother Nature's way of protecting us from harm. At work, however, when there are no bears for miles around, the fight-or-flight response induced by social anxiety is a burden, not a life saver. To those who don't suffer from social anxiety, a networking function, a team meeting, an important presentation, or a telephone call to a client is a simple professional situation engendering no cause for alarm. Only those who suffer social anxiety can see the threat; only they experience the same physiological response that arises when we are faced by a bear.

Approximately 15 million people in the U. S.—the majority of whom are introverts—experience social anxiety each year, making it the third most common psychological problem. Put simply, social anxiety is a fear arising in response to interactions (or even the anticipation of interactions) with others. Although it can be misdiagnosed as depression, panic disorder, or some other malady, social anxiety happens to people who are quite normal when they are alone.

If you experience social anxiety, you may appear withdrawn, aloof, or unfriendly, but what you feel inside is a fear (which you know is irrational) of being watched or judged by others. You may feel trapped by this fear. It may keep you from being more outgoing and seeking leadership roles or other professional opportunities that require interactions with others. You are likely to dislike networking and introductions, speaking out in meetings, being observed at your work, making small talk with colleagues, or negotiating a host of other similar social encounters. Your dislike is similar to what many other introverts feel. But *your* feelings in these situations can range from a racing heartbeat to dry mouth, blushing, sweating, tremors, tightness of breath, shaky speech, an inability to think, and outright terror.

If you've experienced social anxiety, you know that it can be debilitating. It can combine with your introversion to make a powerful cocktail, and you may feel helpless to deal with its effects. But the good news is that social anxiety can be treated quite successfully. Research shows that cognitive behavioral therapy (CBT) can successfully alter what you feel, think, and do when faced with fearful interactions. Once you initiate that change, the world opens up and you can do virtually anything you want to do that requires social interaction to succeed. Given this high success rate, I believe it's important that you address any social anxiety issues with a professionally qualified CBT psychotherapist.

My own experience with social anxiety is a case in point. As a young adult, I suffered from a severe public-speaking phobia that went beyond normal anxiety. My heart would race, my voice would quiver, I could not catch my breath, my body would shake, and so on. It was embarrassing and difficult, to say the least, but I could not overcome it.

Of course, when we have such reactions, we intensify the problem by avoiding situations that evoke the response. The less we do it, the less chance we have to overcome the fear. As Russ Harris writes in his book *The Happiness Trap,* "The more importance we place on avoiding anxiety, the more we develop anxiety about our anxiety—thereby exacerbating it. It's a vicious cycle..."[1] I did the avoidance and exacerbating parts pretty well.

As a graduate student, however, I had an opportunity to participate in a research study on the use of CBT to deal with such phobias. Under the guidance of a psychologist, I was strapped to monitors and underwent intensive therapy sessions, practicing public speaking under time pressure and visualizing the worst possible situations that scared me. What I learned is that our bodies will *not* stay in fight-or-flight mode for extended periods of time. As I gradually discovered that the physiological arousal would eventually decline, I was able to develop confidence to make presentations. Did I still get nervous? Of course. Any good actor will tell you that a bit of stage fright keeps you at your best. But my fright was no longer so oppressive that it rendered me dysfunctional and unable to perform well. I learned that my symptoms would subside and I could speak with ease.

I cannot adequately convey how positively this discovery changed my life: I was able to learn to be a good speaker, a successful professor, and much more as a result of my CBT experience. I have little doubt that you too can conquer your social anxiety with CBT. If you suffer from this type of intense anxiety in any situation, I urge you to see a psychotherapist for help. Look for someone who specializes in CBT for social anxiety. If the first one doesn't click with you, keep looking until you find someone who does. You can find relief, and it won't take years of psychoanalysis to achieve it.

In the meantime, here are some basic steps to try on your own, adapted from *The Happiness Trap*:

Steps to Manage Anxiety

1. Become more aware of your thoughts and what you're telling yourself about the situation—e.g., "I will screw up, I'm afraid of showing my real personality, etc."

2. Accept your feelings and sensations (e.g., accelerated heart rate, sweating, the knot in your stomach). Pay attention to these sensations and focus on how they feel. Let yourself feel them rather trying not to feel them.

3. Be mindful of the present moment. Keep your attention focused. Pay attention to sounds, smells, taste, temperature, sights.

4. Recognize that you are not your feelings. Recognize that your thoughts and fears are separate from you. You can observe them as they come and go.

5. When you're not in the midst of a stressful situation, take the time to clarify your values and goals. What is important to you in life? Assess whether you're willing to feel some anxiety in order to accomplish these ends. How willing are you to accept some anxiety?

6. Take action. Set goals based on your values and identify some specific incremental steps you can take. Practice, practice, practice!

Milestones Along the Journey

Below are a few of the key ideas related to this chapter with a couple extra bullet points for you to fill in. I'd like to hear other ideas that may have resonated for you or were stimulated by what you read. Go to the website www.TheIntrovertsGuide.com to share with me those that have special meaning for *your* personal journey.

- Social anxiety is a common psychological issue that can hamper the achievement of career goals, chiefly because many people who suffer from it avoid anxiety-provoking situations that might benefit their careers.

- Social anxiety can be successfully alleviated with Cognitive Behavioral Therapy.

- _____

  _____

- _____

  _____

CHAPTER 31

From Internal Capability
to Third Eye Expert

In Part IV of this book, you have learned a variety of ways to build your *internal capability*—the innermost portion of the Third Eye Framework—and allow your quiet competence to come forth. The skills you choose to develop will give you the personal resources to create *impetus*, develop sustainable relationships, and structure your *interfaces* to your advantage.

The three elements of the Third Eye Framework—as set forth in Parts II, III, and IV—work together to help you leverage your introverted strengths to your career advantage. The combined insight you've gained from all three elements of your professional development should allow you to more clearly see the gestalt of your professional challenges and know how to respond. You may go back to the beginning and work at building solid relationships by applying your influence, you may focus on structuring your interfaces better, or you may decide that your skills in key aspects of interpersonal relations have gotten rusty. This ability to more clearly see what else you could do and what actions you might take to advance your career—and how the three layers interrelate to support one another—is what I call becoming a Third Eye Expert.

As you work through this process, go back to the strategic career plan that you created at the outset in Chapter 7. Planning is an iterative process, never quite finished, and it keeps you focused. As you achieve one objective, set another. Your stakeholders (Chapter 15) will no doubt change over time as new people move into and out of your professional life. Stay alert to such changes and reanalyze your network occasionally to pick up on the need to forge new relationships. Use your newly acquired insight and influence skills (Chapter 16) to do so with integrity, always aiming at win-win outcomes. *Use your plan to anchor and center your professional development efforts.*

My hope is that your journey through the Third Eye Framework also reveals to you strengths deriving from your introversion (and from elsewhere) that you didn't know you had. Beyond that, your burgeoning self-awareness, confidence, emotional intelligence, assertiveness, and a host of other attributes will all put you on a trajectory toward your goals that complements the other strategies you undertake to create impetus and structure interfaces.

In Part V you meet some of the choices and challenges you will likely face as an Insightful Expert (now a Third Eye Expert!) as you progress on your path to greatness. These include potential downsides to introversion, dealing with the other introverts in your professional life, changing career paths, finding meaningful work, and being a leader.

Milestones Along the Journey

Below are a few of the key ideas related to this chapter with a couple extra bullet points for you to fill in. I'd like to hear other ideas that may have resonated for you or were stimulated by what you read. Go to the website www.TheIntrovertsGuide.com to share with me those that have special meaning for *your* personal journey.

- Look to the Third Eye Framework to identify future areas where you may wish to focus your professional development and career-building efforts.

- Use your strategic plan (Chapter 7) to continually reassess your efforts and to take a new tack as you mark accomplishments.

- Be proud of your many professional strengths that derive from your introversion.

- _____

  _____

- _____

  _____

PART V

Choices and Challenges

CHAPTER 32

The Dark Side of Introversion?

With the personal knowledge that comes from living as Insightful Experts, most introverts know that their preferred ways of being in the world differ from those of extroverts. Research in cognitive psychology indicates that all people seek ways to remember and understand differences by simplifying information. This makes it all too easy for an Insightful Expert to identify strongly with introversion as the foremost characteristic making him or her unique. This tendency is likely to be even more pronounced because introverts are seemingly "out-grouped" in a professional culture that appears to place greater value on extroverted behavior. People in groups perceived as non-dominant seek a cohesive identity, so it's quite natural for Insightful Experts to see introversion as their defining trait.

At the same time extroverts, generalizing from a single characteristic (recall the halo effect from Chapter 25), are more or less equally as likely to anchor on your introverted behavior and attribute all of your traits to that one dimension of your makeup. In effect, your introversion can distort and minimize the projection and influence of your other characteristics and come to dominate how you are perceived by others. So, for example, if Hillary is a good scientist, her braininess might be attributed by others to her introversion, when in fact she is simply one bright member of a family lineage of above-average IQs.

An acquaintance of mine, Jeannie, mistakenly believes that all introverts are passive-aggressive. That some introverts are insensitive to other people's feelings by no means proves her correct. Insensitivity and introversion are two different traits; it is simply wrong to conclude that they are somehow linked. Such erroneous conclusions are fueled by the misguided stereotyping of introverts as misfits and recluses.

All such generalized characterizations give introversion a bad name. Far from being based on fact, they simply make the world easier to understand for those who lack understanding. The "introversion" label is a convenient one.

Introversion is also one of the most visible and thus more salient human characteristics[1] simply because the Introvert-Extrovert dimension of personality has to do with how you engage with other people. Whether you prefer solitude or being with others is highly visible, and whether you talk a little or a lot is evident to those around you at your first introduction. In contrast, you can discover, for example, whether or not someone is conscientious, emotionally stable, or open to new experiences only by speaking to them at length or perhaps participating on a team with them as colleagues. Because it's so visible, introversion can become a catchall characteristic.

Diversity is like the kaleidoscope you might have played with at the beach when you were a kid. It is a combination of colors and shapes that pleases us. Your unique traits mesh with my unique traits, making a beautiful configuration. But when our traits clash and we fail to see their value in the other, we're less pleased. Neither set of traits is inherently better or worse; it's the fit that's bad.

Suppose that Jon is a detail-oriented introvert, while Jenna is a big-picture extrovert. They seldom see eye to eye. Because introversion and extroversion are both highly visible, it would be natural for Jon to conclude that Jenna's big-picture orientation, which Jon finds frustrating, is due to Jenna's extroversion. Equally, Jenna might decide that Jon's "nitpicking" is due to the fact that he's "one of those introverts." This reaction would be reinforced if it so happened that Jenna's last boss, an introvert whom she hated, was also detail oriented in the extreme.

Yet one trait, however visible, does not paint a whole portrait. Of major personality attributes often cited by psychologists, introversion is but one.[2] Regardless of its power, introversion is—at most—no more than 20% of what defines you as an individual. What's more, it can combine with other personality traits in a myriad of ways.

I know introverts who are compassionate toward others and introverts who view such compassion with disdain. I know introverts who are conscientious and others who could care less about hard work and achievement. What's clear to me is that these other traits have nothing to do with their introversion.

In their book *Type Talk at Work*[3], Otto Kroeger and his coauthors examine leaders' personalities when introversion/extroversion are combined with judging or perceiving—traits related to an individual's tolerance for uncertainty. The combination of extroversion and judging is most strongly associated with success in the role of leader. Introverted judgers are strong, silent people who are second most likely to end up as leaders. Both extroverted and introverted perceivers, on the other hand, are hard to find in leadership roles. Such results support the notion that other traits can override the effects of introversion/extroversion.

So, is there a "dark side of introversion?" Well, maybe. Read on.

Be Aware of Your Story

I've just outlined the tendency on the part of others or even yourself to attribute all your personal foibles and characteristics to the fact that you're an introvert. Such attribution can become how you define yourself; it can write your "story," your identity, if you let it. *If* there is a dark side of introversion, I believe this is it. No matter what professional situation you might struggle with, do poorly in, or discover yourself ill-suited to, you would then attribute it to your introversion, as in, "I'm simply an introvert in an extroverted world."

Well, perhaps—but is that the whole explanation? When you begin to grow through application of the Third Eye Framework and start to leverage the career potential that was there all along, you will also come to understand that your introversion brings with it many positive attributes, strengths, and competencies. You're likely to discover that you can get beyond your "story." You can emerge into the light and let all your positive attributes shine, unhampered by a past that took place before you figured out how to negotiate an extroverted professional world.

And now, since you must work with other introverts as well as extroverts, let's explore how best to get along with them.

Milestones Along the Journey

Below are a few of the key ideas related to this chapter with a couple extra bullet points for you to fill in. I'd like to hear other ideas that may have resonated for you or were stimulated by what you read. Go to the

website www.TheIntrovertsGuide.com to share with me those that have special meaning for *your* personal journey.

- Because introversion is so visible to others, other traits can be ascribed to it inappropriately.

- Introversion is one slice of your personality, not the whole.

- _____

  _____

- _____

  _____

CHAPTER 33

Sandwiched by Introverts: Dealing with Introverted Staff, Bosses, and Colleagues

Have you considered what it must be like for others to adjust to your introversion? One of the outcomes of self-awareness is learning how others, especially but not only extroverts, react to and perceive your introverted traits. You have indisputable strengths of being able to work independently, make thoughtful and careful decisions, project a reserved professionalism, and more. You also have qualities that are not always *perceived* as strengths. Your need for solitude, your preference for privacy, your reticence in lively conversations, your lack of energy after prolonged social interaction, your difficulty with—or at least distaste for—providing immediate responses: such introverted behaviors are hard to accept not just for extroverts, but for other introverts too.

This chapter would not be necessary if the business world were not biased toward extroversion. But since it is, a deliberate awareness of how to make the most of your fellow introverts' qualities and contributions will serve you well in the workplace. How we interact with our fellow introverts says a lot about how much we really understand and respect introversion as an equally valid way of being. We can learn how to have great relationships with other introverts as well as with extroverts in professional situations.

If you have read the earlier chapters in this book, you no doubt have a pretty good idea of what it means to be an introvert in an extroverted professional world. Let's put this knowledge to good use in considering the best ways to work productively with your fellow introverts.

Supervising Introverted Staff

The first condition for success with introverts is recognizing that they are different—in other words, being aware of the diversity generated by this dimension of personality. Introversion falls outside the cultural "norm"; even though half of us are introverts, the business world most often prefers extroversion. For this reason, your first task is to discard mainstream assumptions about how your employee should behave. Once you've crossed this hurdle, it will be easier to adapt. Of course, treating *all* your subordinates as the individuals they are will help your rapport with them, but this is especially important with introverts, since they are perhaps more likely to retreat from an unsympathetic boss, withholding their fullest and best contributions because they never figure out how to get their ideas across to you. Your objective is to bring out the best in your employees, not to change their personalities.

If you have been following along with the Third Eye Framework and know your own Insightful Expert predispositions, you are prepared to manage your introverted workers according to the Golden Rule: do unto others as you would have them do unto you. Sometimes this is easier said than done, but it offers a high standard to which to aspire and a practical guideline when ambiguous situations arise. If you have awakened your self-awareness, your next challenge may be to apply that self-knowledge to the task of managing interactions with your subordinates, with a pronounced dose of empathy.

Begin with clear expectations. Ensure that your introverted worker understands what is expected. With this foundation, you are in a position to coach him/her to achieve the results you seek. Give him time, working alone, to propose some goals, then set the final goals together—truly together—with you listening carefully to what your introvert says. Collaborate. Finally, after a lag of a day or two to allow for second thoughts that might improve the final product, put the goals in writing, but give your worker enough flexibility to figure out how best to meet them and to adapt to circumstances that change, as they always do in one way or another. It's almost always best to leave implementation up to the specialist and to give him or her the autonomy to find the best way.

Meet personally to finalize your mutually agreed expectations. Because introverts are so prone to retreat into their private offices and perhaps to avoid asking questions or challenging your statements, it is especially important that you take the lead with this. You will have to make more effort at this point of your relationship than you would if you were dealing with an extrovert, but it will pay off later.

Once you have mutually agreed expectations, you can step back and let your introvert do her thing, as she will readily do if she's a worthy employee to start with. You must give your introvert time and space to work alone and to accommodate the introverted style. Don't try to micromanage, but you *must* occasionally check in. Whereas an extrovert will be forthcoming with issues and problems, an introvert often won't come forward until much more time has passed. Two introverts working together—you and your subordinate—may exacerbate this potential problem, since both of you may shy away from checking in. As the superior, it's up to you to make the extra effort to check in. Seek an effective way of doing so that accommodates your own style as an Insightful Expert.

Prevent issues from becoming problems. Take the time to check in and provide feedback regularly. Your feedback should be frequent, clear, and focused on the behavior, not the person.

One of the most crucial steps you can take to be successful with introverts is to draw them out. You will forego much that your introverts have to offer if you don't do this, simply because they may not offer up information readily. Checking in serves this purpose one-on-one.

As discussed in Chapter 24, when you are managing a team that includes introverts, you must attend to eliciting the contributions of the introverts. Group problem solving will suffer if introverts are overlooked and underheard. As team manager, it is your job to consistently and conscientiously ensure that people who tend toward introversion are heard. One technique that works is to formalize the process of gathering input in meetings from your team by going around the circle and explicitly soliciting input from each person. If you allow the information-gathering process to occur informally, with individuals speaking up when they get an opening in the conversational flow, your decisions will be weighted more heavily by the input of the extroverts. Informality may seem warm and relaxed, but it's a disaster if you truly desire contributions from all your employees. What's more, it may leave your introverted employees frustrated when the meeting is called to a close and they have yet to speak their minds. In time, their frustration potentially will lead to decreased motivation and increased turnover.

If you establish a rapport with your introverted employee, your need to check in and give feedback may decline over time. What you are doing is creating a stronger social situation for your introvert. In strong social situations, introverts behave much like extroverts. In fact, one would be hard-pressed to tell the difference! So take a long-term perspective. Invest in your relationships with your introverts.

I believe that supervising introverts is much harder for you, an introvert, than it is for extroverts. You must overcome your reticence and need for privacy and so must your worker—just enough to get the job done effectively. An extroverted boss more readily establishes routine contact with introverted workers because extroverts are by nature very social and enjoy interaction with others. On the other hand, you can understand your introvert as no extroverted boss possibly can. You may also find that your similarities lead to working styles that mesh. For example, you both need privacy and time to reflect. This can affect how you meet, perhaps choosing a series of short meetings rather than a less frequent longer meeting.

Consider self-disclosing to your introverted supervisees. As their introverted leader, you are in a unique position to set an example and be a mentor. If something is difficult for you or has been difficult at some other time in your career, consider sharing your experience. By revealing yourself, you also show that introversion is nothing to be ashamed of and that it can flourish in the professional world.

Managing Your Introverted Boss

Much of what I've said about supervising introverts should give you ideas about how to manage your introverted boss. As experts John Gabarro and John Kotter state in their article *"Managing Your Boss,"*[1] managing a boss simply means working with him or her to achieve good outcomes for both of you and for your company. It is pragmatism, not political gamesmanship, to attend to a relationship with someone with whom you are so closely tied and with whom there is such a high degree of mutual interdependence. Each of you needs the other to be successful at what you do. Not surprisingly, the foundation for a strong relationship is a solid understanding of your respective predispositions and working assumptions.

Keep in mind that your introverted boss is an individual, unique in many respects, only one of which is her introversion. Drop your expectation, if you have it, that all bosses should be extroverts! Why in the world should they be? Introverts are just as bright, talented, and ambitious as extroverts. As you drop that expectation, you can more readily see the quiet strengths that an introverted boss possesses. She may be a good listener. She may be reflective. She may rarely be pushy or aggressive. All of these qualities allow you to do your best without a great deal of interference.

But your introverted boss can also seem uncommunicative, remote, and disengaged! Notice that I use the word "seem." You can't really know, because an introvert sometimes presents an impenetrable façade. Similar to when you are supervising an introvert, it's up to you to go the extra mile to communicate with your introverted boss. Since you're also an introvert, this can be hard, but it must be done. Check in regularly but politely. Ask. Ask again if need be.

At this point you would do well to learn the difference between assertiveness and aggressiveness. It is important that you demonstrate some assertiveness in order to open the lines of communication with your boss regularly. (See Chapter 28 for some assertiveness techniques.) One Insightful Expert, Judy, asked her boss for a formal weekly meeting to accomplish this. It can be helpful with some bosses to provide something in writing in advance of such a meeting in order to show respect and, even more important, to allow the introverted boss time to reflect on the upcoming session.

Care must be taken to avoid appearing aggressive. There is a delicate power balance to be struck in dealing with superiors, and if you're used to dealing with extroverts, your body language could be off-putting to an introverted boss. Don't stare or glare; instead, break your gaze and briefly look away when talking with an introverted boss. Don't speak overly loudly or lean too far forward. Give the boss plenty of space. Don't look for immediate replies. Give him time to reflect. Train yourself to identify problems early so that your boss has time to react and reply according to his introverted style. Keep meetings short so that the boss's energy is not depleted by her interactions with you.

Drawing out a superior, introverted or not, who is not clear or forthcoming is a delicate balancing act. Gabarro and Kotter suggest a couple of techniques that some managers use to draw out their superiors. One is to prepare a written memo that outlines your work-plan and send it to your boss for his/her feedback and blessing. This can be followed up with an in-person meeting where every detail from the memo is addressed in order to ensure that everything is fully clarified. Another, more circumspect approach you can use to gain insight to the boss's agenda is to speak with others who have worked for the boss in the past. Also, it can be useful to scan formal commitments the boss has made, such as her own objectives or work-plan.

Another tactic is to look for commonalities with your boss unrelated to your introversion. For example, if you are familiar with the Jungian cognitive style dimensions (explained in Chapter 34), see if you both are intuitive or perhaps detail oriented and logical. Alternatively, possibly you are both visual thinkers. Whatever it is, use that known commonality to establish rapport and to deliberately and carefully tailor your communications to accommodate your boss's style (to the extent that you can do so given your own personality).

The Introverted Colleague

Many of the same actions that you take with superiors and subordinates also apply to getting along with introverted colleagues. Tailored communication is central, as is allowing the introverted colleague space and time to manage her energy and contributions. You should take the lead in voicing your needs for communication frequency, but be flexible in how and where it takes place. Introverts have a different style from extroverts, and it's valuable to negotiate these details so that your colleague is comfortable with your interactions. Be open to give and take.

As with introverted subordinates or superiors, briefer interactions—with intervening time for reflection and preparations—work well for introverts. Don't put your introverted colleague on the spot; allow him to work at his own pace. You will likely have to check in frequently with a colleague, as you do with other introverts. Take the lead in this. Seek the introvert's input for best results. Don't expect instant answers.

Your introverted colleague may be neither above nor below you in the hierarchy of your organization, so issues of power that relate to formal authority apply less in your relations with him or her. Instead, you may have to be sensitive to issues of power derived from relationships with others, from expertise, and from information. You will want to learn to be more inclusive and participatory with your introverted colleagues. Inclusiveness can take the form of:

- *Building a relationship* with a colleague to engender mutual trust. This need not be a personal friendship, but it should be collegial: professional yet friendly and comfortable. You build trust over time by keeping your commitments, being reliable, and otherwise demonstrating your trustworthiness.

- *Seeking your colleague's expertise.* Do this regularly and intentionally. Expertise is the most important exchange a professional offers. For example, only one member of a team of engineers might be a specialist in occupational safety, but if that member is an introvert, he may be less likely to be forthcoming—especially early in his career. You must seek out his expertise to be inclusive.

- *Sharing information.* Just as you may seek expertise and information from an introverted colleague, you show inclusiveness by sharing information as well. In an organization dominated by professionals, up-to-date and timely information is critical to doing a good job. Your introverted colleagues may be less "in the loop" than extroverts because they spend more time in their offices or on the job site focused on the technical aspects of their work rather than interpersonal relations. They can only be at their best if information is consciously shared with them. Is this being overly solicitous and perhaps providing special service to introverts? I don't think so. I see it more as acknowledging the diversity of the human animal in organization life and doing what we each must do to adapt to the working styles of our colleagues. I can think of countless times when I waited for an extrovert to complete a seemingly long-winded, unoriginal assessment of something before someone else could interject a new perspective. I might have been resentful but, in most cases, was not because I believe that diversity demands tolerance and quite a dose of patience, no matter who is being accommodated.

In sum, it doesn't have to be difficult to get along with introverts. It just takes some time to think through how they are different from extroverts and what that means for how you approach them. It does require more "push" to get along initially, but since you are introverted as well, you may find that the effort required is less over the long haul than what's needed to get along with extroverts. You will not be as exhausted, and you will find less to listen to and parse through to get to the heart of issues. That in itself may be enough to motivate you to make the effort to better understand the introverted way of being from the outside looking in.

Now you know how to work with introverts. But what if the work you're doing is not right for you in the first place, or what if you're making a big career decision? Your career choices are up next.

Milestones Along the Journey

Below are a few of the key ideas related to this chapter with a couple extra bullet points for you to fill in. I'd like to hear other ideas that may have resonated for you or were stimulated by what you read. Go to the website www.TheIntrovertsGuide.com to share with me those that have special meaning for *your* personal journey.

- Do not expect introverts to be like extroverts.

- Introverts need autonomy with regular follow-up and check-ins.

- Watch your body language with your introverted boss.

- Seek out your introverted colleagues' expertise and share information with them.

- _____

_____

- _____

_____

CHAPTER 34

Career Choices and Strategies

"Don't get famous doing something you don't like."

—John Hartford, Grammy award winning musician, songwriter, steamboat pilot, author, artist, disc jockey, calligrapher, dancer, folklorist, and historian[1]

Your profession probably represents your primary opportunity to make a contribution to society, and it also provides the circumstances to find deep enjoyment and personal fulfillment doing work that is consonant with your talents, abilities, and predilections. Lawrence Boldt says, "Our task is to somehow tap into the eternal ocean of bliss and somehow express that energy in the world of forms and time."[2]

Some Insightful Experts naturally land in careers that are a good match for their introversion, but others make false starts. It's easy to go through a long and demanding academic program in, say, medicine before you realize that you thoroughly despise the day-to-day demands of your chosen profession. These may be social demands or other requirements that clash with introversion. By social demands, I mean the requirements for interactions with other people: talking, accommodating, listening, reacting to, working alongside, etc. Other demands that rub an introvert raw might include a lack of down time to recharge your energy, a need to constantly be "on" with no time for introspection, a chronic deficit of privacy, situations where form and appearances are more important than substance, a deficit of engaging problems to keep your mind occupied, highly politicized corporate environments, or other situations where your quiet competence simply is not valued.

If you've made a false career start, you have at least three choices, including:

- staying the course in relative misery,
- staying the course and learning to adapt, or
- making a major career change.

Option one above—staying the course in misery—is not a wise strategy for anyone's mental health, and I don't recommend it.

The second option is to learn to adapt. I was well into a doctoral program in business before I realized how unpleasant it was for me, an introvert, to teach a class of 60 Master of Business Administration (MBA) students. Luckily, I learned to adapt and became a respected faculty member before I began to pursue other endeavors and passions, including doing one-on-one consulting with other introverts. Now I love teaching a class or workshop, but I know what works for me and what doesn't. Often what works for me is not what works for the seminar leader down the hall, especially if he's an extrovert.

While the earlier chapters of this book focused on how to adapt, this chapter offers guidance for those of you who realize that perhaps a major career change is in order and option three may be your choice. It is hard enough to adapt, as we all must do even if we make optimal introvert-oriented career choices from the outset. But when you are faced with a simple bad fit between your predispositions and your chosen profession, adapting won't be enough.

If all the adaptation in the world won't make you happy, something else must shift. As you may have discovered, leaving a career for which you have spent most of your life preparing and placed yourself deeply in hock is both emotionally and financially challenging.

Remember that your work is where you spend many of your waking hours. Your life is precious. Make the most of it.

Know Yourself

The first move toward finding a good career fit is to know yourself. Without self-knowledge and self-insight, you'll have a tough time making a decision that leads to a good outcome. Self-assessment tests to help with this abound.[3] I recommend that you start by understanding your cognitive style, which I will explain briefly here, followed by as many other assessments as you need to feel confident of your choices. I find that almost all such tests offer valuable insights.

In simple terms, cognitive style is simply the way you think. Psychoanalyst Carl Jung not only identified introversion, he developed a framework for understanding it along with other characteristics of how we think, often called the Jungian Typology. It is a powerful tool for understanding personality differences among individuals. Jung's Typology is useful for learning more about yourself to make better career decisions.

Jung's concepts have been translated into a number of different assessment measures that are employed in research as well as in practice in organizations to help people build better teams. The most commonly known is the Myers-Briggs Type Indicator® (MBTI®) developed by Isabel Briggs Myers and Katherine Briggs. Despite the dominance of the MBTI, The Personal Style Inventory developed by R. Craig Hogan and David W. Champagne is a valid alternative assessment of the Jungian typology. On the web, you can find assessments that have not been subjected to validity testing, so you will want to use the results with caution. But for fun, try the assessment at www.humanmetrics.com.

Let's briefly review the Jungian Typology. Alongside the Introversion-Extroversion dimension, the Perceiving-Judging dichotomy has to do with how you live out and carry on your life. People with a preference for *perceiving* tend toward flexibility, spontaneity, and openness, while *judging* types tend to prefer stability, planning, and organization.

Two central dichotomies in the Jungian Typology provide additional insight to cognitive style. These are (1) how you take in information (through sensing or intuiting) and (2) how you make choices based on the information you have (via feeling or thinking).

Sensing types tend to prefer hard data and facts when it comes to information gathering. They are concerned with the here and now and want to know what is practical and what will work. *Intuiting* types, on the other hand, prefer possibilities to facts. They focus on the big picture, the gestalt, and the long-range potentials of a situation.

People with a preference as a *thinking* type tend to prefer an objective, impersonal approach to making choices. They take a logical perspective and can readily consider theory and draw conclusions. In contrast, *feeling* types tend to make subjective decisions. They are concerned primarily with human needs and personal values. Less concerned with what is true or false than a thinking type might be, feeling types care more about what is good or bad.

The table below shows the four possible combinations of these core information-processing dimensions. The combinations suggest the abbreviations of ST (senser-thinker), SF (senser-feeler), NT (intuiter-thinker), and NF (intuiter-feeler). ST's focus on facts, efficiency, and getting things done. SF's care about specific other people, getting along, and communicating. NT's emphasize possibilities, new approaches, and out-of-the-box thinking. NF's are concerned with meaningfulness, autonomy, and values-related implications for people in general.

As an Insightful Expert, you will of course not want to put yourself into a career position that demands intense public interaction with others in a fast-paced environment—a scenario that rarely works well for an introvert. Inner-directed and reflective, you would quickly find yourself drained of energy. But when you're choosing a career, begin to pay attention to the other dimensions as well. If you are a big-picture person (an intuiting type), for example, it will be difficult for you to deal with minute mundane details day in and day out. Or if you are a thinking type with a bent for logic and systematic analysis, you are likely to find a job that deals with people's messy day-to-day problems both challenging and quite unsatisfying.

	THINKING		
SENSING	**ST** Facts; Efficiency; Getting things done	**NT** Possibilities; New approaches; Innovative thinking	**INTUITING**
	SF Specific people; Social interaction; Communicating	**NF** Meaningfulness; Autonomy; Values-related implications for all people	
	FEELING		

Cognitive Style Inner Dimensions

Application of the Jungian Typology to analyze your personality fit with careers or other people can lead to unwise generalizations if taken to extremes, but if it is employed simply as another tool to help you know yourself and others a bit better by understanding tendencies, it is helpful. It is always important to remember that no dimension is inherently superior to another; the typology only presents tendencies that are simply different. Assessments that incorporate this model should never be used for employment selection decisions that involve hiring or firing anyone.

A number of books and websites offer detailed explanations of personality types based on the four key dimensions of the typology. The insight gained from understanding your cognitive style is a preparatory step toward choosing an optimal career. It is another piece of information to add to your self-awareness that goes beyond your introversion. The next step is to understand your goals and life trajectory.

Career Path and Goals

It's useful to look first at where you are in your life and career, because this provides a perspective from which to envision your future. Often we take the present and the past for granted, and may not reflect fully on their meaning. Yet this information can be invaluable in making decisions that affect the future.

Try this exercise.[4] First, draw a chart with increasing levels of success on the vertical axis and time on the horizontal axis, from past to present to future. Now draw a line on the chart that represents your own career success over time. Now substitute professional fulfillment for levels of success on the vertical axis of the same chart. Using a different color of ink, draw another line on your chart depicting your professional fulfillment over time. Consider every aspect relevant to you, such as personal growth, values realization, material acquisitions, or other.

In the next step, list ten adjectives that describe you in your career success over time. Also, list ten adjectives describing you in regard to your professional fulfillment over time. Which of these are positive, neutral, or negative? Go back and denote them with a P (positive), N (neutral), or NN (negative).

Finally, examine these charts and your lists. What have you learned about yourself? Where are you now with regard to your career? Where are you with respect to your professional fulfillment?

Bring in the results of your values exercise from Chapter 10, "Values = Meaning (and Motivation)." Does this information change your perspective at all? If it does, revise your conclusions about where you are in your career and professional fulfillment.

Now you are ready to consider the ideal. You have already considered the values that are important to you, how you want to live your life. Now consider what you want to accomplish with your life's work. What attainments do you aspire to? Brainstorm. Consider both your career and professional fulfillment. What goals do you have? Develop a list. Then, in a final step, prioritize your goals in the order of their importance to you. Which are most critical? If you were to die tomorrow, which would you regret not having accomplished? Give each goal a ranking from 4 (highest importance) to 1 (nice, but of relatively little importance).

With the self-insight gained from considering your cognitive style and from knowledge of your personal goals, you are now better able to consider what career choices may help you create a meaningful life.

Strategies for Change

Before you undertake a radical change in the profession for which you have already invested so much time, money, and psychic energy, you may want to consider something less drastic. It's usually prudent to start your consideration of options with what is practical and most doable. Then, if a major alteration of your course turns out to be essential, you will know that it truly is the thing you need to be doing.

Another Specialty Within Your Field. Nearly all professions contain a variety of specializations. These can be good places to begin considering options. For example, the American Board of Medical Specialties lists 145 certified specialties and sub-specialties, running a broad gamut from pain medicine to medical toxicology to nuclear radiology and many more. Some of these specializations are more research oriented, some require more or less patient interaction, some will be practiced only in high-tech large health center settings, and others can be run from a solo practitioner's office. These sorts of differences may be key for you.

Similar specializations exist in the law: bankruptcy, criminal, intellectual property, real estate, and so on. Engineering includes civil, electrical, mechanical, software, ceramics, chemical, environmental, and dozens of other specialties. In accounting, there are specializations in tax, cost, forensics, environmental, and others. Similarly, the physical and social sciences include many specialties, as does management. In administration, you could specialize in supply chains, e-marketing, human resources, operations, etc. Even nursing and education embrace many diverse specializations. In fact, most professions include multiple specialty areas.

Is it easy to switch specialties? Probably not in many cases, since it does involve additional education, training and possibly certification. But it's likely to be easier than training for an altogether new career field. The education and experience you have already accumulated can lessen the time necessary to acquire new credentials.

Research different areas of specialization to find out what is available and how much additional education and training you will need. The important thing is to believe that it's possible to find something that is a better fit with your introversion and your cognitive style. Use the information from examination of your life trajectory in the previous exercise to seek a good fit with your skills and values.

A Different Practice Setting. Sometimes Insightful Experts think that a career is a bad fit when in reality it's the setting, not the career, that clashes with their introversion. Common professional settings range from solo practices and small partnerships of two or three professionals to larger partnerships of up to hundreds of professionals, for-profit companies, nonprofit charitable and philanthropic organizations, and government entities. Some of these may be more hospitable to introverts than others.

For example, a very small practice may require more marketing to get started, and this may not be appealing to an introvert. On the other hand, this may in the long run be balanced by less need to negotiate with partners and supervise employees, and it may also allow more downtime if you wish to conserve energy and achieve goals at your own pace.

In general, for-profit companies will be more oriented toward monetary results, whereas government and not-for-profits will be more mission-oriented and, in the case of government, more bureaucratic. Large partnerships also tend to be oriented to financial results and billable client hours, an emphasis that rewards networking and marketing efforts. Schmoozing is often required. These are not typically strong suits of most introverts. Government settings require virtually no marketing yet may be quite stressful with regard to ambiguous demands and changing budgetary priorities. They offer the advantage of much time to just do what you do. As a professional, you are likely to be left alone to do your job. This can work well for an Insightful Expert, especially if you don't mind the increased paperwork that often accompanies public service accountability.

Consider the various settings within which your profession is practiced to determine if there is a change that could be beneficial to your introversion. Use the Internet to informally poll others in your profession to determine the specific traits called for by different practice settings.

A Different Organization. Related to a different setting, though not identical, is the option of simply switching employers. A given organization may simply not be a good fit for you—perhaps it never was—or perhaps you've outgrown what it has to offer. Some key organizational variables include:

- Size
- Culture
- Your boss, partners, and colleagues

Organization size is something we often don't think much about, except perhaps to assume that larger is better. For an Insightful Expert, however, larger may not be better. Why? Because with size, organizations develop more written rules, plans, procedures, and other formal trappings. This bureaucracy is essential to maintain control of a large organization, but its effect tends to be greater rigidity and less flexibility.

Other dimensions of your personality (e.g., intuiting versus thinking) can help to determine which of these you prefer, but a smaller and thus more flexible organization is more likely to give you the leeway to retire to the privacy of your office when necessary to conserve energy and regroup, and a smaller organization is also more likely to accommodate divergences from the extroverted mainstream of modern business culture. So, for example, you might be able to do less networking in a flexible workplace so long as you do other things well, and you will likely find more openness to different ways of communicating and more informal communications. A flexible work environment may allow you not to be so good at speaking and thinking on your feet. It may allow you more time for important decisions. In general, smaller is more flexible, and that could be an asset to an introvert.

The *culture* of an organization can likewise determine how hospitable it is to Insightful Experts. Broadly speaking, an organization's culture is the sum of the assumptions held in common by its members, whether it's a partnership of two or a multinational corporation. These assumptions determine what people value and how they behave toward one another and toward their work, clients, and colleagues—whether information is shared or hoarded, whether excellence is valued over mediocrity, whether people are polite or rude to one another, or even whether clients are treated with respect or simply tolerated. These working assumptions determine how day-to-day life in the organization is experienced. It may be that your current organization's culture is simply not a good fit for you.

Because culture is learned over time in response to threats to an organization's survival, it is relatively immutable. It also tends to be pervasive and difficult to escape, with the possible exception of a very large corporation that occupies multiple geographic locations, each of which may indeed have a different culture. In general, an organization's culture defines its very nature, and if that culture is extremely extroverted, you might be better off to leave that organization and seek a company that offers a better fit.

In their ground-breaking examination of cultural values in organizations, business culture experts Ralph Kilmann and Mary Jane Saxton[5] identified four groupings frequently cited by survey respondents. Their empirical analysis, which looked at gaps between desired and actual norms for behavior, uncovered these four categories of norms:

- Task-support norms that have to do with workplace supportiveness and sharing;

- Task-innovation norms that have to do with innovation and creativity;

- Social-relationship norms that have to do with professional interpersonal relations; and

- Personal-freedom norms having to do with individuality and personal choices.

What norms support your needs as an introvert? What kind of work environment would serve your needs? Begin by considering the task-support and innovation norms. Do the task norms in your present or future workplace provide you with the space you need to think and work in solitude? Do you or will you have private projects or your own workload, allowing you to work at your own pace, or is everything a team effort with reciprocal interaction throughout all phases of the work? Are you able to follow your own muse and devise innovative ways of practicing your profession?

The social aspects of culture are especially important from the perspective of introvert/extrovert differences. As an introverted individual, you tend to experience a strong need to conserve energy. You are likely to have a preference for smaller groups and one-on-one interactions and meetings. You no doubt prefer electronic over face-to-face and written over oral communications.

You may find that a different organization has completely different cultural values than you currently experience. Look for a fit. Be aware of cultural norms as you consider other companies or practice settings. Research culture by asking people who work in other settings and by observing the physical, visible artifacts of a company. The bottom line is: Is it okay to be an introvert in this professional environment? Do introverts thrive here?

Your Boss. Even highly skilled professionals have issues with the boss. The most common one I hear is that the boss is extroverted and simply does not understand introversion. The preceding chapter provides guidance on working with your boss and developing a better working relationship (whether that person is introverted or not), but if that doesn't work, you may wish to consider that simply getting a new boss could help you forego major career disruption.

Influential colleagues with whom you are unsuccessful at developing rapport may also be impediments to staying with your current organization. A new set of colleagues in a different setting and organizational culture might make the world seem very different. Consider this variable before undertaking a reluctant career change.

Use Your Professional Knowledge in a New Field. Another strategy that falls shy of full career change is to seek a way to leverage your existing professional qualifications in another field. For example, Emily, a lawyer who doesn't want to practice law, loves to write. She found a job in a law firm writing legal briefs for its partners. A physician might find a position as a researcher in a pharmaceutical company. If you're an executive in an educational institution, you might find a niche in another type of managerial role in another industry. Again, the key is to look for places and positions where your introversion is an asset or at least neutral. It's no fun to spend your working life being miserable, so it's important that you seek and find a fit that works. At the same time, you have invested significant portions of your life to your profession. It makes sense to leverage what you have if possible. If it's not possible, then by all means go back to school and pursue your dream job, because now you have the experience to know what your introverted nature can stand and what it can't.

Start Over. You may choose to undertake a major career change. For example, Nick is a veterinarian who decided to go to art school at age 45. Major changes are the most difficult if you are at an advanced career stage because they frequently require significant lifestyle changes. You'll often need to negotiate roles and enlist the support of your family. If you are currently unhappy and half measures will not work for you, then you should leap at the opportunity to finally find work that matches your aspirations!

Among the possibilities to consider is a job that enables you to work virtually. With the lightning-like advances that are occurring in information technology and the natural suitability of such work to the introverted temperament, it may be worth exploring how your capabilities and interests might be exercised and fulfilled in a virtual setting if that is something that appeals to you. As we discovered in Chapter 5, introverts appear to be less disadvantaged in virtual work settings, a theme echoed in my final note to this chapter that reports one book's perspective on the best jobs for introverts.

Much of the above information on finding a good fit will apply to you as you consider a new career altogether. In addition to this, I have listed a few excellent resources in the Notes that should help you get started.[6]

Interviewing Tips

In this section, I have pulled together some hints for the interview process, because this can be the most difficult part of the job search process for an Insightful Expert. You're pretty good at researching positions and writing a strong cover letter, curriculum vitae (CV), and resume, but an interview just might trip you up. It's that not so "good on your feet" thing! I don't have a miracle cure for it, but here are some ways to compensate by leveraging your strengths in the interview process.

Focus. Keep your overall focus on the employer's needs, not your own. Show that what you offer is an outstanding match to solve their problems and lead them to success. This is a marketing rather than a selling perspective. In marketing, you identify a need and find a way to fulfill it. In selling, you have a need to sell something so you find a way to convince someone that they need it. This is a subtle but important difference in how you approach the process that will affect how you come across to a prospective employer.

First Impressions. First impressions are critical, as discussed earlier (Chapter 20), and this is especially so during an interview because you may never have a second chance to impress your interviewer. Some research shows that the first 30 seconds determine someone's assessment of you much, much later. It may be necessary to be slightly more extroverted during your introduction with a warm smile, a firm handshake, and body language that leans in with direct eye contact. A crisp hello is great! After this, you can simply be yourself by following the other tips here.

Demeanor. Smile a lot, unless of course the discussion is serious. Be friendly in your own quiet way. Show your ability to appreciate humor. Because you are not extroverted and thus may lack the warmth and openness that can unconsciously draw a stranger to your personality, it is valuable to show that you are a congenial human being who will be a pleasure to have around the office and collaborate well with colleagues.

It's not necessary for you to fake it. If you are confident in your expertise and your experience, you can be calm and collected. You need not pretend to be bubbly and energetic *if you have this assurance and are genuinely interested.* Do make an effort to express your interest by the questions you ask and by outright disclosures that you find the position attractive. Often Insightful Experts hide their true feelings behind an expressionless face but your face can be misinterpreted as a lack of enthusiasm so make sure that what you say makes up for it.

Body Language and Speech. Watch your body language. Use erect posture. Size up the interviewer. Be careful not to intimidate an introvert by leaning into their private space or speaking too loudly. Use your mindfulness training (see Chapter 9) to take a deep breath and calm yourself before speaking. Speak clearly at a moderate volume and tone. Don't fidget. If your interviewer appears extroverted, you can show more animation and lean into them more. Don't cross your arms or legs—it makes you appear standoffish rather than open. Make eye contact. This is likely to be hard for you as an introvert, but keep reminding yourself and do it again and again throughout the interview.

Talking Points. In an interview, focus on two areas: (1) your professional expertise and accomplishments and (2) strengths that are grounded in your introversion.

Your professional expertise is the sum of your training, residencies, prior positions, certifications, continuing education credentials, and your successes. Your accomplishments or successes should be quantifiable if at all possible. The best ones are outcomes such as lives saved, cases won, companies turned around, disasters averted, students mentored, revenues generated, patents, research papers, grants funded, and so on. Like many job seekers, however, you may lack such dramatic results from your efforts. The next best accomplishments are process-oriented ones that show your productivity: cases handled, classes taught, projects completed, employees supervised, books catalogued, years of experience, etc. The important thing is that you try to quantify your successes.

The second area to highlight is competencies that derive from your introversion. As noted in Chapter 3 and elsewhere in this guide, you bring a number of desirable qualities to your profession and to any given employment situation. These include your careful attention to detail, your engagement and dedication to your work, your inventiveness, your ability to be autonomous, your professional decorum, your writing and research skills, your thoughtfulness, and more. Build on these to identify those of your characteristics that match the needs of the position.

At a Loss for Words. Do not be afraid to stall for time by taking a sip of water to collect your thoughts. Self-disclose if need be, saying that you hesitate to make snap judgments because you have a more deliberative decision-making style. Ask if you can contact your interviewers the next day with additional thoughts that come up for you. Talk about diversity, and make clear that you are sensitive to different work styles. Take the opportunity to say that your own style is careful but that your decisions are good ones.

How Much to Say. Because you may be nervous, you run the risk of saying too much, so watch out for that tendency. Instead, ask questions. Research has shown that interviewers who talk more during the interview rate applicants more highly than when the tables are turned and the applicant talks a lot. Use this to your advantage by researching the position and company and asking good questions. Let the interviewers talk as much as they like. When you do that, the comments you do make may just be viewed more favorably. And, as an Insightful Expert, you will feel less pressured to be something you are not—that is, a talkative candidate!

Introversion. Even though introversion as a trait may never be explicitly discussed (see my comment below), be prepared to address the downsides of introversion in your interview. If you are implementing the Third Eye Framework, you should be able to talk about how you are able to build solid one-on-one relationships with others and how you are reserved but enthusiastic, even if your enthusiasm doesn't show as much as it does in some other people. You might also mention how you have honed your communication skills.

Because of stereotypes, I would refrain from offering the information that you are an introvert unless the interviewer brings it up, but use your judgment on that. If you are interviewing with another introvert, it might give you an edge to show that you're sensitive to different types! Regardless, be careful not to reveal any disdain for extroverts. Respect for differences must run both ways.

Logistics. Make sure the interviewer is comfortable. Just as it might be uncomfortable for you to have to squint into glaring sunlight from the window over your interviewer's shoulder, consider how it is for him or her! Do you want her to see your face or to be irritated by a glare? Take the marketing perspective and focus on the employer's needs rather than your own, while also not compromising yourself if possible. Let the interviewer find the seat that serves him best, and then find one that also works for you.

Confidence. Always remember that you bring great things to any organization. The interview process is simply to assess whether there is a good fit. If there is not a good fit, then you wouldn't want to be there anyway. Just keep looking until you find a match. A myriad of factors can determine how you are perceived—everything from your skills and background to the personality of the interviewer to the group dynamics and politics of the search committee to the weather the day you interview. Sooner or later, you will find what you are looking for! Even if you make a choice you later regret, it will lead you to something else.

Final Note: Careers That Suit Introverts

When I discovered the book *200 Best Jobs for Introverts*, I thought, "Great—now I can give my readers a list of jobs that can help them find their new careers." Well, maybe. I'll discuss the methodology used in a moment; it can help you decide if this is *the* list for you. It's an interesting read because it presents lots of diverse lists of jobs (all from the 200 but sorted in different ways) to get your juices flowing.

The book reports that the top jobs requiring a bachelor's degree are computer applications and systems software engineers and computer systems analysts. The top three jobs requiring a master's degree are hydrologists, environmental scientists/specialists, and geoscientists. There is only one top choice for a professional degree: lawyers. To round it out, the top three jobs requiring a doctorate are medical scientists, biochemists/biophysicists, and physicists. In the overall listing (drum roll, please!), the three best jobs match the bachelor's degree list: computer applications and systems software engineers and computer systems analysts. Read the book to learn of all the many jobs that are *not* in the top three.

200 Best Jobs for Introverts uses an interesting method to identify the jobs that will be most appealing to reserved people. First, jobs are rated from 1 to 5 on a measure of *independence*—i.e., being on one's own to do the work—a lower score denoting a job that provides more independence. Second, jobs are rated from 1 to 5 on a measure called *contact with others*, which is defined as the extent to which the worker has to deal with others by telephone, in person, etc. A score of 5 denotes a job that requires constant interaction with others. The scores for independence and interpersonal contact are then averaged, and the result is a rating of the degree to which an occupation will appeal to an introverted disposition.

Following this process, all of the jobs in the database are placed in descending order in three different rankings—growth potential, median earnings, and projected annual vacancies. An overall score for each job is calculated by summing these numerical rankings.

Whew! That's quite a process. I've taken the time to explain it because it's interesting to note what has *not* been considered in this calculation. I'm not criticizing the authors' approach—after all, no ranking is going to appeal to everyone—but lists are beneficial only if they are compiled on the basis of criteria that *you* care about. And everyone is unique. So it pays to pay attention!

For example, the 200 best jobs were selected on the basis of independence and contact with others, but what if you are also concerned with being "good on your feet," which introverts typically are not? What if you love independence but hate networking? Even if the job doesn't require contact with people—say for example, an animal handler—if you have to market your services and network to get customers, this ranking won't accommodate your needs. What if, like most introverts, you're analytical and thoughtful? Those qualities are not reflected in this ranking.

Further, the ranking then considers job characteristics such as growth, earnings, and vacancies, but what if you're more concerned with staying in a rural community or avoiding the need to earn yet *another* degree in order to be eligible? What if you want a job that is socially responsible or deeply and personally meaningful? Nope. None of these are considered. To be fair, the authors of *200 Best Jobs for Introverts* do sort the 200 into categories based on how much training is required, personality types, interests, etc., but these factors are not among the screening criteria for determining which jobs end up among the 200 to begin with.

Take advantage of lists like these—any ranking based on best-guess criteria can help you think about the issues involved in a career change—but be aware that you'll never find the perfect ranking compiled by someone else, no matter how well and how hard they've worked at it. What's important is that you do your own self-reflection followed by careful study of various jobs that might fill all your highest-priority needs. And the best way to study jobs is both to read about them and to conduct some interviews (even casual online conversations on list serves) with people who do them.

Milestones Along the Journey

Below are a few of the key ideas related to this chapter with a couple extra bullet points for you to fill in. I'd like to hear other ideas that may have resonated for you or were stimulated by what you read. Go to the website www.TheIntrovertsGuide.com to share with me those that have special meaning for *your* personal journey.

- Self-awareness lays the foundation for good career choices.

- A new professional specialty, a different practice setting, a new organization, or a different boss is sometimes all that is needed to revitalize a career.

- One of the keys to finding a new career is to look for roles where your introversion is an asset. Research job interests by talking to people who actually hold those jobs.

- _____

  _____

- _____

  _____

CHAPTER 35

Right Livelihood

The concept of right livelihood comes from Buddhist practice, where it is one of the elements of the Eightfold Path. It is an important moral principle stating that the work we do should not harm others. This implies that your life will be most enriched to the extent that the vocation you choose to practice is consistent with values of respect and consideration for others. Even more broadly, this principle suggests that your work must reflect your values.

Consonance between our work—especially work for pay—and our values leads to a sense of purpose and meaning in the work itself. Without this, work becomes drudgery. Victor Frankl, in the now-classic book *Man's Search for Meaning*[1], wrote of how prisoners in Nazi concentration camps during World War II survived by finding meaning and life purpose under horrific circumstances. Frankl went on to develop a theory of mental health called *logotherapy* on the premise that meaningfulness is essential to living a healthy life.

Choosing work that is meaningful to you (and that avoids harm) may be the best decision you make as you consider a new career or new career goals. With this as a foundation, you will find it easy to take the steps outlined in this book to thrive as an introvert, because you'll be motivated by your innermost goals and aspirations.

Milestones Along the Journey

Below is a key idea related to this chapter with a couple extra bullet points for you to fill in. I'd like to hear other ideas that may have resonated for you or were stimulated by what you read. Go to the website www.TheIntrovertsGuide.com to share with me those that have special meaning for *your* personal journey.

- Finding work that simultaneously gives meaning to your life and causes no harm to others can support your efforts to achieve professional success.

- _____

  _____

- _____

  _____

CHAPTER 36

Behold Your Leadership

Is your goal to be a leader? When most people think of leadership, they conceive of it as a formal role. A leader is often taken for granted as the individual who has authority over people, objects, and situations. Yet consider how a fledgling, democratically organized group selects its first leader when there is no preexisting authority structure. When the members choose a leader, they anoint someone who moves them in some way. They are willing to accede power to a leader whom they believe is worthy of their trust.

Mother Teresa, winner of the Nobel Peace Prize in 1979, was such a leader. A nun who worked with the poor in the streets of Calcutta, she attracted a following of young women eager to become Missionaries of Charity, who worked alongside her. Other people donated money, buildings, food, and other goods to help. Her mission grew and grew, leading to hospitals, orphanages, and various refuges for suffering people.[1] Her leadership emerged in an organic fashion as increasing numbers of people believed in her vision for the impoverished people of Calcutta.

Even someone who has attained a formal leadership role—a CEO, or divisional chief, for example—must earn the continued loyalty and respect of the people around him or her in order to be effective. I suspect we've all known people with leadership titles who didn't fare well in our private assessments.

Some years ago, I taught leadership classes to MBA students, all of whom were working professionals. In one assignment I asked them to interview someone whom they knew personally, and whom they felt epitomized the ideals of leadership, and to write a paper exploring the connection between their interview findings and leadership theories. The results were enlightening. The people chosen were sometimes bosses, sometimes friends, and sometimes colleagues. Occasionally, they were executives. What the interviewees tended to have in common was an uncommon quality to connect with others by articulating problems and situations in ways that engendered solutions and motivated those around them. They often functioned with quiet self-assurance. Many were Insightful Experts.

The assignment confirmed for me that leadership is about creating a way for us to view or see our experiences. Leadership experts Linda Smircich and Gareth Morgan have called this "the management of meaning."[2] A leader defines situations for us in a manner that enables us to get things done. Often this may be by getting us to see old things in new ways, such as Mother Teresa shaping others' views of the impoverished of Calcutta—they were human, and she (and they) could help them one at a time. It is no coincidence that the word "vision" is often used with respect to leadership.

But vision is not enough in itself. One of the central reasons why leaders are able to get us to view our experiences differently is because we learn to trust them. Their actions match their vision, and they treat others around them with integrity. Often a leader's world-view, like Mother Teresa's, is characterized by values or moral principles that resonate with those around them. For example, honesty is the top-ranking attribute identified in James Kouzes and Barry Posner's survey of the characteristics that people think of as "leadership."[3] Humility also fosters trust and perceptions of integrity.

As you undertake the journey in *The Introvert's Guide to Professional Success*, you prepare yourself for leadership. The Third Eye Framework sets the conditions for you to *be* a leader. Whether you simply perform your present role, choose a new path, or take on a formal leadership position, you will be perceived as a leader by others around you in your professional life.

The ingredients are in place. Beginning with the first phase, creating impetus for yourself, you can develop greater clarity for your goals and, even more important, your values. These drive the world-view you communicate to others in your day-to-day professional dealings. The second major part of creating impetus is developing self-awareness and confidence and beginning to connect with others by self-disclosing more often. These and other aspects of emotional intelligence build momentum, enabling you to focus on your individual stakeholders and to begin the process of using reciprocity principles to make exchanges. Exchanges based on expertise and personal connections culminate in strong relationships that are built on a foundation of integrity and honest community. You do this by learning to exercise power and influence as an Insightful Expert—one person at a time, and with genuine goodwill aimed at mutual gain.

If this approach is unsettling to you at first, it is only because the traditional model of getting ahead in an organization and a career has been framed from an extrovert's point of view, in which only the strongest survive. The hierarchy is to be climbed, pushing others aside if need be. Force is a given, because acting in the world is an extrovert's strength. But when you come at the problem from an introvert's point of view, it is transformed from a Machiavellian dog-eat-dog process into one of mutual gain—a classic win-win scenario. We introverts approach the problem from our inner world and employ our strengths of introspection and ability to focus on the task at hand. An introvert has no problem at all identifying inner values, formulating a vision, and connecting one-on-one—that's the introvert's forte!

In the second phase of the Third Eye Framework, as you structure your interfaces, you begin to take control of the human side of your career on a daily basis. By learning and implementing the 3 R's of researching, deciding on rules, and rehearsing before interactions, you seize your potency as an Insightful Expert—shaping your work life on your own terms. Structuring situations to better fit your personality traits and predispositions is a proactive response in accord with your limits rather than the ideals of extroverts. By doing this, Insightful Experts gain confidence and begin to be seen and heard, necessary preconditions for leadership roles. But the way you are seen and heard is not as an extrovert would be—instead, the 3 R's help you bring quiet competence to your meetings, your daily interchanges with coworkers and clients, and your other interpersonal dealings. It is the kind of visibility that fosters respect and trust.

You develop even more hands-on leadership skills to further facilitate the expression of your values and vision by building your internal capabilities in the third and final phase of the Third Eye Framework. You learn to manage your energy, construct a strong network of trusting relationships, work productively with a team, and communicate with assertiveness and genuine interest. These skills are like oil in an engine—they keep your interpersonal relations lubricated and running. They enable you to continue to connect with others and share your weltanschauung—your world-view. By doing so, you are able to carve out a more meaningful professional career—whether you are a leader in name or simply by your actions.

So, whether you have been aware of it or not, in following the Third Eye Framework and developing your abilities to shine as an introvert, you also have been preparing yourself to be a leader. You already had a world-view resulting from your professional training and your technical qualifications. Connecting with others *as an introvert on an introvert's terms* enables you to reveal it and incorporate it more fully as an integral element of your professional life because you are now trusted and *known* for your competence, integrity, and humility.

Milestones Along the Journey

Below are a few of the key ideas related to this chapter with a couple extra bullet points for you to fill in. I'd like to hear other ideas that may have resonated for you or were stimulated by what you read. Go to the website www.TheIntrovertsGuide.com to share with me those that have special meaning for *your* personal journey.

- Because leadership is a set of behaviors and traits rather than a position, it is useful in any role and accessible to anyone.

- Leadership is founded on integrity, trust, competence, humility, and vision.

- In the process of becoming a Third Eye Expert, you simultaneously develop your leadership capabilities.

- _____

  _____

- _____

  _____

Afterword

The path that guides you from an Insightful Expert to a Third Eye Expert enables you to realize your highest career aspirations, and to do so as a member of the half of humanity that is introverted. Following it does not require you to disguise or abandon your essential nature behind a facade of extroversion. It does, however, require you to tune into your strengths and to put concentrated effort into building the gestalt of your professional career—to develop your human expertise and combine it with the substantial technical expertise you already possess. This process is not difficult, though it does take time, and The Third Eye Framework offers the step-by-step program that guides you to your goal.

As we have seen, you begin by building sustainable relationships that create *impetus*. Then you structure your *interfaces* to better accommodate your introversion. Finally, you develop the strategic skills that will nurture your *internal* capabilities to function in an extroverted world. Each phase of the process builds on the foregoing one in synergistic fashion.

Implementation Issues

Planning is a great thing, but putting plans into action often leads to unanticipated issues and problems. As you undertake the process outlined in *The Introvert's Guide to Professional Success*, you are likely to run into a bump or two along your road, the most common of which follow. I'd like to leave you with some guidance for those times. If you run into obstacles I have failed to address here, go to the website for this book, www.TheIntrovertsGuide.com, for a list of frequently asked questions (FAQs) and my replies.

We all have times when motivation wanes. It's easy to become discouraged in the absence of positive feedback from others or a strong sense of self-esteem, or when the initial results of your efforts aren't yet apparent. You also can reach a plateau when early progress seems to stall, when acknowledgements and visible signs from others that your efforts are paying off seem to dry up. There may be still other times when you are unsure what to do next or you perceive a lack time or energy to do all that you believe should be done to boost your career efforts. You may need more specific guidance than that offered in this book. For example, you could be uncertain what follow-up actions are needed to build your influence among some of your stakeholders.

To move forward despite such setbacks, here are some action steps you can take to renew your momentum.

Check Your Time Frame. First, consider whether your initial time frame might have been overly optimistic. If necessary, adjust your expectations. Just as you needed many years to complete the technical preparation for your profession, it takes time to develop human expertise. Recall the gestalt and view your current efforts from the standpoint of this longer term perspective. It's possible that achieving your goals could require more time than you initially expected.

Take a Deep Breath and Take Heart. Second, review Chapter 9, "Muster Courage to Take Action." Practice the suggestions there for calming your mind, and let some time pass. You're likely to find that you break through a plateau and find the motivation to keep going. Insights about how to move forward are also more likely to come when you relax. You may also wish to reread the chapters that pertain most specifically to the actions on which you feel stuck. When your goals seem elusive, find pursuits that divert you from worrying. Activities requiring intense concentration—such as music, painting, woodworking, physical exercise, or bird watching—build your reserves by producing pleasurable feelings akin to what psychologist Mihaly Csikszentmihalyi calls flow. Nurture your inner introvert with solitude and quiet pursuits. You will come back refreshed, ready to engage people in your professional arena with renewed vigor and optimism.

Seek Support. Third, look for support from others. The simple sharing of ideas and camaraderie with a peer—a trusted colleague or sympathetic friend—can sustain you. This can be exceedingly helpful, and I highly recommend it. Another form of support is what you gain from a mentor, an experienced hand at a senior level who takes a special interest in helping you navigate your challenges. If you are fortunate enough to have such a mentor, your much needed moral support will come wrapped in sage wisdom specific to your profession or organization.

A final form of support is the expert guidance you can obtain from a professional who specializes in working with introverts' career and workplace issues. This support will be more objective than the first two types, and, if you choose carefully, can offer you in-depth knowledge and real-time ongoing consultation and expert analysis of your particular situation. This individual should give you feedback along with specific behavioral strategies to break through logjams and resolve unique interpersonal issues or problems with organizational politics. Carefully consider the qualifications of the professional help you seek, and comparison shop for quality. You will find more information on the various types of professional support on the website for this book, www.TheIntrovertsGuide.com.

Thank You for Taking This Journey with Me to Make Third Eye Expertise a Way of Life

When you complete the steps outlined in this guide and accomplish the goals you set for yourself, the deep blue sky is your limit. You will have developed a higher level of confidence and personal fulfillment than you ever expected. You can be especially proud that you did it while remaining true to yourself.

Now you are no longer seemingly constrained by your introverted nature but instead realize—as you may have known intuitively all along—that it is your *greatest asset*. It allowed you to develop your in depth technical expertise, and assists you in your quiet way of forging deep and honest relationships on the human side of your career ascendance. And close on that realization comes another: that understanding the rules of the game and making a concerted effort is most of what is required to make your mark in an extrovert's world.

With these realizations, you may find yourself at a new juncture in your career. You could be satisfied with the meaningful achievements you originally sought or looking ahead to new goals. Whichever the case, as a Third Eye Expert, you have finally arrived. You have emerged from the shadow of false professional choices, from the presumption that you must either force yourself into an extrovert's mold or simply abandon your aspirations. You have found a new way, one that venerates *your* spirit, acknowledges your quiet competence, and accommodates your needs for solitude, reflection, and authentic integrity.

> *"However daunting a situation may seem, as soon as we say or do something, it is suddenly transformed. When the door of hesitation is unlocked, we enter a dynamic, fluid world, which challenges us to act and act again."*[1]

Connect Online

For additional resources, updates, and more,
visit Dr. Shelleman at
www.TheIntrovertsGuide.com

To connect for advising on your career, please visit
www.TheIntrovertsGuide.com/advising.html

Join her e-newsletter, *Insights for Today's Leaders* by visiting
www.TheIntrovertsGuide.com/newsletter.html

For more information about workshops for introverted professionals
and those who work with introverts, visit
www.TheIntrovertsGuide.com/workshops.html

Acknowledgments

Describing my conceptual framework in guidebook form has been an enormous undertaking. When I began this project in 2007, I had no idea how it would evolve. It has been largely a solo journey but I have benefited from the indirect support of some exceptional people, not all of whom are mentioned here.

First, I am grateful to my clients, my workshop participants and students, and my teachers for all that they have taught me. I admire the courage of the introverted professionals who are unafraid to seek help to actively take on the dominant culture in order to achieve their goals. My perspective has been shaped especially by my professional training —which reinforced my big-picture orientation, my personal experience, and my observations. I see organizations and workplace situations as systems of human interactions, interwoven with diverse histories, personalities, emotions, brilliance, and foibles. An individual is never isolated from these effects and they are in constant motion. The work is complex and never done.

Greg Gull, Bob Priddy, and Pam Robson offered valuable feedback on introductory passages of the manuscript. From the beginning, Bob has been a champion of the value of this project for those in the professions.

Karina Drumheller at the University of New Hampshire enthusiastically invited me to present my early model in a workshop for introverted professionals. Unlike many, she's not afraid to do something new. I am grateful for her faith in me.

Terry Cookson offered moral support that helped me keep the project moving.

Jeff Shields was an unconditional advocate as I brought this book to life. I'm especially grateful for his last minute reading and incisive critique of the final draft that made it a much stronger manuscript. He and Joel Guarna contributed important ideas that influenced my thinking and my approach to this material. I am profoundly indebted to both.

Thanks to Jane Karker for her friendly assistance, Jonathan Eaton for editing the manuscript, and designer David Allen for his artistic eye and care.

I am grateful to my mother Alice for her wonderful encouragement of this project and to my late father Ben for his intellect, penetrating insight, and other gifts to me.

Notes

Introduction

1 Organizational behavior is an applied field of study that examines "what people think, feel, and do in and around organizations" (McShane, S. and M. A. Von Glinow, 2010. *Organizational Behavior* (5th ed.). New York: McGraw-Hill Irwin, p. 4). My individual program of study of organizational behavior included explicit attention to the role of professionals—as distinct from other workers—in organizations and to professional careers.

2 Support for the approach here comes from empirical research in business, psychology, sociology, anthropology, and political science; it includes both laboratory evidence and field studies of many hundreds of people in a range of occupations and types of organizations. It also derives from my personal experiences and those of my clients, my students, and others.

Chapter 1

1 Bryn and Justin are pseudonyms for composite characters based on real people. Identifying features have been changed throughout all the personal accounts in this book to protect the privacy of individuals and the confidentiality of the consultant-client relationship. Any resemblance of the people in this book to actual individuals is accidental.

2 This story is based on one told to me by Ralph Kilmann, PhD, a valued mentor.

3 Leadership is "the management of meaning", a phrase coined by Linda Smircich and Gareth Morgan. An effective leader is able to not only articulate a direction but also is politically adept at convincing others that it's a desirable direction. It is my conviction that personal trust and integrity are vital to this—much more so than "on your feet" communication skills.

4 Seibert, S.E. and M.L. Kraimer. 2001. "The five factor model of personality and career success," *Journal of Vocational Behavior*, February, pp. 121.

5 Psychology treats introversion and shyness as two separate phenomena that need not even occur together, though they sometimes do. Generally speaking, introverts often simply dislike social interaction, while shy people typically experience anxiety from the conduct or even the prospect of interaction. Nor do all introverts experience the professional challenges that

are typical of their cohorts; what's important is optimizing your unique situation. My focus is on imparting effective behavioral strategies for the workplace regardless of underlying causes. For this reason, unless they are especially relevant, this book does not concern itself with distinctions between shyness and introversion, even though such distinctions may be quite useful in other contexts.

Chapter 2

1   Marvin Thomas's book *Personal Village: How to Have People in Your Life by Choice, Not Chance* (Seattle: Milestone Books, 2004) offers a systematic program to help build or rebuild a community of relationships with others. According to the guide laid out so clearly by Thomas in this excellent book, it's not hard to do with a little sustained effort, and sustained effort is something I know you can do! I highly recommend this book if you are seeking to build a personal or professional community.

Chapter 3

1   Jung's theory of psychological types was based heavily in his understanding of Taoism and his belief that humans are a microcosm for the unity of opposing psychological tendencies. I have presented the complementary nature of introversion and extroversion as yin and yang on my website since 2008 as a way of helping others understand the spirit of Jung's original concepts.

2   Cowgil, C. (1997). *Carl Jung.* Retrieved September 24, 2008 from http://www.muskingum.edu/~psych/psycweb/history/jung.htm

3   Helgoe, Laurie. 2010. Revenge of the introvert, *Psychology Today*, 43(5), p. 60.

4   Laney, M.O. 2002. *The Introvert Advantage.* New York: Workman Publishing.

5   Laney, M.O. 2002. *The Introvert Advantage.* New York: Workman Publishing, pp. 49, 51, and 52.

6   Ibid.

Chapter 4

1   International Personality Item Pool: A Scientific Collaboratory for the Development of Advanced Measures of Personality and Other Individual Differences (2008). Retrieved September 24, 2008 from http://ipip.ori.org/.

2   International Personality Item Pool: A Scientific Collaboratory for the Development of Advanced Measures of Personality and Other Individual Differences. (2008). Retrieved September 24, 2008 from http://ipip.ori.org/.

Chapter 5

1   Jones, Del. 2006. Not all successful CEOs are extraverts. *USA Today*, 6/7/2006. Retrieved online at http://www.usatoday.com/money/companies/management/20060606shyceousat_x.htm

2   The other 47% were neutral.

3   Capretz, L. F. 2002. Personality types in software engineering, *International Journal of Human-Computer Studies*, 58 (2003), pp. 207-214.

Clack, G.B., Allen, J., Cooper, D., and Head, J.O. 2004. Personality differences between doctors and their patients: implications for the teaching of communication skills, *Medical Education*, 38, pp. 177-186.

Culp, G. and Smith, A. 2001. Understanding psychological type to improve project team performance, *Journal of Management in Engineering*, 17 (1), pp. 24-33.

Jones, Del. 2006. Not all successful CEOs are extraverts. USA Today, 6/7/2006. Retrieved online at http://www.usatoday.com/money/companies/management/2006-06-06-shy-ceo-usat_x.htm

Satava, D. and Hallock, D. 2006. Extraversion-introversion personality traits of local firm CPAs who previously worked for a national CPA firm: An Empirical Study, *Journal of Applied Business Research*, 22 (1), pp. 81-88.

Randall, V. 1995. The Myers-Briggs Type Indicator, first year law students and performance, *Cumberland Law Review*, 26, pp. 63-101.

4   Brightman, H. Undated. GSU Master Teacher Program: On Learning Styles. Retrieved online at http://www2.gsu.edu/~dschjb/wwwmbti.html, August 31, 2010.

5 For a review, see Langford, J. and Clance, P.R. 1993. "The imposter phenomenon: recent research findings regarding dynamics, personality and family patterns and their implications for treatment," *Psychotherapy*, 30(3), pp. 495-501.

6 Clack, G.B., Allen, J., Cooper, D., and Head, J.O. 2004. Personality differences between doctors and their patients: implications for the teaching of communication skills, *Medical Education*, 38, pp. 177-186.

7 Ramsey, A., Hanlon, D., and Smith, D. 2000. The association between cognitive style and accounting students' preference for cooperative learning: an empirical investigation, *Journal of Accounting Education*, 18 (2000), pp. 215-228.

8 Judge, T.A. and Cable, D.M. 1997. Applicant personality, organizational culture, and organization attraction, *Personnel Psychology*, 50, pp. 359-394.

9 Yellen, R.E., Winniford, MA., and Sanford, C.C. 1995. Extraversion and introversion in electronically-supported meetings, *Information & Management*, 28 (1995), pp. 63-74.

10 Moon, H., Hollenbeck, J., Marinova, S. and Humphrey, S. 2008. Beneath the surface: uncovering the relationship between extraversion and organizational citizenship behavior through a facet approach, *International Journal of Selection and Assessment*, 16(2), pp. 143-154.

11 Tokar, D.M., Fischer, A.R. and Subich, L.M. 1998. Personality and vocational behavior: a selective review of the literature, 19931997, *Journal of Vocational Behavior*, 53, pp. 115-153.

12 Barrick, M.R. and Mount, M.K. 1991. The big five personality dimensions and job performance: a metaanalysis. *Personnel Psychology*, 44, pp. 126.

13 Stewart, G.L. 1996. Reward structure as a moderator of the relationship between extraversion and sales performance, *Journal of Applied Psychology*, 81, pp. 619-627.

14 Gray, J.A. 1973. Causal theories of personality and how to test them. In J.R. Royce (Ed.), *Multivariate Analysis and Psychological Theory*. New York: Academic Press, pp. 409-464.

15 Judge, T.A. and Erez, A. 2007. Interaction and intersection: the constellation of emotional stability and extraversion in predicting performance, *Personnel Psychology*, 60 (3), pp. 573-596.

16 Turban, D., Stevens, C., and Lee, F. 2009. Effects of conscientiousness and extraversion on new labor market entrants' job search: the mediating role of

meta-cognitive activities and positive emotions, *Personnel Psychology*, 62, pp. 553-573.

17 Dunn, W., Mount, M.K., Barrick, M., and Ones, D. 1995. Relative importance of personality and general mental ability in managers' judgments of applicant qualifications. *Journal of Applied Psychology*, 80(4): 500-509.

18 I cannot help but wonder to what extent gender plays a role since traditionally most nurses have been female and business leaders male. Is it expected that incumbents in traditionally male occupations should display greater extroversion than those in traditionally female professions?

19 Moutafi, Joanna, Furnham, Adrian, and Crump, John. 2007. Is managerial level related to personality? *British Journal of Management*, 18, pp. 272-280.

Gardner, William and Martinko, Mark. 1996. Using the Myers-Briggs Type Indicator to study managers: a literature review and research agenda. *Journal of Management*, 22(1): 72.

20 Brewer, Edward. 2006. Extroversion/Introversion communication patterns: A determinant of success in business, *Business Quest*. Retrieved online at: http://www.westga.edu/~bquest/2006/research06.htm on August 31, 2010.

21 Robbins, S.P. and Judge, T.A. 2009. *Organizational Behavior*. Upper Saddle River: Pearson Prentice Hall.

22 Agle, Bradley, Nagarajan, Nandu, Sonnenfeld, Jeffrey, and Srinivasan. 2006. Does CEO charisma matter? An empirical analysis of the relationships among organizational performance, environmental uncertainty, and top management team perceptions of CEO charisma. *Academy of Management Journal*, 49 (1): 161-174.

23 Extroverted qualities are apparent in one of the five dimensions used to measure charismatic leadership, so-called "dynamic leadership."

24 Crant, J. Michael and Thomas Bateman. 2000. Charismatic leadership viewed from above: the impact of proactive personality. *Journal of Organizational Behavior*, 21: 63-75.

25 Balthazard, P., Waldman, D., and Warren, J. 2009. Predictors of the emergence of transformational leadership in virtual decision teams, *The Leadership Quarterly*, 20 (2009), pp. 651-663.

26 Berr, S., Church, A., and Wsclaswki, J. 2000. The right relationship is everything: linking personality preferences to managerial behaviors, *Human Resource Development Quarterly*, 11(2): 133-157.

27 Gardner, William and Martinko, Mark. 1990. The relationship between psychological type, managerial behavior, and managerial effectiveness: an empirical study. *Journal of Psychological Type*, 19: 35-43.

28 Thal, Alfred and John Bedingfield. 2010. Successful project managers: an exploratory study into the impact of Personality. *Technology Analysis & Strategic Management*, 22 (1): 243-259.

29 Berr, S., Church, A., and Wsclaswki, J. 2000. The right relationship is everything: linking personality preferences to managerial behaviors, *Human Resource Development Quarterly*, 11(2): 133-157.

30 Minbashian, A., Bright, J.E.H., Bird, K.D. 2009. Complexity in the relationships among the subdimensions of extraversion and job performance in managerial occupations, *Journal of Occupational and Organizational Psychology*, (2009), 82, pp. 537-549.

31 Agle, Bradley, Nagarajan, Nandu, Sonnenfeld, Jeffrey, and Srinivasan. 2006. Does CEO charisma matter? An empirical analysis of the relationships among organizational performance, environmental uncertainty, and top management team perceptions of CEO charisma. *Academy of Management Journal*, 49 (1): 161174.

32 Bauer, T., Erdogan, B., Liden, R., Wayne, S. 2006. A longitudinal study of the moderating role of extraversion: Leadermember exchange, performance, and turnover during new executive development, *Journal of Applied Psychology*, 91(2), pp. 298-310.

33 Siebert, Scott and Maria Kraimer. 2001. The five-factor model of personality and career success. *Journal of Vocational Behavior*, 58: 121.

34 Judge, T., Heller, D., and Mount, K. 2002. Five-factor model of personality and job satisfaction: A metaanalysis, *Journal of Applied Psychology*, 87(2), pp. 530-541.

35 Melamed, T. 1995. Career success: the moderating effect of gender. *Journal of Vocational Behavior*, 47: 35-60.

36 Moutafi, J., Furnham, A., and Crump, J. 2007. Is managerial level related to personality?, *British Journal of Management*, 18, pp. 272-280.

37 Judge, T., Higgins, C., Thoresen, C., and Barrick, M. 1999. The Big Five personality traits and career success across the life span. *Personnel Psychology*, 52: 621-652.

38 Dunn, W., Mount, M.K., Barrick, M., and Ones, D. 1995. Relative importance of personality and general mental ability in managers' judgments of applicant qualifications. *Journal of Applied Psychology*, 80(4): 500-509.

39 Gardner, William and Martinko, Mark. 1996. Using the Myers-Briggs Type Indicator to study managers: a literature review and research agenda. *Journal of Management*, 22(1): 72.

40 Jennings, D. and Disney, J. 2006. The strategic planning process and its context: the role of psychological type. *Journal of General Management*, 31(3): 71-93.

41 In contrast to applied management literature, most research in psychology on extraversion/introversion (apart from applied psychology) seeks scientific understanding of the general principles of personality and fulfills that purpose quite well. Because its purpose is not application, it fails to shed much insight on career dynamics.

42 Bolman, L. and Deal, T. 2008. *Reframing Organizations* (4th ed.). San Francisco: Jossey Bass. Morgan, G. 2006. *Images of Organization* (Updated ed.). Thousand Oaks: Sage.

43 See for example Doucet, Cynthia and Stelmack, Robert. 2000. "An event-related potential analysis of extraversion and individual differences in cognitive processing speed and response execution," *Journal of Personality and Social Psychology*, 78(5), pp. 956-964.

44 Power and influence are discussed in Chapter 16. All the major sources of power are relevant in any organization but the point here is that certain sources are more central in one organization design archetype than in another.

45 Hezlett, Sarah and Sharon Gibson. 2007. Linking mentoring and social capital: implications for career and organization development. *Advances in Developing Human Resources*, Vol. 9: 384.

46 Opt, S.K. and D.A. Loffredo. 2000. Rethinking communication apprehension: a Myers-Briggs perspective. *Journal of Psychology: Interdisciplinary and Applied*, 134: 556-570.

47 MeyerGriffith, Katie, Reardon, Robert and Sarah Harley. 2009. An examination of the relationship between career thoughts and communication apprehension. *The Career Development Quarterly*, December 2009, Vol. 58: 171-180.

Chapter 6

1 impetus. (n.d.). *Online Etymology Dictionary.* Retrieved January 11, 2011, from Dictionary.com website: http://dictionary.reference.com/browse/impetus

Chapter 8

1 For example, the widely employed transtheoretical model of individual change.

2 A professional organizational consultant, just like your physician or your attorney, will have an approach that he or she prefers to use with clients, based on his/her past experience, including preferred assessment instruments.

Chapter 9

1 This approach, called by the acronym ACT (pronounced *act*) which stands for Acceptance and Commitment Therapy, is based on the work of Steven Hayes, PhD, and others in the field of clinical psychology. It is an empirically supported cognitive behavioral practice that is readily learned and applied to your professional life. It offers principles for living that apply to anyone, anywhere, in contrast to its origins in clinical settings.

2 **For additional reading, see:**

> Ajaya, Swami. 1976. *Yoga Psychology: A Practical Guide to Meditation.* Honesdale, PA: The Himalayan International Institute of Yoga Science and Philosophy of the USA.

> Cohen, Kenneth. 1997. *The Way of Qigong: The Art and Science of Chinese Energy Healing.* NY: Ballantine Books.

> Easwaran, Eknath. 1993. *The Unstruck Bell: Powerful New Strategies for Using a Mantram.* Tomales, CA: Nilgiri Press.

> Nhat Hanh, Thich. 1993. *The Blooming of a Lotus: Guided Meditation Exercises for Healing and Transformation.* Boston: Beacon Press.

> Nhat Hanh, Thich. 1976. *The Miracle of Mindfulness: A Manual on Meditation.* Boston: Beacon Press.

Chapter 11

1 Multi-source feedback, sometimes called 360° feedback, is information about someone's performance gathered from a wide circle of others, such as colleagues, subordinates, clients, and supervisors.

2 For example, www.surveymonkey.com which is free for a minimalist version at this writing.

3 Visit my web site, www.TheIntrovertsGuide.com for more information.

4 Throughout this guide, when I use the term "qualified professional" or make recommendations with regard to obtaining professional guidance for you as you implement the Third Eye Framework, in general I am referring to someone who is trained in applied behavioral science workplace issues. Less important than the title someone uses is his or her background and qualifications. Visit my web site, www.TheIntrovertsGuide.com for a guide to the types of professionals who offer services.

5 Breen, Bill. 2000. What's your intuition? *Fast Company*, 38, August 31.

6 Thich Nhat Hanh. 1999. *The Miracle of Mindfulness*. Beacon Press.

Chapter 13

1 Luft, J. and Ingham, H. 1955. "The Johari Window: a graphic model for interpersonal relations", University of California Western Training Lab.

Chapter 14

1 Mayer, J., Roberts, R., and Barsade, S. 2008. Human abilities: emotional intelligence, *Annual Review of Psychology*, 59, pp. 507-536.

2 Chapter 11 identified self-awareness as one aspect of emotional intelligence that can help you.

3 Mayer, J., Salovey, P., and Caruso, D. 2008. Emotional intelligence: new ability or eclectic traits? *American Psychologist*, 63 (6), pp. 503-517.

4 Feist and Barron, 1996, as cited in Webb, K.S. 2009. Why emotional intelligence should matter to management: a survey of the literature, *SAM Advanced Management Journal*, Spring 2009, pp. 32-41.

5 Goleman, D. 1998. *Working with Emotional Intelligence*. New York: Bantam Books; Mayer, Salovey, and Caruso, 1998 as cited in Webb, 2009.

6 Goleman's statement appears to contradict the research cited in Chapter 5 showing that many CEOs of large companies have little involvement in day to day operations requiring high levels of contact with others. It's important to recognize that the majority of leaders are not CEOs of large companies with the capacity to delegate operational tasks; most leaders must interact with many others both within and outside their organizations. However, it's not clear what the differences were between Goleman's sample and the other study.

7 Boyatzis, Richard. 2000. How and why individuals are able to develop emotional intelligence. In *The Emotionally Intelligent Workplace* by Cherniss, Gary and Daniel Goleman (Eds.). San Francisco: Jossey Bass, 234-253.

8 Ballou, R., Bowers, D., Boyatzis, R., and Kolb, D. 1999. Fellowship in life-long learning: an executive development program for advanced professionals, *Journal of Management Education*, 23 (4), pp. 338-354.

Chapter 16

1 The tales of these accidents and their implications are detailed in Bolman, Lee. G. and Terrence E. Deal. 2008. *Reframing Organizations* (4th Ed.). San Francisco: Jossey Bass. I based this description on their account.

2 One of the earliest studies of the types of power was conducted by John French and Bertram Raven, who described five bases of power. See French, J.R.P. and Raven, B. 1968. "The Bases of Social Power" in *Group Dynamics*, 3rd ed., 259269. D. Cartwright and A. Zander (eds.). New York: Harper and Row. A number of others have built on these concepts and developed our current understanding of power dynamics at work. One of the better treatments of using power and influence is Linda Hill's work, which I draw upon for many of the concepts in this chapter, along with other sources. See, for example, Hill, Linda A. 1994. *Power Dynamics in Organizations*. Harvard Business School, Prod. # 494083PDFENG; and Hill, Linda A. 2009. "Exercising Influence Without Formal Authority" in *Becoming a Manager: How New Managers Master the Challenges of Leadership*. Boston: Harvard Business Press. Other long-standing resources include Kotter, John P. 1985. *Power and Influence*. NY: The Free Press; and Pfeffer, Jeffrey. 1981. *Power in Organizations*. Boston: Pitman. For another view, see Pfeffer's article entitled "Power Play" in *Harvard Business Review*, July-August 2010.

3   In Chapter 23 you will find an expanded discussion of building a network that goes beyond your current workplace to include others in your field and elsewhere who can affect your success.

4   Hill, Linda. 1994. *Exercising Influence.* Harvard Business School Press. For more on how to build trust, see Chapter 23, Networking Made Simple.

5   Cohen, A.R. and Bradford, D.L. 2005. *Influence without Authority*, 2nd Ed. New York: John Wiley and Sons. If you consult one other resource about the process of influence, this is the one that I recommend.

6   Logrolling also explains why lobbyists currently hold so much influence in the U.S. Congress. The high cost of running a successful political campaign coupled with the huge dollars offered by special interests for a Congressperson's vote means that legislators are far more likely to serve the lobbyists' interests rather than to compromise with a political opponent (the origin of the term logrolling). The good will and quid pro quo from the opponent ends up being worth much less than the (lobbyist provided) dollars needed to win an election.

7   A number of the concepts in this section are based on Cialdini, Robert B. 1993. *Influence: Science and Practice* (3rd ed.). NY: HarperCollins College Publishers. This book is a fascinating read and highly recommended. Cialdini offers the research support and logic that explains how and why influence behaviors work.

8   The principles outlined here are drawn from Hill, Linda A. 1998. *Managing Your Career.* Harvard Business School Press.

Chapter 19

1   Gladwell, M. 2008. *Outliers: The Story of Success.* Boston: Little Brown and Co.

2   Tannen, Deborah. 2002. The power of talk: who gets heard and why, *HBR OnPoint*.

3   Part IV of this book includes several chapters that discuss communication skills. These may help you redress any of your communication weaknesses, but they are no substitute for paying attention to how you structure your interfaces at the outset.

Chapter 20

1 A few of the suggestions here are drawn from *Get Your Way!* by Noelle Nelson (Prentice Hall, 1997). She offers a lot of other great advice as well. Highly recommended reading.

Chapter 23

1 This chapter expands beyond the discussion of Growing a Network at Work in Chapter 16 to include networks outside your workplace as well.

2 schmooze. Dictionary.com. *Collins English Dictionary—Complete & Unabridged 10th Edition.* HarperCollins Publishers. http://dictionary.reference.com/browse/schmooze (accessed: July 31, 2010).

3 Uzzi, Brian and Dunlap, S. 2005. How to build your network, *Harvard Business Review,* November. Much of the first section of this chapter is based on Uzzi and Dunlap's research findings and recommendations and I am indebted to them.

4 Bartolome, Fernando. 1989. Nobody trusts the boss completely—now what? *Harvard Business Review,* March-April.

5 Thomas, Marvin. 2004. *Personal Village: How to Have People in Your Life by Choice, Not Chance.* Seattle: Milestone Books. I am indebted to Thomas for some of the ideas in this section.

Chapter 24

1 A team is a special type of work group that is responsible for a shared goal and involves mutual accountability. For simplicity's sake, however, I use the word "team" in this chapter to refer to all groups that work together on some task or activity.

2 Cohesive groups are healthy but only in moderation. If cohesiveness is so intense that members fail to surface conflict and confront disagreements, group performance will decline.

3 Guidelines are based on Hall, Jay. 1971. Decisions, Decisions, Decisions, *Psychology Today,* November.

Chapter 25

1   Tannen, Deborah. 2002. The power of talk: who gets heard and why, *HBR OnPoint.*

2   DeVito, J. 2008. *The Interpersonal Communication Book.* New York: Allyn & Bacon.

3   McShane, Steven and Von Glinow, Mary Ann. 2010. *Organizational Behavior* (5th ed.). Boston: McGraw-Hill Irwin.

Chapter 28

1   Thomas-Kilmann Conflict Mode Instrument. 2002. Consulting Psychologists Press, Inc.

2   Smith, M. 1985. *When I Say No, I Feel Guilty.* New York: Bantam.

Chapter 30

1   Harris, Russ. 2008. *The Happiness Trap: How to Stop Struggling and Start Living.* Boston: Trumpeter Books, p. 4. *The Happiness Trap* outlines an empowering program to achieve genuine peace on your life's journey, bypassing illusive pursuit of happiness. The ideas of Dr. Harris and others in his field have been a tremendous influence on my approach to managing introversion in an extroverted culture and thus many of the ideas in this book. I highly recommend this helpful, insightful, and highly readable book.

Chapter 32

1   Watson, D. 1989. Strangers' ratings of the five robust personality factors: evidence of a surprising convergence with self report, *Journal of Personality and Social Psychology*, 57(1), pp. 120-128.

2   In recent years, psychological research has supported some major dimensions to personality called the "Big 5". These were derived empirically by statistical factor analysis and are tendencies, not firm categories. They help our understanding of personality but do not explain it in its entirety. The Big 5 are: 1. Extraversion, 2. Agreeableness, 3. Conscientiousness, 4. Emotional stability, and 5. Openness to experience. The Big 5 dimension of personal-

ity labeled "Extraversion" incorporates both introversion and extraversion. Agreeableness is the degree to which someone is trusting, goodnatured, cooperative, and flexible. Conscientiousness refers to characteristics around dependability, responsibility, achievement orientation, and persistence. Emotional stability has to do with how much someone is relaxed, secure, and unworried rather than anxious, depressed, and insecure (neuroticism). Openness to experience deals with the degree to which someone is intellectual, imaginative, curious, and broadminded. In this context, we can see that the introversion/extraversion dichotomy is an important personality factor among five major dimensions of the Big 5. At the same time, there are many other important personality traits *not* represented by the Big 5 model. (Recall those 1500 + adjectives!).

3   Kroeger, O. with Thuesen, J.M. and Rutledge, H. 2002. *Type Talk at Work: How the 16 Personality Types Determine Your Success on the Job.* New York: Dell.

Chapter 33

1   Gabarro, John J. and John P. Kotter. 2005. Best of HBR 1980: Managing your boss, *Harvard Business Review*, January.

Chapter 34

1   The late John Hartford's roles are listed on his website: http://www.johnhartford.com/index.cfm

2   Boldt, Lawrence G. 1993. *Zen and the Art of Making a Living: A Practical Guide to Career Design.* New York: Penguin/Arkana, p. xli.

3   Among others, they include the Strong Interest Inventory® and the Birkman Method®.

4   This exercise is based on "Life Planning: A Programmed Approach" from *A Handbook of Structured Experiences for Human Relations Training.* J. William Pfeiffer and John E. Jones (Eds.), San Diego: University Associates Publishers and Consultants, 1974 (Vol. II).

5   Kilmann, R.H. and Saxton, M.J. 1983. *The Kilmann-Saxton Culture Gap Survey.* Pittsburgh, PA: Organizational Design Consultants.

6   **Recommended resources for career change include the following:**

Boldt, Lawrence. 2009. *Zen and the Art of Making a Living: A Practical Guide to Creative Career Design.* NY: Penguin.

Bolles, Richard N. 2009. *What Color Is Your Parachute? 2010: A Practical Manual for Job-Hunters and Career-Changers.* Berkeley: Ten Speed Press.

Sher, Barbara. 1998. *It's Only Too Late if You don't Start Now: How to Create Your Second Life at Any Age.* NY: Dell.

Sher, Barbara. 1994. *I Could Do Anything If I Only Knew What It Was: How to Discover What You Really Want and How to Get It.* NY: Dell.

Chapter 35

1   Frankl, Viktor E. 1959. *Man's Search for Meaning.* New York: Pocket Books.

Chapter 36

1   Guntzelman, Joan. "Who Was Blessed Mother Teresa?" Accessed online at:http://www.americancatholic.org/features/teresa/whowasteresa.asp. December 20, 2010.

2   Smircich, Linda and Morgan, Gareth. 1982. Leadership: the management of meaning, *The Journal of Applied Behavioral Science*, 18 (3), pp. 257-273.

3   Kouzes, James and Posner, Barry. 2007. *The Leadership Challenge* (4th ed.). San Francisco: Jossey Bass.

Afterword

1   Steven Batchelor. 1997. *Buddhism Without Beliefs: A Contemporary Guide to Awakening.* London: Bloomsbury, p. 47.

Index

286

292

About the Author

JOYCE SHELLEMAN, Ph.D., maintains a professional practice specializing in workplace issues faced by introverted professionals and leaders. A graduate of the Katz Graduate School of Business at the University of Pittsburgh with a doctorate in organizational behavior and more than two decades of experience, she is an authoritative advisor, a popular teacher, and an unabashed introvert. She lives near the coast of Maine.

Visit www.TheIntrovertsGuide.com.

CPSIA information can be obtained at www.ICGtesting.com
Printed in the USA
LVOW100747021011

248674LV00003B/8/P